"If you are hoping that your church will thrive but have always found an emphasis on church growth distasteful, then this is the book for you. It is not about slick techniques, but rather messy testimonies. If you are looking to learn the right way for you to grow your church, you will not find it spelled out here. If, however, you are willing to gain insights from a basketful of right ways for others, then read on. This is a sharply observed, narrative-driven account by a wise and good minister-scholar-journalist who has seen up close what is working among the mainliners, evangelicals, liberals, and high church—not to mention a wide range of creative and productive misfits. I came away inspired."

—TIMOTHY LARSEN
McManis Professor of Christian Thought, Wheaton College

"Jason Byassee has written an excellent account of Christian faith in contemporary England, specifically in areas that we might have thought deeply hostile to faith. The result is an insightful account of churches, parachurch networks, and church planting in a modern secular society, and it is far more relevant to current US conditions than we might initially think. His book is very well-written, and often really entertaining. Heartily recommended!"

—PHILIP JENKINS
Distinguished Professor of History, Institute for Studies of Religion, Baylor University

"Byassee takes up the pen with the mind of a theologian, the heart of pastor, and the eye of a journalist. He recently walked into the strange and beautiful world of England's Christ-haunted North East, fell in love with the place, and started asking questions. He has discerned with wisdom and articulated with skill what those of us who live here experience consciously and unconsciously every week. His account of divine patterns and cultural trends in the North East's particulars bear wisdom for the wider church at the dawn (or mid-morning?) of post-Christendom."

—ANDREW J. BYERS
Director of the Free Church Track in Missional Leadership and Lecturer in New Testament,
Cranmer Hall, St John's College, Durham University

"In *Northern Lights*, Byassee brings together the investigative skills of a journalist, the storytelling craft of a preacher, and the intellect of a scholar to paint a compelling portrait of Christian mission for the twenty-first century. With humor and honesty, Byassee explores how a diverse set of communities in northern England works at the center and the edges of society inspired by the Spirit, distilling insights for churches in North America and elsewhere. The book pulses with a colorful cast of characters brought to life—from the formidable former Archbishop of York to a tattooed barber who accidentally started a church to the down and out. Above all, Byassee brings the freshness of an outsider who refuses to take sides, listening to a diversity of voices and shining light on the raw energy, diversity, and innovation he encounters. This is a book I wish I had read years ago, crackling with insight not only into the English church, but asking bigger questions about what the church's mission might look like as a community of communities inviting people into God's work of making all things new. I can highly recommend it for anyone interested in the future of the church."

—JENNIFER ADAMS-MASSMANN

Chaplain, Peterhouse, University of Cambridge

NORTHERN LIGHTS

NORTHERN LIGHTS

*Resurrecting Church in
the North of England*

By
Jason Byassee

Foreword by Sam Wells

CASCADE *Books* · Eugene, Oregon

NORTHERN LIGHTS
Resurrecting Church in the North of England

Copyright © 2020 Jason Byassee. All rights reserved. Except for brief quotations in critical publications or reviews, no part of this book may be reproduced in any manner without prior written permission from the publisher. Write: Permissions, Wipf and Stock Publishers, 199 W. 8th Ave., Suite 3, Eugene, OR 97401.

Cascade Books
An Imprint of Wipf and Stock Publishers
199 W. 8th Ave., Suite 3
Eugene, OR 97401

www.wipfandstock.com

PAPERBACK ISBN: 978-1-7252-6445-8
HARDCOVER ISBN: 978-1-7252-6446-5
EBOOK ISBN: 978-1-7252-6447-2

Cataloguing-in-Publication data:

Names: Byassee, Jason, author. | Wells, Samuel, 1965–, foreword writer

Title: Northern lights : resurrecting church in the North of England / Jason Byassee with a foreword by Sam Wells

Description: Eugene, OR: Cascade Books, 2020 | Includes bibliographical references.

Identifiers: ISBN 978-1-7252-6445-8 (paperback) | ISBN 978-1-7252-6446-5 (hardcover) | ISBN 978-1-7252-6447-2 (ebook)

Subjects: LCSH: England, North East—Christianity | Church growth | Church development, New | Small churches | Missions

Classification: BV652.25 B93 2020 (print) | BV652.25 (ebook)

Manufactured in the U.S.A.   NOVEMBER 2, 2020

For Sarah Coakley, doctor of the church.
And for Luke Edwards, fisher for people. And fish.
And for Ann Conway, brave and inspiring pilgrim.

CONTENTS

Foreword by Sam Wells | ix
Acknowledgements | xi

1 Introduction: Churches that intend to grow . . . | 1
2 Bishops with bullhorns | 10
3 Durham City: Growing churches where churches can't grow | 36
4 Durham Cathedral: This massive fascination | 59
5 Alpha: We're from London, here to help | 82
6 Desperate in Newcastle | 94
7 BCP in Farsi: The nations come to the North | 116
8 Fresh Expressions: Church growth writ small | 134
9 Can churches still *do* that!? | 151

Bibliography | 165

FOREWORD

Jason Byassee has given us an Odyssey around islands of church growth in the northeast of England. With the wit of Bill Bryson and the innocence of David Copperfield, he introduces us to a gallery of the passionate and the disarming, and leaves us, like him, with a hard-won admiration for the love that won't let Jesus go.

Byassee walks into a debate that seems tilted in one direction. Here's the case for the cynical, led by Ricky Gervais, but with armies of the indifferent clustering on his shoulder. This is a story about a lonely prophet in an uninteresting backwater of the Roman Empire two thousand years ago. It should be treated as yet another example of pathetic, if tragic, failure. Yet by a series of happenstances, some remarkable, others calculated, this figure became divested of his obscure Jewish context and clothed as the poster child of empire, validation of the powerful, and opium of the weak. Where he remained, until the undertow of rational logic (read the Enlightenment), scientific scrutiny (read Galileo and Darwin), and social transformation (read Marx and the industrial/technological revolution) finally toppled him off his perch. Yet still nefarious advocates abide, apparently oblivious to the destructive power of passionate truth, and today responsible for the large majority of the world's ills, from clerical child abuse to global warming. Never quite sure if the problem with Christianity is that it's evil or idle, dangerous or boring, the cynical cite the northeast of England as the wasteland of faith that anticipates the overdue secularization of northern Europe.

What could be the case for faith, in the face of such rampant and confident unbelief? Byassee resists launching an abstract argument. Instead he offers us an investigation that becomes a pilgrimage. Jesus changes lives. Small movements of Christians, like Methodists of yesteryear, become communities where ordinary, often broken people, find their gifts surface, their energy released, their shortcomings redeemed, their potential harnessed, their imagination empowered. At the start of the book our author is saying,

"Can anything good come out of Nazareth?" By the end, he's saying "Did I not feel my heart on fire as I talked with these people?" Christianity is manifested in all shapes and sizes: those who believe in buildings, none greater than Durham Cathedral; those who believe in small-group enquiry and Spirit-infused weekends, in the style of Alpha; those who like their evangelists tattooed, those who prefer them to be doyennes of social entrepreneurship. Some are filling old wineskins with new wine, others are pouring in rather familiar-looking wine into new wineskins. Charles Dickens would be proud of such a parade, and like Byassee would retain his sharp wit in order to reassure the reader that enthusiasm hadn't clouded judgement.

Byassee's appreciative enquiry has something to teach the UK, and something to teach North America. For the UK, the lesson is simple: nothing changes people like seeing change in people. The most powerful form of evangelism is testimony. Byassee's own testimony is made up of the testimony of the humble folk to whom he's taken time to listen, through which attention this book is littered with examples that cumulatively persuade the reader to do some serious listening too. There's no triumph of technique or medium; what shines through is ordinary people witnessing to how their lives have been transformed. As the man born blind said in John 9, "I do not know whether he is a sinner. One thing I do know, that though I was blind, now I see." This cloud of witnesses are a little coy about the torrent of disdain the Enlightenment and its cultured successors have poured upon Christianity and the church. But they speak of what they know, and have seen.

For North America, the lesson is more complex: Europe ("Yurp") is not a single entity; the UK is not a single country; England is not a homogeneous whole—even the Northeast has great diversity of class and race. (But when the Church of England has been deemed to have backed the landowners since 1381, you've got some listening to do.) None of these units is a template for North America. The point is not to take a model and make it work anywhere. It's to be enchanted by the way the Holy Spirit works.

For in the end, this is a book not about a church, or a region, or even an investigator-turned pilgrim. It's a book about the Holy Spirit. Not a Spirit who has self-isolated into tongues and healings, but one who constantly, relentlessly, astonishingly makes the risen Christ present where all seemed lost, forlorn, forsaken. The hope of the church lies not in a discipleship course, or even in the catalogue of saints this book unearths; but in the Holy Spirit, which continues to moves stones from tombs and give frightened people tongues of fire.

Revd Dr Sam Wells
Vicar of St Martin-in-the-Fields
Trafalgar Square, London

ACKNOWLEDGEMENTS

THERE ARE MANY PEOPLE I need to thank for their help in approaching this work. One is Presbyterian Innovative Ministries and its intrepid leader, David Jennings. PIM's grant made this trip and this research possible and I am grateful. I need to thank friends such as Richard Topping at the Vancouver School of Theology and Ross Lockhart of St. Andrew's Hall for helping me understand the PCC in its context in Canada, as well as hundreds of Presbyterian and other students and listeners at workshops and lectures and sermons over the years. I need to thank David Wilkinson, Principle of St. John's College in Durham, for the visiting fellowship at John's and warm hospitality there, Philip Plyming, Warden of Cranmer Hall, for a home in a theological training institution, and Lewis Ayres, former Chair of the Department of Theology and Religion at Durham University, for a visiting fellowship there. Friends at Durham Cathedral, like canon (now bishop) Sophie Jelley and canon Simon Oliver, helped me understand the ecclesial landscape and opened doors to me; friends among clergy in town, like David Day at St. Nick's, did the same. Dozens of people provided interviews, sifted through what I was seeing, showed me patterns I couldn't see, occasionally were brave enough to disagree with me strongly—I thank each one of them. I hope I have told enough of the truth well enough here that they recognize themselves and that others can benefit. I fear any one of these folks may still disagree strongly with what I have to say here. That is their right. I have tried to honour each one as a sibling in Christ and coworker in the gospel. Where I have failed it is my fault alone. Our life depends on grace, does it not?

I am grateful to Richard Topping, Principal of the Vancouver School of Theology, for a semester of leave from VST to work on this project in Durham, and for his entrepreneurial work to set up the partnership between VST and Durham University to offer Durham PhDs on the west coast of Canada. I am grateful to my family—Jaylynn, Jack, Sam, and Will—for traveling with me, enduring British uniforms in schools and accents and foods and weather. We are grateful to the Byers' for their hospitality. And to my dedicatees—thank you to Sarah Coakley for her wisdom and hospitality, and to Luke Edwards and Ann Conway for coming to Britain and traveling along with us. Et soli deo Gloria.

NORTHEAST ENGLAND

BERWICK
LINDISFARNE
ALMWICK
NORTHUMBERLAND COUNTY
MORPETH
TYNE AND WEAR
NEWCASTLE UPON TYNE
JARROW
GATESHEAD
SUNDERLAND
CHESTER-LE-STREET
DURHAM
DURHAM COUNTY
STOCKTON-UPON-TEES
HARTLEPOOL
MIDDLESBROUGH
CLEVELAND

UNITED KINGDOM

- NEWCASTLE-UPON-TYNE
- DURHAM

CUMBRIA (COUNTY)

MERSEYSIDE (COUNTY)
- BRADFORD
- HALIFAX
- YORK
- LEEDS
- WAKEFIELD
- OLDHAM
- FITTON HILL
- LIVERPOOL
- WARRINGTON
- MANCHESTER
- SHEFFIELD
- LEICESTER
- ELY
- DUNWICH
- CAMBRIDGE
- OXFORD
- WATFORD
- CHELMSFORD
- LONDON
- SALISBURY
- PORTSMOUTH
- CANTERBURY

1

INTRODUCTION
Churches that intend to grow . . .

Not all growth is good. If you don't believe me, have a look at my yard—what Brits call a "garden."

I grew up in a complex with no individual yards, so I have no skills in gardening, nor any desire to learn them. This is a problem living in the UK, as we did in the first half of 2019, since Brits love their gardens. As England started to happily green and grow when winter turned to spring, our garden grew. And grew. It's still growing. We occasionally hack away branches so we can pass through on the walk up to the house. But we're not tending anything. "Love what you've done with the place," one American friend commented upon visiting. There are flowers in there, and weeds too, and I'm sure someone who knew what they were doing could make more of the former and less of the latter. I'm just not sure how to tell which is which.

I was sent here on a grant from Canadian Presbyterians to see what North Americans can stand to learn from growing churches in Europe. We Americans aren't great in geography, so learning that Europe is sort of a big place, I narrowed things to the United Kingdom. Learning this was still too large for seven months (!), I narrowed things to the Northeast of England. We spent our time in Durham, a small medieval university city in the midst of an otherwise fairly economically challenged region. The Northeast was England's mining and shipbuilding hub, but there has been little mining and less shipbuilding since England grew close to the rest of Europe and Margaret Thatcher closed the mines. Durham can feel like a little island of Oxbridge in a region that is otherwise a desert for economic opportunities.

And so, we thought, it was perfect. As a southerner from the US, I recognize a region that feels looked down on by the rest of its country. A Yorkshireman originally taught me theology, and commenting on the similarity between the US South and the North of England, he said "We're the hicks of our country too." When Americans think of England, we imagine an accent like Hugh Grant or Benedict Cumberbatch's Sherlock. We don't imagine the Geordie, Makem, or Pitmatic accents of the North. For pop culture references, think not so much *The Crown* or *Downton Abbey* as *Billy Elliot*.

As a transplant to the west coast of Canada from the US South, I also thought the Northeast of England was perfect. BC is hyper-aware of itself as a post-Christian place, registering some of the highest levels of religious disaffiliation and antipathy anywhere in the West. Nobody just wakes up and goes looking for a church anymore. So too with the UK generally and the Northeast in particular. Church attendance levels are in the single digits. There is very little cultural pressure to attend church, identify as a Christian, or seek some ulterior gain through church membership. Some theorize this is good—those who do worship do so for more genuine reasons. Maybe. I'm just aware of the demoralizing effect that lower church attendance can have on churches, ministers, and neighbourhoods. There may be more residual religiosity in the Northeast of England than the southwest of Canada—more of what one scholar calls "fuzzy fidelity"[1]—but England and Canada are more culturally akin than I had realized. Lots of Canadians are just a generation away from migration from the UK; lots of Brits tell me they had an aunt or cousin migrate to Canada after World War II whom they like to visit (though they seem to fear the snow and the bears out of all proportion to the actual danger!). And Canadians can be a little more willing to learn from the UK than they are from Americans. They're often tired of being dependent on some expert from south of the 49th parallel claiming to turn up with "the answers." Brits are a little less likely to trumpet themselves as having answers. So the cultural exchange from the Northeast of England to the southwest of Canada might just work—even though it represents learning from one niche to illuminate things for another. Everywhere is a niche. Every local is distinct, even if that local is as big as London or Toronto. There is no church in general, just as there is no God in general—God is always the one who elects Israel and raises Jesus from the dead. God has a taste for particular places (think: Bethlehem and Nazareth), and doesn't seek to obliterate their specificity in order to reach a more general audience (think: televised and web-based church). "Jesus loves the Geordies!" I heard one pastor yell into the microphone one Sunday in Newcastle. And Jesus

---

1. It's David Voas's term. See his "The Rise and Fall of Fuzzy Fidelity in Europe," 155.

loves Cascadia. He's alive and well and working in both places. What do they stand to learn from one another?

Growing churches carry a sort of fascination. How, in an age of aggressive secularism (or worse, oblivious ignorance), does a congregation get people to turn up, worship, grow as disciples, and serve their communities? There are wrong approaches to this question, of course. Donald McGavran's "homogenous unit principle" (HUP) suggested that people want to worship with people like themselves.[2] It grew giant congregations in many suburbs—because McGavran was right. I heard Peter Storey, the great anti-apartheid leader in South Africa, say of HUPs that they'd been tried in his country. It was called apartheid. It took a lot of blood and treasure to get rid of HUPs and South Africa is still trying to heal. While people may like to go to the mall, the restaurant, or even church with people just like them, the church of Jesus Christ is a calling into a Jew-plus-gentile community, where the enemy you'd rather avoid is always sitting right next to you. You may not "like" it, but it's the only way to salvation, according to the savior who hangs on a cross between thieves.

Early in my career as a Methodist preacher I noticed at annual conference these award signs stabbed into the earth outside the meeting indicating the churches that had grown the fastest in the previous year. I wanted to rip them all down. They looked like for-sale signs in front of houses. And they celebrated shininess, success. How is a church supposed to feel that experienced no such thing, whatever it tried? Annual Conference (Methodists' version of a diocesan convention) is meant to encourage those who need it, not those who don't. A church doing just fine on its own has no need of a risen savior. No tombs here, just healthy things and shiny signs. No resurrection needed, thanks.

But then I spent some years pastoring a rural church in a struggling area. And I found the arguments against church growth less compelling. Some would say that courageous pastors preach prophetically and their demands for justice cause less courageous people to leave. There are memories of the civil rights movement in the US South to fortify this. Thing is, I never saw it. Pastors might preach prophetically, but churches are made up of grown-ups. The situation is rarely as clear as a brave pastor and a craven bunch of cowardly parishioners who'd rather be coddled than served with the truth. I did, however, notice pastors tell themselves that flattering story as a way to justify their church's lack of growth. I felt the undertow of young families leaving my little, rural, and old church for something flashier, wealthier, and

---

2. See McGavran, *Understanding Church Growth*. McGavran is the thinker without whom we would not have had the gigachurch movement that birthed such behemoths as Saddleback and Willow Creek.

more kid-friendly in the city nearby. That hurt. But something else happened too. Other people came. Not the people we would have thought to invite, were we in charge of the guest list. Jesus always goes around inviting all the "wrong" people. What we did was welcome the surprising ones Jesus brought. And the church grew. The thing about a small congregation is you can add a single person and it's like a bonanza of growth. Add a family and its 5 percent growth. You should throw a party, take the rest of the year off. A large church can add a family and forget it ever happened. Small churches have wonderful advantages in many ways, not least when it comes to growth. A church full of grandparents may not seem cool or sexy, but as our cultures drift into moral anomie, and our cities become more unaffordable, and folks want to grow their own crops again, it wouldn't surprise me at all to see folks find their way back to these grandparent-filled chapels. At their best, they are sources of wisdom and kindness, of the sort that make us more human for being a part of them.

Later in ministry I pastored a larger church. And I found that growth was crucial. New people coming was like a skin graft onto a wound—it added health to the whole body. Growth also kept us listening to our community. What are folks after? Where do things hurt? How can the church respond? Without growth we turned inward quickly, caring for our own little holy club, while the world around us burned. But a desire to see new people come to faith in Christ and membership in the church kept us listening. Now, I speak as a Methodist, and Methodism is a revivalist sect. If Methodists aren't reviving anybody, what good are we? Boone Methodist knew that in its bones. They'd long ago done a formative Bible study on *Experiencing God*, and taught me an adage from that study that I repeated every chance I got: "God speaks to the church by who God sends to the church."[3] New people were not then marks to hit, givers to fill the budget, currency to bandy about at pastor conferences. No—they were *messengers from God*. They may not know this, or at its suggestion they might even strongly object. But they are. They are a claim on our community. We have to listen carefully: what is God asking of us? So when refugees came from a local conservative Christian missionary organization, we had to learn to talk about Jesus without the politics that drove them away from their previous home. When the local university brought internationals from another faith, we had to welcome across cultures. When grief made its unwelcome knock on our community's door, we had to help a whole town grieve well.

---

3. Henry Blackaby, *Experiencing God*. Now that I teach on the campus of University of British Columbia, Blackaby's alma mater, I often wonder whether any other UBC graduate has ever sold so many books as this Baptist minister and evangelist. I'm betting not.

And when we learned that some folks wouldn't come to our church no matter how nice we were, we had to figure out how to go to them. We didn't seek to grow in order to save people from hell, though in the South that language is always in the mix. We didn't even do it because Jesus commanded it, though that's a better reason. We emphasized it because as a people in mission, driven out by the Holy Spirit, we had no choice. And when we went, we were delighted to find God anew there, just beyond our borders, on the edges, renewing things, bringing life, making us and others new.

I had a mantra at Boone Methodist around the offering that I only later realized is true more broadly. God has no gifts that are not Israel-shaped. God doesn't choose Israel for Israel's sake. God chooses Israel so that *through* Israel God can bless all the others (Gen 12:1–4). So it is with us. God has no gifts to give to us. God only gives gifts *through* us *for* other people. A church that doesn't give is like a garden hose with a kink in it (see? I *have* been in a garden! Briefly and unsuccessfully . . .). No water can come through it. Untangle it and water flows just fine. God's gifts are like manna—try and store them up, and they rot. But give them away, and God will replenish them faster than you can give them. Boone Methodist taught me all that.

And so lots of the arguments against caring about church growth started to fall away. Isn't this just an effort for, as North Americans say, bricks and butts and budgets? Or as Brits say, bums in the seats? Well, no. Nothing is "just" anything. Bread and wine are not "just" bread and wine. New growth of churches in London are not "just" immigrants. On a Christian accounting, nothing is "just" anything. Everything means something else, and God's self-giving is only ever mediated through other, unexpected means. On the particulars, bricks and budgets matter. Holy places matter, as the world relearned watching Notre Dame burn that spring of 2019, as worshipers in Durham Cathedral know in their bones. Budgets matter. We give to what we care about. To pretend money doesn't matter in church or life is a gnostic conceit. To think we can have spirituality without money is like thinking you can have dinner without food. And butts matter. Bums matter. They have this consistent habit of being attached to people. No bums, no hearts. Now, bums don't have to be sitting in a pew—churches didn't do that until the Reformation. But bums are bodies, which are people. Not to care about them is to blaspheme. To put it crudely, in Christ, *God* has a bum. Jesus followed Jewish kosher laws, which include what you can eat and cannot. We go on encountering him in bread and wine. Stanley Hauerwas likes to recount a rabbi friend saying "any religion that doesn't tell you what to do with your pots and pans and genitals fails to be interesting." And pots and pans and genitals and bums are inseparable from one another.

There are wrong ways to speak of and to pursue church growth. Ever since the publication of Dean Kelley's *Why Conservative Churches Are Growing* in 1972, church growth has been a kind of political currency in North America.[4] The loose argument has run like this: only conservative churches can grow, and only church growth demonstrates faithfulness to the gospel, which is the same thing as success. Church growth is a kind of credentialing in this way of thinking, not just within the church, but in the public sphere. Supporting and opposing Kelley's thesis has made many a sociologist's career. There is clearly something to it, especially in America, where "success" of a superficial kind is prized so highly, whatever the cost. But, of course, many one-time "successful" churches have toppled over and brought great harm. And the pursuit of growth at the expense of other goods has done even further harm. "The more people, the less truth," Eugene Peterson liked to say, quoting Kierkegaard.[5] A teacher of mine joked that it was easy to get people into church: just post a banner promising "free beer!" and get ready to implement crowd control measures.

The absolutism of the argument that "only" conservative churches can grow is a mistake. One only needs a single counter-example to prove it wrong. And often liberal churches grow. It seems to me the keys for growth are several: a clear and compelling mission, able and energetic leadership (preferably in place for a long period of time), a welcoming congregation engaged in mission, attention paid to discipleship and growth. In short, Christianity as such is compelling. Practice it well and others will be attracted to it. Oh, and it helps to have people around. Andy Crouch likes to greet stories of "miraculous" church growth by asking the simple question, "So when did the new highway go in?"

The flip side of the Kelley argument is the impression that liberals can give: Christianity is for influencing the social order (Rauschenbusch), for comforting the afflicted and afflicting the comfortable (Niebuhr), for bringing about greater justice in the world. The straplines from the early-to-mid-twentieth century assumed that mainline churches had power and influence to lean on Congress to bring about greater justice. But when our numbers decline or vanish, there is no weight to bring to bear, and so less justice to bring about. I'm a sceptic of the whole approach. It's not clear to me we ever brought about much good this way, and the method is practiced just as effectively or more so by fundamentalist churches—Jerry Falwell changed politics in the US more, and for the worse, than the Niebuhrs ever imagined

---

4. Diana Butler Bass's career has largely been about overturning Dean M. Kelly's thesis. Mine has too, in a rather different way.

5. Peterson, *Run with the Horses*, 130.

possible. Christians have been influential vastly beyond our numbers when we have practiced faith beautifully. Desert fathers and mothers rejected the twinning of political power and Christian faith in the ancient church and that rejection has left its mark. Just a few people pursuing holiness can turn heads or change the world. Or not! And yet their faithfulness will be blessed by God and attractive to their neighbours. Shane Claiborne speaks of the gospel's power to change being greater when we rely "not on force but on fascination."[6] The goal of a big church is not to change the world. It is to change the neighbourhood. And the agency is God's, not ours.

My hypothesis going into this study is that growth is something you get not by aiming at it, but by aiming at something else. Aim at growth and you may get it, you may not, but it's not the goal. The goal is faithfulness to Jesus Christ, a community's life shaped around him, taking part in his redemption of the world. Clear and winsome devotion to that—alignment of a church's budget and hiring and liturgy and attention around Jesus—will fascinate and draw others. Not always. There are exceptions. But even if it "fails" on worldly grounds of success and failure, it will have been done the right way. "There is no waste in God's economy," a saint of the church I served taught me. That can't be counted statistically, but I'll go to the mat for it. I'm not interested in cheap tricks or techniques for growth. Several churches profiled here have been over-studied. They have seen success of a sort, but they don't have shortcuts for it, and they tend to insist that all they have done is try to be faithful; God has blessed them, and folks come and grow and bless the world beyond them. There is no shortcut around the gospel.

My conclusion amends the hypothesis. Growth is something to aim for. Not as a good in itself. There are lots of qualifications. But the churches I studied wanted to grow. They tried new things. They failed, a lot, and learned, and tried new things. A friend says "any diet works." Nearly any approach to eating better and exercising more can do you good. Nearly any approach to growth can work. An adage I picked up in England: churches that intend to grow tend to grow. Not always. It's not automatic. But intent matters.

As a journalist I've come to count on something: if a church is growing, something interesting is happening there. That doesn't mean it's something *good*. Joel Osteen's prosperity gospel is particularly odious to me. But then look again. A former student of mine, Jason Morriss, served on Osteen's staff, and insists there is more rigorous goodness in that room than in many mainline churches. There is certainly more multicultural and multiracial representation. And there is a rigorous insistence that the gospel is

---

6. Shane Claiborne says this often. See, for example, his article "What If Jesus Meant All That Stuff?" in *Esquire*, 18 November 2009: https://www.esquire.com/news-politics/a6646/shane-claiborne-1209/.

good news for its hearers. As I write, a church in northern Virginia is in the news for praying over President Trump. The pastor tried to avoid glorifying him, though the images of a pastor with hands on the faithless boor of a president will certainly be played for partisan gain for years. But I'm sympathetic. What would I say if Caesar turned up and asked me to pray? Would I have the courage of, say, John Chrysostom, regularly railing on his imperial sermon-listeners? Probably not. Big churches matter. Not because they always get it right, God no! But more people go to them than go to small ones. People go for a reason—no one goes to church to fight for a parking place—they're there because they're finding something good. What is it? And some mainline churches are growing. Not a lot. But some. What are they doing differently than the rest of us? There is energy there, something worth detecting, either for good or ill. What is it exactly?

I work as a kind of impressionistic researcher. I don't do hard research or sociology or ethnography. I'm a journalist, following my nose and asking nosy questions. I'm also a theologian, trying to make sense of my impressions. But I make no pretention in these pages or anywhere else to any claim to comprehensiveness or objective data-gathering. Lucky for me these are present in abundance already in the church in the Northeast of England. The Church Army Research Unit in Sheffield is an outstanding resource for hard, objective data on church growth in the UK. If it's going on in England, these folks have found it, tested it, catalogued it, shown the rest of us what it means (churcharmy.org). While I was in Durham, I had David Goodhew as a colleague briefly at St. John's College. David is now back in parish ministry in Middlesbrough, but remains the best academic source for church growth UK-wide, especially in the Northeast.[7] These folks' much more exacting and scientific work undergirds everything I say in this book. But just as when I draw on patristic scholarship I make no claim to find anything original—I don't know the languages, I can't go and check the manuscripts—so here I make no claim to do anything scientific on numbers. Others have done that work. I'm writing about places that interest me and trying to discern patterns.

I am doing so from and for a particular people: Presbyterians in British Columbia. This is not a large group. Presbyterians in Canada are those who held themselves out of church union in the 1925 merger of Methodists, Congregationalists, and two thirds of Presbyterians. They know who they are by holding out. I admire their grit. It also means they are not large, and they do not have massive buildings or impressive historical pedigrees. They are, of course, part of the family of Reformed churches worldwide, with

---

7. See David Goodhew's books *Church Growth in Britain: 1980 to the Present*, *Towards a Theology of Church Growth*, and most recently, *The Desecularization of the City*.

historic origins not only in Scotland and Switzerland and the Netherlands, but roots in the entire church of Jesus Christ back to the apostles. They have a great pedigree of teaching doctrine, rooted in John Calvin himself, going back through Augustine to Paul and John. And, like all mainline churches in North America, they struggle in an era of declining numbers and influence, and are divided over questions of social inclusion. But I love this little scrappy bunch. They are determined to show God is not done with them yet. Often what draws my attention in the UK is determined by what I think will be helpful to them. You can only attend to a particular from the vantage of other particulars, and this is the particularity from which I've viewed the other—hopefully the fruit will be helpful to you wherever you stand.

I also practice a kind of immersive journalism. I write about places I worship in. I only occasionally make reference to an ecclesial community where I've not worshiped. We've made our spiritual home at Wearside Parish Church in Durham and my kids have been involved in youth ministry at King's. I see things by being part of churches that more objective, neutral, disinterested observers would miss. I find it more honest to be up front about this, rather than pretend it were otherwise. And I interview pastors about their own work and their peers' work across town. This is an undeniably parochial approach (in multiple senses!). I'm only one person with my own set of ideas and preconceptions. It's why I couldn't get across the length of the UK, let alone Europe. It also makes for awkwardness. I try to write about places by name and face, and try to make hard judgments about what I see. Not everyone has appreciated what I've said about them or to them or recorded from them. I have tried, with their help and permission, to tell the truth about their work insofar as I can see it. The limits of my approach are obvious, I hope. If there are any assets to it we'll see in the future health and growth of Presbyterian churches in Canada, and far beyond.[8]

---

8. A version of this chapter appeared previously as Jason Byassee, "Not All Growth Is Good," *Lutheran Forum* 53.4 (2019) 56–61.

2

BISHOPS WITH BULLHORNS

IF YOU HAVE HEARD of only one of the active bishops in the Church of England during the time I was studying the UK, chances are it was John Sentamu.[1] That is, his grace the Rt. Rev. John Sentamu, Archbishop of York and Primate of England from 2006 to 2020, "the number two man in the Church of England," as I often heard him described by pointing and whispering outsiders. He is as close a thing as the C of E has to a celebrity among its active clergy, with some 75,000 Twitter followers, a regular column at one time in the *Sun* tabloid, and an entire wing of very capable media people responding to unending requests for his time and attention.

There's some chance you heard of him because of games of chance. There is a very active betting industry in the UK, and when the Archbishop of Canterbury's job is open, as it was in 2012, there are odds set as to who will fill it. Sentamu was a good bet. And so as if he were a candidate running for office, his life and ministry were picked apart in the press. Reporters went to his native Uganda and interviewed his brother, a megachurch pastor there. His gifts and flaws were batted around by onetime friends and prognosticators. This was not only ungenerous in the extreme, it was based on a false premise. He is not a politician. He is a priest: "a Christian with you and a priest for you," he often says. He says publicly that the archbishopric of York is not a job, it is a calling: "I received a letter from the queen, summoning me."

---

1. Sentamu was nearing the end of his time as archbishop when I was in Durham, spring 2019. His successor, Stephen Cottrell, was announced at the end of the year.

Such is the peril of leading in an establishment church, still intertwined with politics, for the sake of the church of Jesus Christ, which has no politics but Christ and the kingdom. Like war, it's messy, and there are casualties, but we keep doing it.

If you are a theologian, priest, or otherwise theologically inclined person, Sentamu is not "the number two man in the church of England." The head of the C of E, humanly speaking, is the monarch, but the number one is Jesus Christ, head of the church in all time and space.[2] There are two primates in the Church of England, Sentamu and Justin Welby, Archbishop of Canterbury, Primate of *All* England (catch that "all"?) and many of the church's missives go out in both of their names. Welby is a former oil executive and is well-known in Durham, which we will hear much more about in the next two chapters. Welby trained for ministry in Durham and returned as Bishop of Durham for a year before becoming ABC. He is well-admired among the church leaders I speak with. He's an evangelical from Holy Trinity Brompton (see chapter 5), supportive of new and pioneering forms of ministry, and open in the press about such outlandish expressions of charismatic gifts as speaking in tongues (that is, outlandish to outsiders, but not unexpected for those who read the Bible).

I previously knew of Sentamu because of his prophetic work. While traveling in Uganda in 2008 I learned of his appearance on British television, where he was asked about Robert Mugabe, then-dictator of Zimbabwe. Mugabe was well-known to be corrupt, his country in a free-fall economically and morally, keeping power only by an iron fist. Yet every time international condemnation came, Mugabe played his key card. He was once a hero, in lock step with Nelson Mandela, a freedom fighter against British oppression. His opponents were simply riled up by England, motivated only by racism. The perfect counter to this was Sentamu, the only bishop of African descent among the C of E's bishops at the time. Asked about Mugabe, he removed his clerical collar, produced a pair of scissors, and proceeded to cut it to shreds on live TV. He promised he would not wear it again until Mugabe was out of power. Sentamu was true to his word, and after Mugabe was driven from power in 2017, the same television host presented his grace with the shreds from the collar he had previously cut up. Sentamu, perhaps envisioning this, took out a pristine new collar and put it on, wearing a clerical collar for the first time in a decade (if you are C of E, this is a serious fast!). No one else could have done this, no one else would have thought of

---

2. I know, Anglicans, I know! The sovereign was only spoken of as "head" of the church for about ten minutes, until someone pointed out that scripture describes only Jesus Christ that way, so the monarch of England is the *"supreme governor"* or some other such dodge....

it, no one else would have gotten attention for it. It was a massive public relations success, not just for the C of E, but for the church in Europe generally, where the word "massive" usually only appears in headlines just before the word "failure." And more importantly, it was a powerful civic figure advocating for the oppressed.

I remember wondering on my way to the UK in 2019, "How on earth am I going to get an interview with this man?" That's too strong. I didn't wonder. I *knew* it wouldn't happen. But then, just my luck, he was preaching at Cranmer Hall, the nearby evangelical Anglican training college. Maybe I could catch a word with him, quote him in whatever I would write, catch a bit of celebrity, er, I mean episcopal wisdom, in a bottle.

I had an "in." I had heard Dr. Ruth Perrin speak of her research in progress on ministry in Anglican cathedrals. For reasons no one fully understands, choral Evensong is thriving in the Church of England. People who might "never go to church" still have a need for beauty in their lives, and some find it, in candlelight, the elegant English of the Book of Common Prayer, and a choir (often paid) singing beautifully. There is nothing to catch your breath like a glorious gothic space in the dark. Something *happens* in there. These services are especially full, of course, at Christmas. York Minster Cathedral, where Sentamu's throne is, seats some three thousand people comfortably. As England's second ecclesial city, York's cathedral is massive, built over the course of some 250 years in the Middle Ages, still presiding over the north of a country not now much interested in Christianity. So why are folks interested in a candlelight Christmas service? Perrin reported that the York Minster was full. They had to open a second, unplanned candlelight service at another church nearby.

This is not the image that churchly observers in North Americans have of the church in England. We imagine only great buildings sitting empty. Here a great building was past fire code and another great building filled to the gills too. What's happening?! David Goodhew, the expert on church growth in this country, writes of cathedral worship as the high church success story in the C of E. If Alpha and HTB are filling churches down South with a more evangelical and charismatic expression of worship, and Fresh Expressions are launching countless mini-churches, cathedral worship and choral evensong are growing in a high-church way. Much, much less work has been done on this side of the ledger (Perrin's is in progress). Evangelicals know how media works and tell their stories well in video and song-writing and church planting and with extravagant funding. To speak overly broadly, liberals and high church folk do none of these things naturally. They are slightly allergic to tales of church growth, fearing it will seem tawdry, manipulative, and they are often right. And yet, of course, *someone* spent money to build those magnificent buildings, to train those musicians and choristers, to design liturgical architecture that would evoke awe. The Tractarian movement in the C of E in the 1800s reacquainted itself with the ancient church's legacy in this country. The "success" of this expression of worship today, and its massively under-sold story, is no spontaneous accident. It is one of the treasures the Church of England stewards, occasionally rediscovered and noticed anew. While in the UK, I heard often of the effort to launch events around Anglo-Catholic church growth. The thing is, this wing of the church doesn't "launch" "events." They go to church. "Mass" some of them call it.[3]

This would be my question to Sentamu. "Your grace: I hear that your cathedral was filled to overflowing on Christmas, that someone had to open another church to hold all the people, why is that?"

"One reason is the minster," he says. I'm sure he's right, but this is irrelevant. Many magnificent gothic buildings sit empty year-round. "We have an excellent choir," he offers as a second reason. This is also true, I'm sure, and equally irrelevant. Choral music has its fans, but not three thousand of them on the same night. There are other reasons, I don't doubt, that also tell partial truths. A residually Christian place still has people who go to church once or twice a year to make "Gran" happy. There are not a few tourists in there anytime the doors open. Another key reason is the one that he, of all people, cannot name. It's *him*. He's a magnificent preacher, a significant public figure. I went to church *that very day* just to hear him, and I'm sure I'm not alone. All of this is obvious and unstated and unnecessary to state. And irrelevant to explaining an overflowing Minster on Christmas.

I offer a third, one that warms his heart I think, if I can put it in Methodist terms: "One hallmark of your ministry is an openness to signs and wonders. Can that be part of it?"

"Yes, I think so," he responds, with more of an English accent than I expected of a man born in Uganda (he draws out his "o"s: "saooo . . ."). In one way, he is not as tall as I expected in person—more Yoda than Gandalf. In another, he is taller. He gives off something like grandeur, not elegance so much as holiness. He tells me of a man who came to the minster from Germany, his heart broken at his and his wife's inability to conceive. Sentamu laid hands on him and prayed. The next year he came with his wife and a baby. The next year with another baby. Each year now they come with their several children (though not always a new one every year!), saying thanks. Sentamu believes in miracles, as he often makes clear. He has seen them.

3. John Henry Newman, pioneer of the Oxford Movement, wherever he is, is pleased. The question is, where?! Eamon Duffy's new biography is the gold standard: *John Henry Newman*. The exhaustive account is Ian Ker, *John Henry Newman*.

They are not his power, that would be magic. And they are not automatic and cannot be presumed. They are signs of the goodness of God.

I'm enough of a journalist to know this is when to ask the question, if ever. We've connected. It's natural. "Is there any way I could come and interview you . . . ." He tunes out the rest, I can tell. "I retire next year. The diary is crazy." Oh well, no harm in trying.

A week later I get an email from one of his assistants, inviting me on an evangelistic mission to Liverpool. More access than I ever asked for or could imagine. I say yes immediately, and soon we're off.

This is not a job. I was summoned—by the Archbishop of York.

Better than the way I'm *not* doing it

Sentamu originally trained to be a lawyer in Uganda. When Idi Amin came to power there, he was among those who resisted the dictator's inhumanity—not with arms, but with laws. Amin rallied indigenous Ugandan resentment of the Indian diaspora and its business acumen in East Africa and summarily expelled all Indians from Uganda. This was, of course, illegal and immoral. Sentamu could do something about the former. He protested his government's expulsion of Ugandan citizens. Then Amin did what tyrants and dictators do: he turned to extra-legal violence. Sentamu wound up in a prison cell, watching friends and colleagues beaten to death, and was beaten badly enough himself he assumed he would be next. "He was properly tortured," one of his staff tells me. He spent months in the hospital, and when he recovered, he left his life there and became a refugee to Great Britain. England took him in, and he retrained for a new profession, studying theology at Cambridge and eventually working as a chaplain there. He rose in the ranks of the Church of England, first to be a suffragan bishop in London, then a diocesan one in Birmingham before eventually being summoned by Her Majesty to York.

This origin story is crucial to Sentamu's ministry in York. David Goodhew explains in an interview: "For years he has been the most prominent black person in the United Kingdom." Not cleric—*person*. The four chief cabinet posts in Britain were not filled by a daughter or son of Africa until years after Sentamu held the office of Primate of England. Rowan Williams spoke with courage and conviction against Mugabe's repression in Zimbabwe, but a white Archbishop of Canterbury passing judgment played right into that dictator's hands: "British racists being British racists." Mugabe had no such easy defense against Sentamu's prophetic actions.

The other piece of the story is that Sentamu has suffered. There is a long tradition in the church of Christians being oppressed for speaking the truth to power. In the order of things, martyrs are the most highly honoured for their defiance of tyranny, but just after them are confessors. That is, folks who suffer, but survive, undoubtedly scarred, and so remade more deeply in Jesus' image. After the triumph of orthodoxy at the Council of Nicaea in 325 CE, the fathers of the church took turns reverencing the scars of the confessors: kissing mauled limbs and missing eyes. This is not just macabre fascination (though I confess to some of that myself). It is a sign of the kingdom of God sitting at odds with every kingdom of this world, and ultimately, in this world or the next, triumphing.

White Christians in the West may imagine themselves oppressed when someone smirks or writes a less-than-glowing tweet. This is—does it have to be said?—not persecution. By contrast, Sentamu possesses an unending reservoir of credibility. He has suffered "properly." It's enough to make one reconsider one's easy alliance with the state, the market—forces that still wield deadly power, but seem entirely satisfied that we Christians pose no threat.

The cutting up of the dog collar on television shows another facet of Sentamu's ministry: he has a feel for the prophetic public action. That most well-known example is not the lone example. While I am with him on mission in cavernous Liverpool Cathedral, he reads a famous Lenten passage from the Bible: "Rend your hearts, not your garments" (Joel 2:13). By calling it a "famous" passage, I mean professional religious types have all heard it, preached it, considered it, and are now bored by it. That was true for me until Sentamu got hold of the passage. He took with him into the pulpit a purple clergy shirt, sign of episcopal power and authority. He said very little. He just acted. He held the shirt up, and ripped it. The tear reverberated through the cathedral—a familiar sound in a place we'd never heard it. He took his time. Rip. Rip. Rip. Rip. Rip. Then he let the two sides of the now divided garment float to the floor from his pulpit's elevated height.

Sentamu didn't talk his illustration to death, as I would be tempted to, making it a patronizing children's sermon, or otherwise drowning the newborn image in the murky pool of moralistic voiceover. He let the action linger. I'll never forget it.

Several of us, his "team" on the mission, asked him later: had he done that before? Never. Had he planned that in advance? It was more of a whim. Was it an old shirt?! One he was nearly done with anyway? No! he laughed. A perfectly good shirt! Here he is in line with the biblical prophets. Jeremiah smashed jars. Ezekiel laid on his side for a year and ate food cooked over dung. Jonah wandered into an enemy's city preaching a sermon without good Anglican taste: "forty days and you'll be dead!" This is biblical preaching, done with one's whole person. And wardrobe.

Just to name the obvious, not every illustration works so well. They can come off as more stunt than prophetic action. He turns several times to an illustration with a flashlight (called a "torch" in Britspeak) where he has a child come and try to turn it on, it won't work, he opens it, it's full of rubbish, which the child removes, and the flashlight works. By the fifth or sixth time he pulls out the flashlight I'm rolling my eyes (did I do that out loud?). It's a children's sermon, it works ok in church, but not in public, and *requires* being talked to death. He has a congregation turn around in our places to illustrate repentance, but of course to repent is to turn 180°, not the 360° we have to turn to see him again. These illustrations run the risk of being trite, "cheesy" as we say in America, "naff" as they say in the UK.

And that's the point. Sentamu is willing to risk all those judgments, which he surely has heard muttered by his fellow English when they thought they were just out of his hearing. I hear another pastor joke to colleagues about the eleventh commandment of the church in England, "Thou shalt not be naff." It is an inevitable risk if one is trying *anything*. The eyeroll, the patronizing cluck of the tongue. The first minority in any position has had to endure the disgraceful inference that he or she is "only" there because of their status as a non-white-person. Don't think for a minute Sentamu is naïve to this. He uses the power that his office brings while holding it lightly. And he uses is for *the* key thing the Church of England needs in the next generation of its life: for evangelism.

These British islands have been evangelized before. Every Christian church exists because someone took the risk of being an obvious outsider in a new place, entirely dependent on the hospitality of non-believers, opening their mouth and suffering, being mocked, or more simply, being rejected. Jesus preaches and demonstrates this himself: he sends out seventy in mission, then he sends out the forgiven and restored twelve as apostles, and he promises to return only when the whole world has heard. The church outside the West has a living memory of this missionary imperative in a way that churches grown fat and lazy intellectually (though thin in the pews) in North Atlantic countries do not. The great East Africa revivals of the early 1900s in places like Uganda are comparatively not that long ago. In the church where I serve, it is often implied, or outright stated, that evangelism is necessarily "just" colonialism, the faith in the poor Jew extra-judicially murdered by an empire turned into a cudgel for white male capitalistic dominance and repression of racial and religious minorities. Sentamu isn't having it. We've already seen the immense integrity he carries in the wounds on his body. And he has put them to use making this claim unmissable: the church must evangelize England again. And everywhere else as well.

Anglicans in Canada and Episcopalians in the United States were some of the first to tell me the story of the evangelism of the British Isles this way: Pope St. Gregory the Great saw slaves in Rome who impressed him with this odd fact: they were white, their hair blond, their eyes blue. Asking, he learned they were "Angles." Not just Angles, but angels, he said, in an alliteration that still works in English. Gregory sent the future Augustine of Canterbury to evangelize what is now the South of England. A pagan king just happened to have a Christian wife. He listened, gave Augustine permission to build a church, he converted, his subjects, having little choice in the matter, followed suit, and there is now one of the great churches in the world in Canterbury, though Augustine's heirs fear that telling the story the way I just have can turn into white supremacy and racism. It often has in modernity. Add a scientific revolution on top of the superiority in most cultures' stories and you have Britannia ruling the waves, singing how they "never never never will be slaves." Other people can, that's fine. Packed in the hulls of English ships, sent to living hells in the Caribbean and US South in exchange for rum and sugar, the "sweet" taste of death.

Here's a question: where'd that Christian queen come from?

Christianity was not new to these islands with Augustine or Gregory. It had come centuries before. When Christianity in Rome became aligned with state power and then inseparable from it, monks protested with their bodies. They left. Some went to the desert in Egypt and Palestine and Syria, seeking places where Christian faith was still costly. Poverty, chastity, and obedience became their cross. Some went farther away, seeking the same. The missionary imperative that St. Paul drives in the New Testament as he seeks to preach all the way at the end of the known world (Spain, on his map) keeps going. To notice that history, and position oneself within it, is to be a catholic Christian. Monks arrive at the end of the world, completing Paul's desired journey. Little islands that dot the edge of what is now Ireland had Christians living and praying there as far back as we can discern. Those little islands were their "desert." The world learned of these islands from *Star Wars: The Force Awakens* and *The Last Jedi*. Skellig Michael, where Luke Skywalker hid himself in the films, was the inhospitable home of Christian monks before Gregory or Augustine were born. By centuries. They prayed, met God, and did what Christians are commanded to do: they offered hospitality to whatever strangers were hardy enough to find their way there. They preached the gospel by word and deed. They communed with nature. They sought not vain worldly power but peace with people and creation. Some who tend their story speak of "Celtic Christianity"—a label I had come to loathe as synonymous with nature worship and Catholic-bashing. I was wrong. Irish monks bashed no one, nothing, except their own sins.

Some came to what is now Iona, some came to what is now Lindisfarne—then unimaginably remote islands, now tourist meccas. Some have names we know, like Aidan, Hilda, Caedmon, Etheldreda, and in the Northeast of what is now England, one Cuthbert of Lindisfarne. That's *Bishop* of Lindisfarne to you, thank you very much. He wanted to pray, and as folks heard of his healing powers over nature and sin and disease, they came. He left. He did not want fame, he wanted to pray, to be with God, and God's most gentle creatures. The irony of those who leave is that people follow them, and the fame they flee finds them. He was prevailed upon by King Oswald of Northumbria to become Bishop of Lindisfarne. The desert fathers say "flee from women and bishops"—they should've added kings. Cuthbert did not want to take the job, and after a year or so they let him flee again back to island remoteness and solitude. You'll hear the rest of the story in chapter 4—the most impressive parts of Cuthbert's ministry happened *after he died.*

As someone said, the past is a foreign country. They do things differently there.

Evangelism can happen without violence. It has happened peacefully before in the North of England. Sentamu, inspired by these stories, set out to do something radical: to imitate them (the peace-filled ones that is, not the conquering ones). He set out on foot across Yorkshire for six months in 2015–16, slightly south of where Cuthbert still lays in Durham, traveling some 1,800 miles on foot. "God said, three times, 'on the road,' so I went," for six months. He met people in shops, in public squares, people in need of healing, and good news. "Jesus did not come to bring religion," Sentamu often says. "He came to bring life, in all its fullness." That's good news. This is where Sentamu's own personal touch comes in: he is magical with people; funny, compelling, encouraging. He prays with fellow believers and tells of oneness with God and others and creation with those who do not believe (yet). And some came to believe. Some were healed. "Miracles happened," one member of his staff tells me. This being the Twitter age, and 75,000 people at least potentially looking in, the stories were told on social media. And being Archbishop of York carries the privilege (and burden) of being in charge of all the dioceses in the North of England. He summoned his fellow bishops to go on retreat at Lindisfarne, and after praying in the ruins of Cuthbert's monastery, he suggested all the bishops go on pilgrimage in one another's diocese. They would call them "missions." Local churches would organize events, as Billy Graham's pre-crusade volunteers once labored away for years in obscurity before the famous evangelist showed up. This would not be just the bishop in his or her diocese. All the bishops would come. And these events would not be one-offs, but new initiatives that could be ongoing once supercharged by the bishops' presence. Folks would have an excuse to invite neighbours. A step beyond debating evangelism is . . . doing it. Sentamu would lead. His church would follow. All the way to Liverpool, where I joined in, now near the end of these missions and of Sentamu's tenure.

It would be, in short, all the glory of Anglicanism: broad, open, inviting, with all the energy of evangelicalism: exciting, insistent, vibrant. What could go wrong?

Former Archbishop of Canterbury Michael Ramsey had an allergic reaction to Billy Graham coming to England. So he did what academically trained, master's degreed, and PhDd churchmen do when evangelism comes up. He critiqued. Ramsey, also a former Bishop of Durham, where he retired and is still beloved, came around on Graham to some degree. Graham's brother-in-law, Leighton Ford, reports to me Ramsey's concession, "I like the way Graham is doing evangelism better than the way I'm *not* doing it." Anybody can talk evangelism to the proverbial death by a thousand papercuts. Some want to defend its importance. Few want to do it. Fewer still do it well.

Sentamu does it well. He has put his body on the line before. When I ask him privately about his torture, he calls it "nothing, compared to the man on the cross."

I have argued many times that Christians must do evangelism again, however awkward it may feel. I have noticed in England that when I see Christian street preachers I roll my eyes. When I see Muslims in the street offering me literature, I smile before not accepting a Qur'an. Hypocrite. Go and be brave. I have done evangelism cold-calling before, and felt really, really stupid. I was converted at a Baptist camp that I can't now send my own kids to—too much talk of hell and the rapture, meant to scare the kids into the loving arms of Jesus. It's not just embarrassing, it's wrong; it's not good news for most of the world God creates and dies to save. I took refuge from evangelicalism at its manipulative worst by joining a mainline church and getting as educated as I could before there was no more education to be had. And suddenly I'm on the streets of Liverpool, a city I do not know, holding little booklets explaining the gospel, as a bishop in a purple shirt with a megaphone at a city square squawks that God loves people. It's Ash Wednesday and we are distributing "ashes to go." And no one is coming. I am standing there with a box of booklets, feeling more self-conscious than I ever have (which is saying something). One great Catholic scholar of the twentieth century is reputed to have said "I am required to believe there is a hell. I am not required to believe there is anyone in it." I now have incontrovertible counter-evidence. This street evangelism in Liverpool is *hell*. And someone is in it. *I* am.

At another event on the Liverpool mission, we gather on a beach, as a notably older congregation sings "Shine Jesus Shine." I remember my evangelical megachurch as a teenager saying the song had been overplayed and was being retired from the song rota. That was in 1990! The beach event outside Liverpool was evangelism for church people to reassure themselves they are still doing evangelism. It has no affect on anyone not already inside the camp.

One thing it has meant to be mainline in North America is to be *not*-evangelical. More of us come from evangelical origins than you would think from the vehemence of our denunciation. Some have been scarred, not just embarrassed. Others have been women. Or gay. Or divorced. Or otherwise disqualified in some way in contrived acts of meanness. Wounded people found refuge, and maybe the saving of their life, among Christians who were kind instead of mean or cruel or stupid. The mainline church assumed it would never have to toot its own horn. But now we're going away. The money and the people are gone. And we are panicking. So some of us take to the streets. And we find, to our surprise, that the streets are a hard place to talk about Jesus. I wince as one bishop, now another (not Sentamu, whether out of wisdom or because of a cold he's nursing is not clear), blasts away on a megaphone at passersby just trying to get to lunch. Sure, they're saying nicer things than the loonier people, but no one is listening. This is evangelism done badly. As if we remember when we've seen it done badly and then try to imitate it as badly as we can. Sure, we don't mention the untrue parts: whole classes of people whose certain banishment to hell we will delight in. But we are still religious people on bullhorns (what the Brits call megaphones). If we have taught England anything, it is that these people are *very bad*. And now, whether out of panic or misplaced enthusiasm, we is they.

"I'm not sure Ash Wednesday is a great place to start with the gospel," one team member muses afterwards. Others report successes: some people took ashes. In a heavily Catholic city like Liverpool, there are lots of Catholic people who have fallen away from the life of the church for one reason or other, but they miss some of it. Ash Wednesday is the only day we ask all baptized people to *look* visibly Christian, like Muslim women in hijabs or Jewish men in their headgear. I am comforted noticing that others with signs are also out. Pax Christi has just protested a nuclear submarine. Good for them, I feel, standing up for what they think is right. Some other group of more fundamentalist Christians has signs about hell. Less good for them, I think. Yet another batch of protestors has rainbow flags, pushing for inclusion. I smile at them too. Some man is following us around with a cane and a frock coat and top hat, like he just walked off a stage somewhere. Is he with us or against us or just a bystander? He's undoubtedly weird. Here we are, all us visibly identifiable crazies in the square, pushing our views on folks ignoring us.

Alasdair MacIntyre says that protest is the prototypically modern form of speech. It is not an argument. It seeks not to persuade, but to emote. More recently we have come to call this "virtue signaling": we are reassuring our "side" that we are still on side, and this is partly accomplished by pushing the other side away. That's what the signs say. Meanwhile the shopping behemoths on either side of us at Paradise (!) and Church Streets (!!) shout to hawk their wares, silently with multi-story adverts, and less silently with commercials we can't cut off on our phones. They are in our faces in all public places, and we have all adjusted and come to accept them. Somehow religious people's messages are unwelcome, but Marks & Spencer's are normal.

This is also evangelism done badly.

That's better than evangelism not done at all. But only if evangelists learn from the experience and adjust their approach accordingly. As I stand there, miserably critiquing, I remember that this is why I'm here. I was asked to wear a clergy collar and work the crowd, passing out booklets, praying with people moved by what they are seeing. I would rather melt back into the crowd and join their avoidance of the whole scene and critique in safety. The church once built these streets and named them things like "Paradise" and "Church." Now we can't even get a hearing on a corner we once owned. Except from religious leaders in collars, photographers paid to record their presence, and fellow weird people and freaks.

It's not the first or last time Jesus draws only strange people to himself, and only in strange ways.

What's your Jerusalem, Judea, Samaria, and the ends of the earth?

In the book of Acts, just before he ascends back into heaven, Jesus announces the apostolic mission that his followers will undertake after the descent of the Holy Spirit. They will preach the gospel and be his body in all places, starting in Jerusalem, then Judea, next Samaria, and on to the ends of the earth (Acts 1:8). Christians have often taken this as a frame for the theology of mission. The church is to do ministry where it already is (Jerusalem), among its own people and nearby neighbours (Judea), among enemies and outcasts (Samaria), and in every other place on and beyond the edges of its knowledge as well. Acts 1:8 can be a frame for understanding the church in the North of England (Liverpool is actually in England's Northwest; much of the rest of this project is focused on the Northeast, but bear with me). Like lots of magisterial Protestant churches in Europe and North America, the C of E does good ministry within the walls of churches (Jerusalem), within affiliate institutions such as schools (Judea). It struggles to name any enemies at all. And it grows deeply anxious in discussion of going to the ends of the earth. It is a clarifying question for any church: who is represented by each of these circles radiating out from Jerusalem? If "churches that intend to grow tend to grow," we must attend to where we're growing, and with whom.

First, Jerusalem. While on pilgrimage with my fellow Pharisees in Liverpool, I am impressed at how good Christianity can be within the walls of the church. Rowan Williams was once asked what could provoke interest from him in any of the claims of the "new atheists." He suggested they produce a work of comparable beauty to Dante's *Divine Comedy*. Having heard Gregorio Allegri's *Miserere* in Liverpool Cathedral, I can understand his comment.[4]

Allegri wrote the work for Holy Week in the early 1600s, based on Psalm 51, King David's great psalm of repentance: "Have mercy on me, oh God, according to thy unfailing love." Upon hearing the work, the pope supposedly insisted it only ever be sung in the Sistine Chapel. I respect this. The most beautiful piece of music should be played in the world's most beautiful place of worship. And so it stayed, until a century and a half later, when Mozart heard the work, then went and wrote it down from memory. It was soon produced everywhere, and even the pope of his time praised Mozart's work of popularization.

In Liverpool, a boys' choir sings the work for us on Ash Wednesday. The *Miserere* includes a note so high it can only be sung by a few professionals or really, really gifted angels. The choir in the cathedral has a few singers positioned so high in the building's rafters that when they hit the note, I have trouble telling which it is. Wait, they're behind us? Above us? From the heavens? In our midst? That note for me is like Williams' comment on the *Divine Comedy*. Its beauty is enough to make you believe that all this Christian stuff might all be true. Not that there is no ugliness in the world, or that you forget it, even for a moment, or that unbelievers can't produce beauty—God is not stingy with divine gifts. But all people desire beauty.

---

4. Just for the record, I don't care at all about "classical" music. I was more impressed meeting Paul McCartney's cousin.

Is that just mass human collusion in a meaningless delusion? Or was that desire put in us by some One, for some reason?

On another occasion we visit Liverpool Parish Church, a very active congregation with high sacramental proclivities in the heart of the great city, near its port. That port was once bustling with Irish migrant workers whose arrival brought historic divisions between Catholics and Anglicans to town with new force. But in this case, Anglican and Catholic bishops befriended one another, working hard for reconciliation, leading the way for the service I attend. The Catholic bishop is there. Nearly every Anglican bishop alive, it seems, is there. The Methodist circuit steward is there. Such ecumenism is a glimpse of faith as it should be, enabled by the non-sacramental nature of the gathering. Ashing is not a sacrament, so Christians of all stripes can be told we're dirt together. Sentamu preaches, of course, and speaks of the woman caught in adultery in John 8. He hardly has to mention the differences in the room: Catholic, Protestant, male, female, celibate, married, gay, straight. Sentamu spreads the healing cloak of the gospel over all of them: Jesus writes on the sand, recording, as some in the ancient church once speculated, the sins of each one. They are in sand, Sentamu adds, so Jesus can erase them all. Many use this passage to quote Jesus' words, "Go and sin no more." But we have no authority to say that to anyone. Only Jesus can separate anyone from sin. Our job is only to bring our friends to Jesus and leave them with him: "He knows what to do." We come forward for ashes, that rare liturgical event that sacramentally divided Christians can join in together.

Pondering this sermon, waiting to go forward for grit on the brow, I look, and the new Bishop of Warrington, Beverly Mason, is bathed in light. It streams in at that hour through the window under which she imposes ashes. She looks haloed, resplendent, an image of the Holy Spirit herself. I mention this vision to her later, and she tells me how powerful it was to dispense ashes and tell strangers they are dust and to dust they will return. "I said, 'turn away from sin and be faithful to Christ,' and they nodded, as if to say, 'Ok, that's a good idea.'" This is Christianity in gestures more than words; in visions, not mere ideas. We do it really, really well in church buildings. And even just outside our buildings: Bishop Bev excuses herself from our conversation and crouches down to speak with a beggar on the sidewalk. She seems perfectly natural not rushing past with a coin or a look of pity or aggressive avoidance (my preferred tactics). She bends low, and really *sees* the person, as Christians are commanded to do. Whatever she said or did next was not for me to hear or see—it was for the beggar and the bishop alone.

Second, Judea. The church performs Christianity well in schools, a way that hardly seems possible in North America, but seems so normal in the UK that folks are surprised when I tell them I've never seen it before. UK schools mandate Religious Education (RE), which seeks to inform students of all the religions practiced here. And I did say "mandate." I remember a legal battle over whether my high school in the US could offer a non-required religious *elective*. Many schools in the UK are founded and often still affiliated with the Church of England or the Roman Catholic Church (my Methodists have a few too, but not many). Bishop Paul Bayes of Liverpool tells me that for all the C of E's troubles, they still have some twenty-seven thousand people in worship in his diocese week to week, and some thirty-three thousand students in schools. Catholics in Liverpool are twice as numerous. A vicar in a parish is often pastorally responsible for a school, in addition to his or her congregation. So there is a natural "in" for priests to be present, to "loiter with intent," as folks tell me, to minister to the staff and administration. They cannot proselytize, and they do not, but they do build relationships of trust between church and school. When Archbishop Sentamu visits schools in Liverpool, they roll out the red carpet: special assemblies, visits to classroom, local photographers present, the chance to tell his story, even pass out literature, right there in class. I can hardly believe what I'm seeing. Neither can his team. A former teacher says, "I could never have gotten away with this." He's not "proselytizing." He is sharing his perspective. Everyone can do that in RE.

This can help or hurt the faith, of course. One really efficient way to kill a faith is to study it—splaying it open on the autopsy table to cut up its insides rather than watch it alive and in its native habitat. I watch students from an RE class at the Ash Wednesday service at Liverpool Parish Church where Bishop Bev was illuminated. Do they see what I see? They are there, but they haven't been prepared for any of it, presumably being taught by instructors as uninformed about Christianity as Christian clergy once were about Islam (and maybe as hostile). I notice through the whispers that one knows more than another. She points to a place in the service bulletin and says, "This is where they think the bread becomes the body and blood of Christ." The other student is genuinely baffled by this. She asks the right question, maybe the only question:

"How?!"

One could tell the whole history of Christianity in all its glory and all its sordidness in response to that question. I can't resist at this point. I have to interrupt. I'm wearing a collar in a church—when else are they going to hear an answer to this that comes from a believing perspective?

"We don't know," I say, trying to gloss the word "mystery." "But it's cool, though, right?" I go forward. They do not. I wish they would come with me. The Lord Jesus is sharing himself with his people, all his people, whether we believe or not yet. This desire to commune with others and with Jesus is evangelism. They don't come with me. Maybe one day?

The bishop's team rejoices as we leave one school. Christians there had been praying for the chance to establish a Christian Union—Britain's equivalent of InterVarsity Christian Fellowship.[5] The school could hardly invite the Archbishop of York and then say someone else cannot have a Christian organization. The story I hear Sentamu tell more than any other is of the friend of his father's who told him about Jesus Christ. Sentamu was born prematurely and was often sick as a child. A physician told his father that if John lived to be ten years old, he could expect a normal life span. The tenth birthday bash was a blowout celebration of new life, even greater than a normal birthday. And yet more life came. Sentamu learned that day from his father's friend that Jesus wanted to be his friend, that he could befriend him in turn. I hear him work this story into every single Q&A session in Liverpool. Who's the most famous person Sentamu has met? (expecting a story about the royal family or Elton John perhaps?): Jesus Christ. The greatest achievement in his career? Meeting Jesus Christ. The best day of his life? Meeting Jesus Christ. Whether religion does more harm or good in the world? Well, let me tell you of when I met Jesus Christ, . . . Sentamu has a genius for being sure he bears witness to his faith at every single gathering. Not to religion in general, as might be expected in more polite settings: "Religious people scare me," he often says. But to the new life that Jesus brings.

And need I say this? None of this would happen in a public school in the US or Canada.

Of course, Judea can be a place of pain as well. The church has a long history of anti-Judaism, especially pronounced in the Middle Ages, re-erupting in modernity at times. There were medieval cults to "saints" supposedly ritually murdered by Jews here in England, struck from the modern calendar of course, but the scars remain. Jewish people harmed or killed in reprisal for such scurrilous fabrications cannot be brought back. Such historical events are often left ignored. As a preacher I bring up the church's tradition for edifying stories, not miserable ones. But the whole gospel starts with a call, from John the Baptist, to repent! If any people can lead the way in repenting, it should be the church of Jesus Christ. Sentamu has shown this. He and rabbi Jonathan Sacks visited a cemetery desecrated by pro-Nazi

---

5. Sentamu's ecumenism extends even to Christians more evangelical than Anglican—he has participated in baptismal services for non-Anglicans, begging canon law questions. He seems delighted to confuse the lawyers.

sympathizers before World War II, praying together, on the way to its reconsecration. Sacks has told synagogues that having the Archbishop of York visit the Chief Rabbi of Great Britain to learn about Sabbath observance is a genuinely new thing, in a world often convinced there can be nothing new under the sun. Sentamu and a rabbi colleague journeyed together to the site of a massacre of Jews in York in 1190, one seeking forgiveness, the other indicating that York is a good place for Jews to live in again. It is hard to imagine who would lead in such pilgrimages of penance if not a church leader like Sentamu. It took a church to do such serious harm. It takes a church to do such serious repentance.

There can be danger here in Judea too, of course. Often the church gets the penalties of establishment without the benefits. When headlines announce that the church apologizes for this or that, the perlocutionary effect of such an announcement is to reconfirm the public's assumption of the church's bigotry: "there go the bigoted Christians, doing bad things as they always do." But those acts of violence were perpetrated by whole societies, not just Christians, but *all* of England—government, business, education, the courts—the works. And all of England is appropriately horrified at them now.[6] The church, in claiming to repent on behalf of all people, may be overstating other English people's sense of guilt. Most of us, facing outrages from centuries ago, do not recoil in personal horror. *We* here, breathing now, didn't do it. Nobody we're related to did either, going back nearly a millennium. Lillian Daniel's book title proclaims that she is done apologizing for a church she doesn't belong to.[7] The United Church of Christ is not now guilty for its pilgrim forebears burning witches in the 1600s. These apology tours can result in what I call the "sacrament of feeling vaguely shitty." What *are* people supposed to do about it? Yet we claim the spiritual treasures of the past very quickly. We are still heirs to the financial largesse of years past, including property ill-gotten, by these and other means. Others suffer from the loss of what could have been eras of prosperity. Sentamu and other church leaders are right to name our neuralgic points of history. But for the purposes of this book, it is hard to imagine such constant penitence *growing* a church—and so may show the limits of desiring growth. It may, however, be required of ministry done well in Judea—the larger neighbourhood, and indeed among our Jewish elder siblings in faith.

---

6. There are, of course, racist and neo-Nazi groups in England, as there are always crazy people on fringes. The internet amplifies their voices. They are not influential here, though similar groups have gone from the fringe toward the centre at other times in history, as some are now in central and eastern Europe.

7. Lillian Daniel, *Tired of Apologizing for a Church I Don't Belong To*.

Third, Samaria. Who are the Church of England's *enemies*? The Church owns and runs thousands of ministries of mercy throughout the country, doing work that anyone short of social Darwinists would have to applaud. Anglicans do ministry with refugees, migrants, and asylum seekers, as we will see in chapter 7 on the C of E's welcome to Farsi-speakers. The people ignoring our evangelical efforts in the square are not enemies any more than they are enemies of Nike or Pax Christi—they have no opinion, they're just trying to get into the store, man! Yet the New Testament was largely written from jail. It was written for people on their way to jail, or worse, to execution. There is a deep binary in the New Testament between good and evil—the powers and principalities are defeated by Christ, but his final victory is yet to come. Meanwhile, as the hymn says, "mid toil and tribulation, and tumult of her war, she waits the consummation of peace forevermore." Stanley Hauerwas makes this clear in his lecturing and preaching: "No enemy, no Christianity." Its fundamental shape is warped out of recognition.

Against whom is the Church of England fighting?[8]

At one school assembly, the Archbishop was the keynote speaker for a celebration of an anniversary of the school's founding. In some cultures, a religious leader would turn up for such ribbon-cutting events, or a local politician. In western Canada we often have a dignitary from the local indigenous tribe to come and sing a welcome. Sentamu is both a religious leader and a politician, and even more importantly in our day, he's a celebrity. So he dons a purple alb, originally made for his first pilgrimage in York, and comes to give the keynote. Other schools in town bring their choirs, each of which sings a song. Some are sort of religious. Some are mostly not ("Let it Be"). The event starts late, as the Archbishop's team was scrambling to make our third or fourth event of the day. The students sit in rows, dressed smartly in their school uniforms, remarkably quiet and well-behaved. Then there are the speeches. The leader of this year's class. The president of that club. The head of this organization. The something of somewhere else. Someone designed this event based on some memory of what religion was supposed to feel like, mediated from memories of their grandmother or descriptions of Victorian-era churchgoing. Sit still. Be quiet. Do nothing. Important people are talking. I feel myself melting into my chair out of sheer boredom.

---

8. Some more xenophobic politicians and parties in southern and eastern Europe have managed to blame "do-gooders" for immigration and win votes. I've not heard such claims in political discourse in Britain, blaming the church for increasing immigration. Jason Horowitz, "In Matteo Salvini's Italy, Good is Bad and 'Do-Gooders' Are the Worst," https://www.nytimes.com/2019/04/13/world/europe/italy-do-gooders-buonisti-matteo-salvini.html.

Gentle reader, take note: *I lead religious events for a living*! What do these kids think, who, to read the statistics, *never* go to church?

That it's boring and irrelevant. And who could argue against the patent conclusion? British people, maybe all people, love sticking it to the man, taking the piss out of someone. We, dear religious friends, *are* the man, the someone. The last thing anyone will want to do spending time in this assembly is look for more chances to spend time in similar company doing similar things. Unless they *really* like dressing up and being honoured on stage. Which is even more worrisome.

Sentamu's sheer charisma breaks through the dreariness, as he tells stories and jokes, illustrates with his signature invited participation ("look at this torch!"), and makes a point to speak about Jesus in an inviting way, despite the strictures. But this gathering reminds me that I only care about the church because of Jesus Christ and the promises he makes about it and to it. The church for its own sake, with all the pretention and mixed motives and patent hypocrisy, would send me right to the pub instead. It costs less and you leave happier.

But again, temporarily inflicted boredom is not enough to make an enemy, just a passive avoider.

The questions from high school civics and philosophy students provide more of a clue. Student: Does the House of Lords, un-democratically chosen through peerage or being chosen as a bishop, do enough to include non-Christians, LGBTQ people, people without privilege? Archbishop: Yes, the House should do more. But he's more worried about the democratically elected House of Commons on that score. Student: What does he make of the rash of anti-queer sentiment and legislation in his native Uganda? Archbishop: Yes, it is bad, and he wrote to the president and parliament of his home country to protest laws that would have made homosexuality a capital crime, and was not very popular back home for doing so. But this is a remnant of British colonial rule. Homosexuality was never illegal before the Brits came. The implication is clear—now that British people are demanding these previously British-demanded strictures be removed, their impatience is rich indeed. Sentamu tells of a previous Archbishop of Canterbury, Michael Ramsey, arguing before the Lords that homosexuality in the 1960s may be a sin, but it is not a crime. Student: should Britain open its doors to all asylum seekers? Archbishop: no, not all. Health care and social structure are chronically underfunded as is, and parliament is reluctant to raise taxes on well-off people, so the burden of offering ministry of mercy falls disproportionately on already-poorer communities in the North. Student: hasn't the Archbishop defended Britain's Christian heritage, with all its racist and colonialist baggage? Archbishop: yes, and there should be more Christians, and more Christianity, in politics. The UK is like a man who has climbed high on a ladder who then kicks the ladder away. How did Britain become the country it is, other than Christian faith?

The questions are polite, but there is a radical critique expressed here. The church is racist, sexist, homophobic, colonialist, obscurantist against science, and a promulgator of climate-science denial. As a preacher in the US, I often point out that people go on for the rest of their lives rejecting the version of the Christian faith they first learned when they were nine years old. That's untrue in England. No one learned anything when they were nine. Now they go on rejecting the version of the Christian faith they learned from a Ricky Gervais standup special on Netflix—a vile caricature that makes the new atheists seem charitable by comparison.[9]

Sentamu has often used his convening power, both as a bishop of the church and as a leading figure in the public eye, to lead in the wider world. As Bishop of Birmingham prior to his appointment to York, he founded a weapons amnesty program called Bringing Hope. The police couldn't do it, for those with illegal weapons aren't likely to bring them willingly to police. Only the church could wield the power to insist on no CCTV cameras. Bringing Hope saw more than ten thousand knives turned in and some thirty shotguns. (Thirty shotguns may not sound a lot if you're in the USA, but in the UK, where relatively few people own guns, it is quite a big deal.) He is far from alone. Former Bishop of Liverpool James Jones was several times in the public eye after disasters in his diocese. He chaired an independent panel investigating the Hillsborough football stadium disaster of 1989, in which police blamed Liverpool FC supporters for hooliganism to shift attention from their own negligence at crowd control. Soccer feels like a religion in England, for good or ill, but when nearly a hundred deaths and more than 750 injuries needed investigating by a source independent of the government, the police, or the victims' families, the country turned to an older religion still.

The establishment of the Church of England brings problems, no doubt. But it is hard to see who else in the country could have had this sort of symbolic and convening power to bring about healing.

9. Gervais is a popular repristination of the French Enlightenment quip that religion was born when the first fool met the first knave. I owe to Rev. David Day the observation that Gervais is much more influential than Richard Dawkins. Gervais glosses prayer in God's voice this way: "I know what you want, but I want you to beg for it. Grovel. Ok, I'll think about it." He mocks celebrity "thoughts and prayers" for victims of disasters: "Silly me, I just sent money."

Gervais speaks with the bitterness of a lover spurned—a child of faith at one point who felt betrayed that his family wouldn't tell him the truth, as they finally did about the tooth fairy and Santa Claus.

One Christian leader in Durham tells me that before his conversion, he assumed all Christians behaved like Westboro Baptist Church, which protests the funerals of American soldiers killed overseas, claiming these deaths are divine retribution for an overly gay-tolerant country. He didn't know that no Baptist church or association recognizes Westboro's validity. It's run by one family, filled with hate, to be sure, but no more indicative of what Christianity is as such than ISIS is of Muslims in general, except that ISIS is much, much larger.[10] But secular people genuinely don't know these distinctions, and we've given them little reason to care. In the UK this vague and imprecise and unfair "critique" is exacerbated by the Church of England's alignment with power. Look at those buildings. Look at those flashy meetings with royals. The Archbishop lives in a palace, with a chapel inside it bigger than most churches, and a staff befitting a prince more than a poor preacher of the poor Christ.

Anna Rowlands, a political theologian at Durham, blogs about meeting a man at a pub in Sunderland who is resentful of Muslims coming to his community.[11] They work for wages too low, they won't go to the pub to drink with people, they reject the things that make England great. No wonder this man votes for Brexit. The House of Bishops unanimously opposed Brexit, while two thirds of C of E church-goers supported it.[12] The bishops are out of touch *with their own churchgoers* politically, and they know it. How much more so with the man put out of a job at the pub in the Northeast? And you know those church properties pay no property taxes? Like the royal family they *get* our money *through* the government.

None of this is fair, of course. When secular people *see* religion, it is through the same screens that they see Trump, terrorism, drowning migrants in the Mediterranean, and increasingly angry talking heads fulminating about whose fault it all is. Fulminating back against the ignorance of this misperception only makes things worse. One former C of E publicity person says that when he worked for church communications they tried desperately hard for headlines other than "Church says no." Sentamu often gets more positive headlines: jumping out of airplanes to bring attention and money to healing wounded soldiers, cutting up dog collars, bringing

---

10. For a remarkable piece of journalism on Westboro, see Adrian Chen's "Unfollow: How a Prized Daughter of the Westboro Baptist Church Came to Question Its Beliefs," *The New Yorker*, 23 November 2015: https://www.newyorker.com/magazine/2015/11/23/conversion-via-twitter-westboro-baptist-church-megan-phelps-roper.

11. Anna Rowlands, "The Fragility of Goodness," *Journal of Missional Practice* (Winter 2017): https://journalofmissionalpractice.com/fragility-of-goodness/.

12. See here Gilles Fraser "How the Church Lost Its Flock over Brexit," *UnHerd* (23 November 2018): https://unherd.com/2018/11/church-lost-flock-brexit/.

a larger-than-life personality to spaces that are often deadly dull.[13] I watch in one school as he walks up to snickering older boys and high fives them, poses for selfies, and they run off shouting to their friends "I've just met the Archbishop of York!" Who? I don't know, that famous bloke over there. The best Sentamu can do, and it's a lot, is break through the expectation of sheer boredom and irrelevance and qualify as "one of the good ones," like a rare politician or football star or actor or mafia don who's a decent human being.

That's the C of E's enemy: a media-generated misperception, for which it bears only some responsibility, over which it has nearly no power. Modern liberal Christians fight against that false image with all their might, struggling to be inclusive of every "other" on the grid, denouncing fundamentalists in more strenuous terms than any secular person, advocating for justice with its remaining political might, trying above all to prove we're "not like the bad kind" of Christian. If the opponent were named so clearly—*bigoted Christians, whom we* really *don't like*—non-religious or anti-religious people might respond, "Good. Neither do we." We're a long way from evangelism or church growth here. This is rather a poor sort of "good news," more virtue signaling than evangelism, aiming at best for the milquetoast compliment, "Well, I guess if I went to church it'd be one like yours."

Perhaps then the enemy is simple ignorance. The students asking Sentamu hostile questions "know" about the vague impression of the church's misdoings, but not about its ministry of reconciliation. One can see why the C of E hires as much PR help as it can get. But PR itself is driven by vague impressions. Social media deals not in journalism, nor in headlines even, but often simply in images, especially those that draw outrage, and so clicks, and so advertising revenue.[14] Sentamu has 76,200 followers as of this writing, which is impressive, Paul Bayes 8,698. Ricky Gervais has 14.4 million. Rowan Williams, by contrast, is not on Twitter. Perhaps instead of trying to win, we concede, as desert monastics once did. But then who would bring healing to places like Liverpool after events like Hillsborough? Is Gervais available?

I am not suggesting that any person of good will could not lead a community in healing, of course they could. God has used a donkey, an enemy army, and could use a phone book or a dead dog if God wanted (Karl Barth). But the C of E's genius is that it takes responsibility for the whole of the country. "Every blade of grass in the UK" belongs to a parish, canon Simon

13. Martin Beckford, "Archbishop of York, John Sentamu, Performs Charity Skydive," *The Telegraph* (6 June 2008): https://www.telegraph.co.uk/news/2083754/Archbishop-of-York-John-Sentamu-performs-skydive.html.

14. See here Ben Myers and Scott Stephens, "The Discipline of the Eyes," in *The HTML of Crucified Love*.

Oliver told me. The church is called to pray and advocate on behalf of all affected parties in a disaster—not just for victims, but also perpetrators, not just soccer fans, but also for police and media and first responders. (One still cannot buy *The Sun* tabloid within the city limits of Liverpool, thirty years on—blaming the victims has a way of lingering in the memory.) The Bishop of Liverpool's office had done important reconciliation work across denominational faultlines before, helping Catholic and Protestant Irish migrants live in peace in Liverpool much earlier than the Good Friday accords allowed them to back in Ireland itself. Such credibility has to be earned over multiple generations and can be lost in a nanosecond. And comedians who offend for a living are not likely to earn it or keep it long.

Fourth and finally, the ends of the earth. The church does still have the ability to direct the public's gaze to places most of us ignore, especially places of pain and sorrow. Liverpool Cathedral hosts an art exhibit called Sudarios ("shrouds"), which features striking photos of women in Columbia who have seen family members brutalized or killed. The images fill the front entrance of the nave of the great space, and grief fills their faces, and suddenly one wonders about a part of the world and a set of political commitments that cause such suffering. The church physically will not let the eyes of those in her walls look away.

Another example. Liverpool was the site of a shocking, racially motivated murder in the mid 2000s, as a young black man named Anthony Walker was ambushed by two white men and killed. The church did what the church is supposed to do: stepped in and offered grace. Rev. Malcolm Rogers presided over the funeral, and Gee Walker, Anthony's mother, told the world she refused to hate the murderers—hate is what killed her son. She forgave. Media coverage was intense, awards were given. (Rogers was made a Member of the British Empire, and dedicated the award to Walker's memory.)[15] The world moved on.

The church did not.

Rogers and others got to wondering out loud what motivated the sort of hate that killed an eighteen-year-old man who should have had years of promise ahead of him. As a native Scouser (a reference to the local accent—Liverpudlians have great nicknames), Rogers knew his city was once very wealthy. But where did that wealth come from? Not surprisingly, as a port city, some of Liverpool's riches came from its participation in the Atlantic slave trade, with its triangle of death between Britain, Africa, and the Americas. He hadn't heard of this growing up in Liverpool. So he started

---

15. "Rev Malcolm Walker Dedicates MBE to the Memory of Anthony Walker": http://www.liverpool.anglican.org/index.php?p=2354.

a mission called the Triangle of Hope to raise awareness about where Liverpool's architectural and cultural largesse had found its economic footing. Partner dioceses in Ghana and Virginia join in to make youth mission trips to each others' regions, to explore systemic racism, and to remind the church of the systemic grace she also bears.

Here opponents of Christian mission can get quite loud indeed, especially within the church. We have agreed altogether too quickly and eagerly with the common claim of our cultured despisers that Christian mission is simply colonialism by another name, and a short step from cultural genocide. David Goodhew tells of the reaction of David Martin, one of sociology's most able proponents of secularization thesis—the view that as the West grows more and more economically and technologically advanced, religion must necessarily dissipate: "We didn't expect churches to agree with us!" Some of the most outspoken liberal bishops of the Church of England in decades past would themselves prognosticate that the church would be gone from British cities within a few years. Now the church is back in British cities, perhaps more confidently so in London than it's ever been.[16] And the ends of the earth have now come to us. The Nigerian Redeemed Christian Church of God has gigachurches ringing England's capital and (somewhat smaller) churches in the Northeast. We will look at Farsi-speakers in the Northeast of England in chapter 7.

John Sentamu presaged this sort of surprising reverse mission in his own life and person. While on mission, he offers a piece of exegesis from the book of Acts that I'd never heard before. Those gathered are principals and teachers from the school that had previously not granted permission for a Christian Union to exist on campus. Sentamu preaches in a teachers' lounge, perhaps to some of those very same decision-makers. In Acts 16, Paul went not to the synagogue first, as was his custom, but to a river, where he supposed there would be people praying, and he preached to the women there. These are, note, the "wrong" sort of people—gentiles—but also people of peace and prayer. And some responded. Lydia, a dealer in purple cloth, that is, a wealthy merchant, whose house becomes a hub in Philippi for the church's life and mission (Acts 16:14–15). On his way out, Paul is shouted down by a slave girl possessed by a demon—the most oppressed in society, to whom he brings healing (16:16–18). The church's origins are as a society for all people, from the wealthiest to the most excluded, from the least to greatest, the least to most educated, Jew and gentile alike. It was after this meeting that the school agreed to let a CU meet on campus. For the school is also trying to be a place of welcome and healing for all people.

16. Examples all from Goodhew's *Desecularization of the City*.

Whatever that is, it's not simply secular: a Christian archbishop retelling the gospel to a people who thought they'd heard it and thought better of it, but who might actually have never heard it at all.

Just when you count Christian faith out, put a stone in front of the tomb and consider it dead, it comes right back altogether new, with this odd, recurring, resurrectional habit. We do our best work when accounted the lowest. It can happen again, you know.

Patterns

How do churches generally learn from Archbishop Sentamu and the Church of England's missions in the north? One, Sentamu's pilgrimage and missions are an act of "traditioned innovation."[17] They reach back into the C of E's treasury and pull out something precious, dust it off, and deploy it for a new age. This act of traditioned innovation is quite literal: the bishops wander around the same geography that ancient northern saints did, trying to do the same sorts of things. When St. Aidan would meet a stranger he would ask if they were a Christian. If not, why not? If so, he would offer to pray a blessing. What sort of creative analogies could the church come up with to do something similar, but different? How can we travel over our area with greetings, questions, and blessings? Don't be too technical about it. The joke says that theologians are presented, in heaven, with a fork in the road: this way to heaven, that way to a seminar discussion critiquing the idea of heaven . . . what would it mean for your bunch to hit the road, meet others, and bless them?

Secondly, Sentamu brilliantly incorporates his own story into his evangelism. Some of this is intuitive. He cannot not be who he is, as a son of Africa, and adopted son of England, where he now serves and leads. Some of it is hyper-intentional, such as making sure he bears witness to the time he met Jesus at his ten-year-old birthday party. How do we draw on our own story in similar acts of witness? Some traditions, like my Methodists, have at times been practiced at this. Some traditions, like many Reformed, would be positively appalled—and for some good reasons! The gospel is big, capacious, cosmos-changing. We can't reduce it to the cramped contours of our own souls. Fair enough. But how has your soul, *as an object in the cosmos that God is redeeming*, looked different for Jesus' saving work upon it? And

---

17. Greg Jones coined this language and *Faith & Leadership* has developed it extensively here: https://faithandleadership.com/category/principles-practice-topics/traditioned-innovation

how, without seeming forced, can you bear witness to that in your life? In your congregation? Neighbourhood?

Thirdly, the use of Acts I give here is fairly conventional in Christian circles. Acts 1:8 is a map, with Jerusalem as those close to us, Judea as those farther out, Samaria as enemies, and the ends of the earth as, well, the ends of the earth. How do you identify each rippling circle out from yourself and your congregation? And how do you follow the Lord's command to evangelize in each place? Colonialism is evangelism that tries to control how people receive the gospel. Evangelism proper is giving away the gospel and relinquishing attempts to control its outcome (or even whether you will survive that act of witnessing or become a martyr!). The very act of clarifying who your Jerusalem, Judea, Samaria, and ends are can be enormously clarifying for you, your household, your church. Give it a go.

Fourth and finally, an image from Eugene Peterson.[18] He speaks often of the gospel wisdom to be found in natural phenomena, and drew lessons from a certain tree in Central America. The black sap poisonwood can attack a person's central nervous system just with casual contact, and can be deadly. The antidote to the tree's chemical attack is in trees just nearby it. Sometimes these antidote-providing trees *share the same root system* as the poison. So it is with the church. That place is dangerous. It is full of pharisees, sinners, in short, of people like us. It will harm you. But the cure is also close. Don't flee far, stay close, and find your healing there as well. Evangelism has often been poison, and has led to some of Christians' worst impulses. Do not flee. The antidote is near as well. Sentamu's ministry suggests the antidote is not evangelism ruled out, but evangelism done well, open-handed, no ulterior motive, just a conviction that a life or world filled with more of Jesus will be good news for all involved. How can you find the cure to evangelism amiss very near to the purported poison?

---

18. I take this from Dr. Julie Canlis, a theologian who studied under Peterson and remained a mentee in subsequent years, taken from the Abbey School at Newhaven Parish Church in Edinburgh, UK, 7 June 2019.

3

DURHAM CITY

Growing churches where churches can't grow

CONTRARY TO WHAT YOU'VE heard, the weather can be lovely in England. One particularly sunny day, I was walking down the hill into the city centre. The view below me was the one that led medieval crusaders, fresh home from a little adventure in regime change in the Middle East, to compare Durham to Jerusalem: full of hills, resplendent with spires, and that without the Muslims to kill. The sun radiated off anything bright, fresh after a rain. And a toddler holding his mum's hand on the pavement in front of me pointed to the spire of St. Nic's. "What's on top of that castle, mummy?"

I wanted to jump in. When else can a theologian be helpful? It's actually a church, not a castle. Second, it's a rooster. In the toddler's defense, it's hard to tell. All we could see was a splash of gold, as if Van Gogh's brush splotched it in. The rooster is an obscure reference. Most Christian minds go immediately to St. Peter's denial of the Lord, after which the cock crowed. It took some years and some digging by a friend pastoring a Reformed church to learn otherwise. The rooster became a symbol of the Reformed Church in France because its crow signals that the dawn is coming. The church exists to announce a new day dawning, illumining everyone. It's a resplendent image. Christianity is not a private benefit for its adherents. We announce a new world that no one can stop, slow down, or even hurry—one intended for the benefit of all people, not just its own members.

But the poor mother didn't know this. "That's a weathervane, dear."

We are several generations into post-Christendom in Britain. If you're middle-aged it's not just you who are ignorant about Christianity (no judgment implied in the word "ignorant": you just don't know anything about it). Neither does your mum and maybe your gran. In fact, from my time in Durham, I can say it's more likely your mum and gran are out on the town Saturday night, dressed in fewer clothes than that they would be if they were in church on Sunday. There may have been a day post World War II when most people went to church in Britain. James Woodward of Sarum College in Salisbury grew up in Hartlepool, once a thriving port city, now a down-in-the-mouth post-industrial town in the Northeast. In the 1980s, nearer to the beginning of his career, some 3.7 million people were attending Church of England congregations regularly in the UK. Now the figure is closer to one million, and may have slipped below seven figures. "I don't think it's *all* my fault," he jokes. Church leaders in the Northeast speak of the region between the Wear and the Tyne as the least church-going region in the country, making them some of the least-Christian places in Europe. Apparently several other parts of England claim the same dubious honour.[1]

One benefit of being in a post-Christendom context is that there is a wide mission field. The woman trying to raise a child is being asked questions to which she knows no answer, and can only bluff so long. Parenting is exhausting when you are well-resourced; when you are not . . . There is an absence in life without God, and sometimes we even feel it more keenly when we are failing at parenting, as we all do. One massive success in the Church of England over the last fifteen years has been Fresh Expressions, an effort to launch new forms of church beyond the forbidding confines of Sunday morning liturgy, about which we'll learn much more in chapter 7. As the church learns anew to go in mission to the places where people are already living their lives, rather than expecting people to find their way to us, one people to whom we go is struggling parents. Modernity may be described as an experiment in raising children with only one or two parents in a household, as opposed to the dozens of parents, grandparents, aunts and uncles in any traditional village setting. The results of this experiment are not promising thus far. One keystone to Fresh Expressions' success is called Messy Church. Parents bring their children for several hours of play, an activity around faith, an age-appropriate talk, and food. Parents join in rather than sending kids off to Sunday School, as in a previous generation, and children enjoy. Think of it as Sunday School without the boredom. The woman I saw that day would see her whole life improved with Messy Church in it, and she might even get a chance to meet some Christians and learn about God for herself.

---

1. So claims Martyn Percy in his essay "Paradox and Persuasion: Alternative Perspectives on Liberal and Conservative Church Growth," 75.

Rebuilding the walls

The "weathervane" belongs to a neo-gothic church in Durham's handsome walking downtown area.[2] That may not narrow things down very much, since there seem to be dozens of them. All stately, reaching toward the heavens, aflush with stained glass, replete with statuary outside and wooden beams inside. The architecture and decoration warm the heart of believers. They can chill the heart of non-churched people. What goes on in there? Am I welcome? Is anybody? One study of Church of England websites showed one phrase appearing repeatedly: "Join us!" To the uninitiate, it sounds like a pitch for money. Gyms, food delivery services, do-gooder organizations, magazines, and so on all ask you to join—and charge you through the nose and never let you leave. What we take to be warm and inviting others hear as menacing. Rev. Mark Miller, whom we will meet elsewhere in this study, says the first thing done to turn Stockton Parish Church around was to open the doors. Literally. Restaurants not on street level do poorly: people can't see in. What's it like in there? Can't tell? Move on.

Wearside Parish Church (WPC) has nothing to hide. The first time I ever saw a worship service there, in late 2017, the chairs looked to be overflowing out into the square. I wanted in precisely because there was no room. Contrast this with a stately, neo-gothic church elsewhere in the country. I had been in the place as a tourist and seen plaques to the visit of this monarch, the organ performance of that famous musician. Then I was strolling by right at 10 o'clock on a Sunday morning, when worship was due to start. A rector was out front to welcome people. But there were no people. He was stately, regal even in his robes and stole. They fluttered in the breeze—an arresting image for those strolling by. But none strolled in. He checked his watch, whether in frustration or resignation I could not tell. He turned and slunk inside for what could not have been anything but a dispiriting service.

WPC has undergone a rejuvenation of sorts in the last fifty years. If it had not, it would be as lifeless as the church above. But it has, and there is life there. The architect of that rejuvenation went on to be a well-published bishop in the C of E. Its longtimers still speak in glowing terms of the man who arrested the decline and put the place back on solid footing. You can still see the fruit of his work: this ministry, that liturgical change, the other

---

2. WPC in this chapter is the only church in this book I do not identify by name. I prefer as a reader to know where a specific place is, to look and check on the author's work. This sketch is a composite of several similar places in a variety of cities in the Northeast. What I observe here is true, then, but the specifics are scrambled and cobbled together somewhat.

innovation, a social benefit organization or two with international renown. He has regaled audiences with his success in books and lectures countrywide. Yet there is a problem. This former rector, whom we'll call John, still comes up in conversation at WPC entirely too quickly. He has not been present in the lifetimes of the college students present. He has not been present in the lifetimes of some of the college students' *parents*. Churches can be held captive to a previous generation's successes. This place seems stuck circa 1976. To an arch-traditionalist, it feels too "contemporary," too "evangelical." They just mean guitars are in use. To anyone not born in the 1940s, the music seems so old as to be nostalgic at best, gratingly antiquated at worst. "Thy Word" may have seemed cutting-edge in the 1980s, but it's not now, and it was never good enough to be worthy of "classic" status.

The building John inherited was, as the Brits say, "poorly." Stories are told of a guest luminary preaching away at WPC one Sunday when a piece of masonry crashed to the floor *during the service*! "Someone up there must not like what I'm saying," the perfect quip, was the preacher's response. No one was injured, but clearly the place needed some tending to. The church launched a building program and set about raising six figures. Members made sacrificial gifts, leading local citizens helped beat the drum for the campaign, and the building was restored. Every gathering for worship at WPC gives off cheerfulness. Brits are not nearly as exuberant interpersonally as Americans (in fact, as an expat in Canada, I can always tell when Americans walk into a room. The volume increases considerably). But they're friendly at WPC. It's hard to get out after the service without multiple introductions and invitations to coffee.

But a new day is needed. The church has halved in size from John's day to now. The service I visited with the full house is, unfortunately, an outlier. The church's bells seem to have a mind of their own—peeling at odd times of the night, as though the ghosts were celebrating a wedding. Part of WPC's problem, to put matters in crude, capitalistic terms, is competition. Durham is not a city with a great evangelical pedigree, and there are a dozen or more evangelical church plants of other denominations now that did not exist half a century ago. WPC calls itself an "evangelical" parish. That ought to mean that it has to actually evangelize people well. In reality, it seems simply to mean it doesn't celebrate the Eucharist very often (since that's what Anglo-Catholics do). All the clergy and retired clergy and students-in-training present from the university create another accidental problem. There's a kind of clericalism about. It feels as though one has to be in a collar, or preparing to wear a collar, to do Christianity "right." But of course clerical leadership is only there, biblically speaking, to equip and encourage the ministry of everybody else. Another vicar in the Northeast groused to me about WPC (and pastors everywhere do love to grouse about their peers), reflecting on its built-in advantages of location and heritage: "That church should have a thousand people in it."

It's trying. It has applied for a multi-million pound grant to become a "Resource Church," that is, a local hub of creative mission and ministry for the entire region. One legacy of being the establishment church in Great Britain is that the Church of England still has a little money. Lands once given to the church in tithes or offerings centuries ago still produce huge revenues. The Church Commissioners in London invest this money, and as long as those investments do well, the church has money to spend. In recent years the C of E has taken to spending not just the revenue produced, but some of the principle, on the argument that if it doesn't sell off some of the family silver, there will be no church left to support. The inspiration for resource churches is Holy Trinity Brompton, a gigachurch in London's trendy and crushingly expensive borough of Kensington.[3] HTB's Alpha Course has had an unimaginable impact on growing churches worldwide. As HTB grew and sent people into ministry, it noticed that Oxbridge colleges would turn them into semi-academics, not missionaries committed to church growth. So HTB did what one does: it started its own seminary. St. Mellitus College focuses intensely on missional church planting and replanting, and has had a huge impact in a short period of time across the UK, partly via online and hybrid education. Former Bishop of London Richard Chartres was willing to give a closed church building to HTB to be restarted in a sort of "church graft"—dispatching a few dozen people to relaunch a place from scratch. The problem is he ran out of buildings. Church growth has trended upwards in London for more than twenty years now, where 10 percent of people go to church. It sounds small, but compare it to 1 percent elsewhere in England.[4] In Canada we have seen a spillover effect, as St. Mellitus-trained ordinands come to fill empty buildings with life in decaying Canadian Anglicanism. Chatting with a friend here in Durham about the one-time hit BBC show *Rev*, about a struggling London parish, he said this: "Any idiot can grow a church in London."

Everything I said above could stand nuancing: The C of E has gobs of money in certain places for certain things but not everywhere and for everybody; St. Mellitus is a school for the whole Church of England, not just HTB; Archbishops of Canterbury do not have the power to direct money

3. I'm not sure a "gigachurch" is really a thing, but scholars tend to speak of megachurches as those with two thousand people or more in worship. By "giga" I mean a church approaching something more like ten thousand than a mere, trifling 2K....

4. See David Goodhew's *The Desecularisation of the City*. Jason Fout's book *Learning from London* chronicles this growth in London well.

the way I implied (the Reformation left the C of E like a great hulking ship in which the bridge has been destroyed—it's not only unclear who is at the controls, it seems there are no controls at all). Suffice to say, however, HTB and Alpha are two success stories in terms of church growth in a denomination starved for those. There are others (St. Helen's Bishopsgate in London has done similar church planting work in a more conservative, less charismatic vein; St. Thomas Crookes in Sheffield has as well, and there are others). The point for now is that if one has an idea for church revitalization, and one is Anglican, one can apply to the Strategic Development Fund and gain access to a seemingly endless reservoir of cash. When I asked Sam Wells, vicar of St. Martin in the Fields in London, about resentment over Resource Churches getting all the SDF money he said, "I always respond the same way: 'have you filled out an application? Funny enough, people who get the money tend to be the people who apply for it.'" I often notice a general sense that a church showing ambition, eagerness to grow, desire for a future with hope, has violated some sort of unwritten norm in England.[5] But WPC, with its evangelical pedigree and need for renewal, has a little ambition. And it has applied. Don't be surprised to see it in the news as the recipient of a grant with seven figures in it, part of tens of millions of £s in grants all over the UK from the SDF.

This is the sort of gift that sets non-Anglican English churches to grinding their teeth. Imagine what we could do with that sort of money! It's the sort of gift that can hurt the C of E's reputation also. Anglicanism has always been aligned with the upper classes in Britain (the Queen, the bishops, cathedrals, Oxbridge, even the military) and traditionally struggled with poorer people (British Methodism and then the Salvation Army slid into this vacancy for a short time each). Grants like these don't help the C of E's undeserved reputation for only caring about posh people. Even WPC could be harmed by the awarding of a grant. Folks hear of millions of pounds for a diocese or parish and don't notice—a grant award is spread over multiple years. It is divided among multiple projects in the diocese. Do the math quickly and you'll see WPC's share would be down to low six figures per year. That's tremendous—but it also has the adverse effect of making lay people ask, "well why do we have to give if we have all this cash now?" Of course, that grant is to fund *new initiatives*, taking little to no pressure off the regular operating budget. Other churches in town suspect they're sitting

---

5. Kate Fox, in her brilliant popular work of anthropology, *Watching the English*, argues that the English aren't so much atheist as apatheist. Bothering to care enough to call oneself an atheist requires more energy than most on this island can muster (484–546).

on shrink-wrapped bricks of cash they don't know what to do with. No opportunity is without challenges, and vice-versa.

The very concept of a resource church is compelling: dioceses don't grow or plant churches—thriving parishes do. Churches that struggle to maintain aging infrastructure (fifty years is a long time since the last major reno) and to pay priests and children's ministers and musicians rarely have money set aside for new projects. These investments allow them actually to take a risk, to invite someone new, to open the windows, to meet that mum and her child with grace, offering another image of Christian faith over against the monstrous varieties she sees on the news. David Goodhew, the key researcher of growing churches in England, preaches often that secularism fails to offer three things the gospel succeeds in offering: *purpose*, *pardon*, and *peace at the last*.[6] Such projects are a chance to bless not just the church, but the world outside those glass windows.

On a few recent visits to WPC I caught a glimpse both of its challenges and its opportunities. The church *looks* evangelical enough: "Jesus Christ is Lord" and "Abundant Life" are plastered on banners where the medieval altar would have stood. Prayers are for suitably evangelical things—for the persecuted church in Pakistan, for victims of terrorism at home and abroad, and for more broadly Anglican things, for wisdom amidst the nonsense spewed about Brexit, and, of course, for the Queen. There are no organ pipes visible, just a praise band. Hillsong-style praise music is difficult, and the musicians are struggling. A man is snoring loudly in the back, a reminder of the Church of England being the church for everybody, not just the cool and hip. Another time I visit for worship, the preacher is regularly interrupted by a mentally ill person in the front. He gamely and politely holds her off, and even manages to uncork a fine sermon. The preaching in this parish is excellent, and then some. But it's hard both to be cool and downtown and not be able to afford the best music. On other occasions the music is genuinely good along with the fantastic preaching. With students and faculty from Durham University and Cranmer Hall, the ranks of preachers are full, and WPC can be choosy. There are enormous challenges. The church is just big and beautiful enough to lead worshipers to expect excellence, but just under-resourced enough not to be able to pay for it. And it is, of course, aging. It feels like John has been gone a week, but it's been half a century. "WPC needs a cleaning out somehow," one local observer tells me. Church memories are long. Previous "successes" can become "the way we've

---

6. David Goodhew often says this in speaking about church growth, and repeated it to me in an interview at St. John's College in Durham.

always done it," and just as stuck-making as what came before. Their work is cut out for them.

And so it is too for the rest of the church in the Northeast of England. Churches do not grow by mere competence and kindness anymore, if they ever did. We have enormous disadvantages. Our very buildings can feel like someone else's living room. Why are there all these plaques on the walls to dead soldiers from long ago wars? Why that musty smell from the Union Jacks hanging in the ceiling (and why are there Union Jacks hanging in the ceiling in the first place?!). Why are we singing? Who is this bloke or this chick talking to me? Why from that book? Why are they asking for my money? These are perfectly understandable questions—ones that a church aligned with state power did not have to ask or answer . . . ever. We could count on Christendom homes, villages, schools, and society writ large to "answer" them. Folks had a sense about such things, often a terribly wrong sense, but they didn't *feel* ignorant about them. Look in the faces of folks who happen in for whatever reason and note their terror. Think of the terror you feel when you turn up for the first time in a yoga studio, or a vegan restaurant, or anywhere where you don't know quite what to do, or what they are going to do to you. Now think of your terror at, say, a ski slope just beyond your ability level. Or, say, a gun range. Or a dirtbike trail—doing an activity that could, not inconceivably, kill you. That's how they feel. Our most profound home—the church—is a place that sets off every insecurity alarm they have. There's your task. You may or may not have a little money to help. Go get 'em.

The sacrament of liberal bashing

Less than a three-minute walk from WPC in an idyllic town square is Christchurch, its bête noire. Christchurch used to be even closer than that, meeting opposite WPC, a perfect Anglican standoff. A WPC vicar in between Bishop John and today spent his days and nights muttering about Christchurch's "intrusion" into his parish, parking their howitzers on my lawn. They had no "right" to be there, Anglicanly speaking, but they were there, and stealing all the young people with their conservative theology and their better worship show. For those who like their gospel "neat," several folks tell me, WPC is not nearly evangelical enough. Christchurch announces forthrightly exactly where it stands, and exactly where you should stand too. This is the gospel in black and white, and it's appealing.

Christchurch calls itself "Anglican," but it is not in submission to the Bishop of Durham, since they regard the Church of England as having stepped away from the historic Anglicanism of the 39 Articles of the Reformation. Christchurch is Anglican then via connections in Africa and elsewhere, but not Church of England. They hold an ordination while I am in Durham, but fly in a white Anglican bishop from South Africa to preside. They are the sort of Anglican church who see themselves in the Scriptures' depiction of a faithful remnant. Though most others bow the knee to Baal, they will remain true to Yahweh, alone if necessary. They are also the "cessationist" option in town, meaning they don't go in for the expression of charismatic gifts like speaking in tongues. And they do represent a strand of Anglicanism that is staunchly conservative, worried about the future of the Church of England, but confident the growth of the Anglican communion worldwide is in their direction. Vicar Tony Jones often credits the church's fruitfulness to its expository preaching, that is, to line-by-line unpacking of the Bible. The church has sent more than a hundred graduates into ministry of one form or other in a decade of its existence.

And they are still doing well with students. They count some two hundred among their number, among four hundred or so folks present in total the Sunday I'm there—a large church in the UK, especially the Northeast. Once term time is over and the students are gone they are back down to one to two hundred and the most-attended student service is not held. If Christchurch gets much larger, they try to plant another church quickly. That is, Christchurch tries *not* to grow too big in one place, but as it grows, it plants new communities. It is well-networked with like-minded congregations in Oxford, London, and other metropolitan and academic centres.

Now, if you're a leader at WPC, you imagine those folks could have been in your midst, instead of in a competing congregation. To listen to Sam Herbert, a staffer and lay preacher at Christchurch, "it is not we who have departed from Canterbury, but Canterbury that has departed from the gospel. And that's sad." Contrary to my expectation, Herbert is not at all triumphalist about Christchurch's success with students. If there are some twenty thousand students at Durham University, and two hundred of them worship at Christchurch, that's hardly "success"! "I wish we were thriving more. 1 percent is not thriving. It's not good enough."

Herbert is good enough though, not by his lights, but by mine as a preaching professor. He speaks with conviction and elegance. His sermon is on 2 Corinthians' denunciation of "super apostles," and Paul's elevation of weakness, frailty. In a line I plan on stealing with regularity, Herbert preaches that "God never wastes a weakness." Herbert promises the two hundred or so gathered on a Sunday night that they can have God's power by "praying to be weak." The gospel does not promise prosperity or success, since, for Paul, "the strong don't need a resurrection." The sermon works because it is so biblical. And that is indeed one of the three-fold strands treasured in Anglicanism since the time of Richard Hooker in the sixteenth century, alongside tradition and reason. Conservative Anglicans speak of expository preaching as their goal—meticulous unpacking of the Bible so as to live in its light. To me, at times, this feels like reading the notes of one's Bible study. But they show, as well as tell, that the Bible is important in their life.

"We aim to reach out, build up, and send out with the gospel." Herbert says. And they are doing well at it. Worshiping on Sunday night is one key: "Students say worshiping at night makes it not 'feel like church,'" so folks can invite their friends more easily. And they *sing*! The eighteenth-century building reverberates with voices, not electronically amplified sound. The music is under-programmed. Contrary to stereotypes there are no smoke machines, just a simple musical accompaniment and people singing like they long for God. Christchurch is not selling a cool gospel; if anything they revel in its lack thereof. Herbert's own earnestness shows part of Christchurch's success. He speaks with conviction, he cites Scripture far more regularly than any other interview subject with whom I speak. He knows he is constantly an evangelist—even when speaking with a fellow Christian from outside Christchurch (indeed, perhaps especially then!).

The difficulty comes with Christchurch's elevation of itself over other expressions of Christian faith, its diminution of Hooker's other two strands. My first visit on a Sunday morning, vicar Tony Jones makes not less than three references to hell or judgment in the first fifteen minutes. A man stepping forward for ordination says he "became a Christian" at Christchurch, even though *he grew up in a family that prayed together*. Their problem is they didn't factor Christ into their decisions adequately. One man says he'd been "very churchy" before, and even raised a lot of money for churches, "but I was not a Christian," though he might've thought differently then. Chatting with another student, he tells me he's studying Arabic and German. He wants to go to Italy to work with refugees, since "there are very few good churches there." While talking with Herbert, I bring up a number of fairly evangelical traditions by my lights—Alpha, Hillsong, N. T. Wright (former Bishop of Durham!), confused why these are not evangelical enough. There are good bits in each, he says. In fact, people important to him have become Christians through Alpha. But Alpha led by a liberal will be worse than Alpha. (In other words, liberalism is so bad it'll mess up something otherwise good.) If you're judgment-lite, sin-lite, holiness-lite, cross-lite, you'll be gospel-lite. Christchurch preaches the stuff other churches are embarrassed about, and they revel in it. As observers both sympathetic and unsympathetic tell me, they nail their colours to the mast and others find them flying and are drawn close. Lots of churches, including my own United Methodists, have tried to fudge our position on homosexuality, for example. We have good people and leaders and power on both "sides" of such a question, so we kicked the question down the road as long as we could. Christchurch does not fudge. They are clear in their conservatism. If you find the world too liberal—and who has *not* found that in a university town at times—Christchurch is a refuge. One could even disagree with the position they take and be glad for the clear articulation. While it is hard to avoid the rubbishing of other churches at Christchurch, they do not spare even themselves. To Herbert's credit, he aims this full-blast gospel against Christchurch itself. The CU at Durham has some four hundred to five hundred students in it, higher than most in the UK. "But how many of them are going to be effective in going the distance? I include Christchurch students in that question." Several critics mention to me "research" that suggests Christchurch-going alums from Durham leave their faith behind after university at an alarming rate. I ask a sociologist of religion in Durham University's theology department about this. He's heard of it too, but as far as he can tell it's an urban legend. It seems people *want* such research to exist. We liberals can be intensely envious of the success of those to our right.

Christchurch seems only to know who it is through bashing what it is not, in a sort of mirror image of the liberal/mainline churches for whom being conservative is the only sin there is anymore. If there were no perceived "liberal" Church of England, how would Christchurch get its bearings? The bishop flown in from South Africa, Martin Morrison, had me wondering, are there any *nearer by* Anglican bishops who could be sought out? (like, in walking distance?). He congratulated the ordinand for becoming a "presbyter" (not priest) in the "one, holy, Christian, and apostolic church" (not "catholic"), and then launched into his boilerplate sermon about . . . wait for it . . . hell. Jesus himself insists there is an unsurpassable boundary between heaven and hell (Look it up: Luke 16:26). "The sign over the gate of hell says 'Too late.' Your sins are either paid for by Christ on the cross or they will be by you forever." I can see why students grant this church the courage of their convictions. There are, no doubt, passages of Scripture and traditional hymns and confessions that they can say without crossing their fingers that others cannot. They do not get embarrassed about hard passages. In fact, they run toward passages from which others flee, even on a night when a new ordinand and his family might've expected to be celebrated and blessed a bit more than they were. But perhaps a church that knows who it is through the sacrament of liberal-bashing, a humdinger on hell is the best way to say "welcome."

And then there's the money. If you're at a place like Christchurch, it might seem that WPC and the Church of England have all the money in the world. It certainly has most of the grand old buildings. But Christchurch is up-front about its funding streams from down South, where the serious money is to be raised in England, including for that eighteenth-century building. Folks at WPC scrape to fund a part-time student minister, while Christchurch has several. Christchurch indeed teaches about tithing, and an operations manager who looks half my age explains to students that if they give while in university they'll give all their lives. There are benefits to preaching the unpopular stuff. The week I visit Christchurch, some two thousand Church of England leaders sign a petition asking that the church not allow baptismal services to be used for gender transition liturgies.[7] What seems to some like long and painfully fought-for liberation seems more obviously at Christchurch like the whore of Babylon doing what it does: "polyamory and interfaith stuff will be next," Herbert speculates. There are plenty of biblical resources through which to see oneself as a faithful remnant, the one without the knee bowed to Baal. That's not a bad posture in an age where being aligned with official power brings few benefits and not a few deficits. It is not hard to see why Christchurch is doing well with students where more liberal churches struggle. Of course, Christchurch has powerful friends in and out of town too. Bashing Baal is not just courageous, it can be remunerative.

We can't handle all the new people

The pastor of another student church in Durham, Mark Bonnington, says a pox on both Anglican houses (my language—he's way too nice). Both Anglican churches have reasons to overstate their differences, and dissenting churches in places as Anglican as Durham know who they are by being not-Anglican. "If you ask the two churches to write down their twenty favourite doctrines, eighteen will overlap," Bonnington told me in an interview. King's Church Durham has another approach.

King's grew out of what was then called the "house church movement" in 1970s and 1980s England. Bonnington narrates that eruption of charismatic and independent churches as a rejection of liberal theology and church practice. "The charismatic movement was a reaction to the death of God and a permissive society," Bonnington told a class at Cranmer Hall, the local evangelical Anglican college. No one sought charismatic gifts for their

---

7. Hattie Williams, "Transgender Guidance Was Not Premature," *Church Times* (22 February 2019); https://www.churchtimes.co.uk/articles/2019/22-february/news/uk/transgender-guidance-was-not-premature.

own sake. The question people were actually asking was this: "Why is the church adrift? And the charismatic movement was the answer that came."

All sides would agree that worship at King's *is* more lively than at Christchurch. Students on Sunday night sing at the top of their voices, hands reaching upward for grace, filling a miserable little church hall with song, sweat, and softly mumbled prayers. By contrast, in several services at Christchurch, I counted one raised hand—for a moment only. Those who attend King's speak of its great "balance," and its aim is for consistency, not histrionics. KCD is charismatic, but not "charisbonkers," as one student said.[8] The church's leadership is actually far more charismatic than what is shown on Sundays, but holds itself back because of the denominational breadth of those present. Folks from some thirty different denominational backgrounds have worshiped at King's over the years, including more than one retired Church of England vicar, Bonnington told me. Several leaders tell me King's is among the most successful churches in the country at attracting students—some 170 total as of spring 2019. And 160 of those are in small groups, a 94 percent small-group enrollment rate that any pastor would kill for. The church sees some four hundred people worship there on weekends when the university is in session, it has twenty-five connection groups, mission trips locally and internationally, and a preacher who also teaches at Cranmer Hall (Bonnington's PhD in New Testament is from the University of Nottingham). Several folks tell me he didn't take a salary till a few years ago. "It just didn't seem fair when we were small and the church was poor to take money from it," he explained, noting his wife's work as a physician made it all possible. KCD's first employee was not a pastor, but a part-time administrator and student worker.[9] Now the church pays twelve other people, Bonnington lately included, and thirteen volunteer or full-time interns. One thing KCD doesn't count is membership. "We have seven members," Bonnington told me, speaking of his board. He has little time for cultural Christianity and lots for discipleship: "We try to widen the front door and close the back." The place is booming. Chris Juby, who has worked at King's for fourteen years, first as a student worker and now in worship, media, and the arts, tells me in an interview these words that will sound incredible to many a vicar in England: "We can't handle all the new people. We get students all the time who want to learn about Jesus, international students especially. It's almost too easy."

    8. Mathew Guest, sociologist of religion at Durham University, gave me this wonderful phrase. There are much more intensely charismatic and Pentecostal churches in Durham that students also attend.

    9. It is striking how freeing it is for a church budget not to have to include a pastor's salary and pension.

Why's it working?

One secret is Bonnington himself. The stereotypical American megachurch pastor has skinny jeans and a body that looks sculpted by a personal trainer and bronzed in a tanning bed. Bonnington looks like, well, a middle-aged professor, who lectures like he preaches and vice-versa. Just a hunch, but this may be an advantage in, say, a university town. Ruth Morley, a part-time employee and longtime attender at King's, tells me of growing up in a "liberal Anglican church with seven-minute fuzzy sermons." She found King's, left for a while for a church that doesn't ordain women, came to her senses and returned. "King's is quite liberal," she insists, speaking of its welcoming ethos and breadth of welcome more than its theology. She points to the church's intentionality about women leadership, including her own: "I feel very invested in here." She works at the church's coffee shop next door to its leased space downtown.[10] And she doesn't hesitate to invite others: "It feels safe. I never fear I'll bring a friend here and the person upfront will say something 'off.' Mark is so biblical." For forty-five minutes or more sometimes.

Juby has another, more quotidian answer to why King's is working: "It's because we meet in the Durham student union." This Cold War era bunker, or Brutalist era masterpiece if you prefer, is where students hang out in droves for pool or beer or study. For a suburban church in North America this would be deadly—no parking is anywhere in sight in Durham city, let alone on campus. But for outreach to students, it's ideal. Visiting as a towny, I'm greeted by not less than five greeting teams, two people each, directing me to where to go for kids, worship, washrooms, the works. It's the friendliest set of faces I've seen in England. Imagining the organization required to get this many volunteers stresses me as a pastor! But it pleases me as a worshiper.

Bonnington does have a contrarian streak, and can sound like Christchurch at times. He makes no apology: "In an age of post-modernism, you have to say what you *don't* think as well." This is not just ideology, it's also local geography: "We have to clarify who we are constantly, especially with the transience in this community." Bonnington wants the gospel to be a reconciling presence across every faultline in Durham: financial, ethnic, town/gown, political. When I compliment King's work in one of the poorer parts of Durham County, he says he'd worry if it were unrepresented in its wealthier places as well.

---

10. King's rents from an Anglican church nearby, who, one would think, would love to have that many students.

One secret to King's is the longevity of service of its leadership. Bonnington meant Durham to be a temporary job until he got a "real" one, but has been here a decade and a half. In a town where students finish an undergraduate degree in three years and head south for a lucrative job, fifteen years is some five student generations. The church has started a community called Achor in Gilesgate, a more deprived area in town. Once that neighbourhood had no Kings folks. Now it has some 150, who have intentionally moved with their families to be neighbours and a presence for Jesus. "We've been there thirteen years," Juby said in an interview. "Folks say 'oh you're the church that clears people's gardens,' or 'you're that church that serves coffee and tea at train and bus stops.' We have no problem getting rooms to rent from the town council." Service is a key ingredient in King's mix. It is also clear about its identity on moral questions. King's invests in women leaders but frowns on homosexuality. If the Church of England lurches further left on that, Bonnington expects King's would see an increase in attendance, but the whole church catholic would suffer for it. I do object to Bonnington in class, sensing some of the "sacrament of liberal bashing." "Surely N. T. Wright was orthodox enough for you?" Bonnington grants the point, but wonders what the Church of England's direction will look like the next few years. He suggests it will look less like Wright, and more like the libertine church of the 1960s and 1980s against which house churches first protested.

Bonnington himself has an entrepreneurial spirit, with long expertise in house renovation, a field in which he has trained recent immigrants and rehabilitating prisoners and ex-cons. Between that and his spouse's work, he speaks like a man free from the pressures of grant-writing and pension-building, as that rare pastoral or academic creature who would still eat if the church closed overnight. He notes that the house churches of the 1960s appreciated conservative Prime Minister Margaret Thatcher for her support of business, and also because she cut off government money to schools: "then they had to rent to us," he says.[11] A lazy North American observer might think King's and Christchurch the equivalent of the Republican Party in the USA, and WPC something like the religious left that keeps failing to launch in reprisal. But an American-style left-right grid of politics and theology doesn't work the same way in the UK. People all across the theological, liturgical, and liturgical grids pray for their country amidst the uncertainty of Brexit, for their region and its rustbelt economics, and call people to resist the economic siren call to London to put down roots for Jesus here.

---

11. Note that this is not a popular political slant in northern England as a whole, mind you, where Thatcher closed the mines and shipyards!

One genuine difference between the three churches, however, is in the expression of charismatic gifts. Where Sam Herbert of Christchurch quotes Paul in our interview, Bonnington quotes words of prophesy that key mentors have said over him. He has been in the same small group since 1977, mentored by charismatic luminary Roger Foster, whom he met through Ichthus Christian Fellowship in London. He speaks of a Methodist from Nottinghamshire praying over him, "God will make you into an oak tree, and in the storm folks will gather under you." And, sure enough, on a recent visit to HTB in London, Bonnington was delighted to see some fifteen former students who had come through King's, some of whom lived with his family in seasons of crisis. He tells of a graduate student from Brussels named Hilary who comforted him when they tried to start an evening service and only five people came: "This is going to be great," she insisted, in the teeth of the evidence. For Bonnington, Word and Spirit are dual foci. Word-alone churches tend to dry up, Spirit-alone churches tend to burn up. "Word, works, and wonders" is the formula he learned from Foster. This charismatic emphasis is part of King's secret too. English people are not known for their demonstrativeness with their bodies. That folks raise their hands in worship is, at first, awkward, then maybe objectionable. But if God is really present and changing lives, perhaps in response we could do something as difficult as stepping into what the English call "awks." Priests of all denominations raise their hands at the consecration of the Eucharist to signal Christ's real presence. And for Protestants, I heard somewhere, every believer is a priest, and Christ is always really present.

Some of King's success may say something about the limits of secularization. "The Richard Dawkins bubble has burst," Juby says. There may have been a time when it was cool and edgy to criticize the church. But now we are several generations into British people having no personal familiarity with Christianity at all. What's interesting or edgy about criticizing something no one knows about? "Cultural Christianity has hit a nadir," which means missionary work can start anew. King's is showing us all how. I used to joke, a little bitterly, that people go on rejecting the version of the faith they learned when they were twelve. Now that confirmation as a teenager is no longer on the cultural to-do list, folks go on rejecting the version of the faith they learned from watching a Ricky Gervais standup show on Netflix. It's the cultural battering ram through the open door. Could Christianity be so forbidden, so passé, that it's interesting again?

But it has to be said that some of King's success may be unique to Durham. If 1–2 percent of folks nationwide go to church, in Durham it may be more like London's 10 percent, with spires poking up by the dozen, a Norman cathedral as the can't-miss skyline, and students who are products of Britain's still residually Christian public school system. "If I invite someone to church in Durham I'm likely to get an answer of 'sure.' You'd need to invite a hundred people elsewhere to get that reaction," Juby told me. Bonnington agrees that the local matters: Durham is cut off by beauty on all sides, national parks on three and an ocean on the fourth. But the gospel is universal. What they've done can be done elsewhere. KCD talks "endlessly" (Bonnington) about life and ministry in the Northeast. King's is brave enough to suggest an alternative to making money and yet suffocating under housing prices in London: stay. Invest in the Northeast. Not for money, but for mission. Almost in passing, as I ask about planting churches, they tell me of a man who planted a church by accident. The very thing some churches struggle to do, a barber in Durham did without trying. I soon had a haircut appointment and an earful.[12]

"She went 'round and banged on doors"

Rusty's Barber is the sort of business that Mrs. Thatcher may not have intended to see started. James Rainey, nicknamed "Rusty" for his red hair during a short stint in the Royal Marines, has set up his shop to be the ultimate man cave. Quentin Tarantino soundtracks loop on Spotify, video games are free, leather lounge chairs ring the place. Ads for Jack Daniels and Marvel comics line the walls. It's a frat house without the beer or misogyny. Yet there is no saccharine piety here either. Rusty's employees respect him, but are not necessarily Christians, and can be themselves. The only thing they all have to be is good at cutting hair: the lines are out the door while students are in town. And Rusty talks about his faith more openly than anyone I've met in England. Before I bring up who I am or what I do, he's chatting about playing in a worship band on Sundays in a former mining village outside Durham. It doesn't feel forced. He's genuinely excited.

Oh and he has a tattoo across his throat—the sort that folks in prison and gang members have, designed to freak out respectable middle class people. I've known him a few weeks before thinking to ask about it. It says "Romans 8"—Paul's great chapter on hope. He got it, partly, to hold himself accountable. He wants to stick with this faith thing.

Rusty is an unlikely Christian. He grew up in one of the local villages, mistreated by his mum and dad. He understands homeless people—some choose to sleep outside to avoid addicted and abusive parents. He joined the marines just to spite his father, and being away just six months made him

---

12. Some of this material was published previously as "Monday Night Church," *Christian Century* (4 December 2019), 10–11.

persona non grata to those in his village who think one should be born, live, and die there. The local pub fell quiet when he walked back in.

His outlet was always breakdancing, which he did competitively. It was part of a fast lifestyle fueled by easy 2000s pre-crash debt. It was also how he met his first Christian friend. A "mate" invited him to a dance class at Newcastle University "because the girls were so hot." And the instructor mentioned he was studying physics and that he was a serious Christian. "Don't those two conflict?" Rusty asked. No, he said. "I started to watch him," Rusty told me, intrigued. "And I remember what he said, 'I've seen some things science can't explain.'"

Rusty tried going along to church, "but I couldn't understand a word." He hung out with church guys though, playing soccer and breakdancing. Once his ankle rolled when a "guy weighin' 18 stone" fell on it. For a barber, this is potentially career-ending. He would need surgery. A friend asked to pray for his ankle. Two days later, Rusty was working. He'd lost out on £98.50 in wages for missing two days. An envelope arrived from a family member containing exactly that amount. Once, coming home from a breakdancing gig at 1 am, not eager to go to work at 6 am, Rusty told his church friend, "If your God is real, he'll find a way to get some coffee in my hand." And who appeared but a batch of folks from a church, offering coffee. One was a friend of his from breakdancing, who seemed embarrassed to be seen with church people.

The stereotypes malingering from Victorian establishment are long gone. Christianity has no power to stop anybody through legal or social pressure from drinking, swearing, or wearing too little in public. But being seen in public with church people brings blushes now. Maybe we have a chance, church.

Finally, as debts came due and family stress ratcheted up, Rusty was having panic attacks. His scientist/teacher friend gave him a pile of books to read. Rusty chose the Bible. He drew a bath and read, and found his way to Genesis and Romans. The water soothed him, the gospel of hope calmed him. He sought out baptism, and soon was trying to help his new church reach the sorts of people he came from and understood. He moved away from the village, never to return, got married, had a child, and opened his business. Bootstraps: pulled up. Not by Rusty's own efforts, he insists, but by God's grace.

Now, at this point, Anglicans, Methodists, and other more established church leaders I know might leap, sensing an opportunity. Send that man to university! Make it free! Stuff him in a clergy collar to plant a church! Send him back to his people in the village! But his colleague Dan Northover explains that some people can't go back. Formerly marginalized people, once they establish new patterns in their lives, often want to leave their old lives far behind. Rusty needed to get away. "Durham's great: there are loads of churches here, loads of Christians," and now, thanks to him, there is one more church.

Rusty and Northover invited some of their marginalized friends from the streets to come to the barber shop on Monday nights. They didn't call it church, didn't talk about God, didn't spring faith on anyone. They fed them—a lot. They asked them about their stories. Everyone in the group brought videos from the internet to watch and talk about. And then they did Alpha. The eight-week video program was easy to understand. "It had a bad-joke dad vibe to it," Rusty says, and for folks hurt or abandoned by their own parents, that was no bad thing. The course ended and those attending said "See yous next week," so Northover and Rusty said, "Ok, sure." "That might kill an organizationally minded person!" Rusty said. But for a handful of homeless, ex-cons, on-again-off-again drug users, and otherwise marginalized people, it was church.

Rusty's Barber Shop planted a church without meaning to. No money, no training, just food and stories and God's Story, capital "S."

Rusty's own involvement lasted only a year. It was stressful, he had a business and baby and spouse to tend to, but Northover is still leading it, five years on. Northover undid any guilt Rusty had from leaving this way: there are times and seasons. What Rusty helped launch, Northover continues leading now, week-in and week-out. The group has the sexy title of "Monday Night Group." One early attender changed things. We'll call her Melanie (so women are, apparently, allowed in Rusty's Barber Shop). She was once one of the most notorious offenders in Durham, more than one hundred convictions to her name, banned from being with children in her own family. She met God while contemplating suicide in a prison cell, and after coming on Monday Night, she supercharged the group.

How?

"She literally went 'round and banged on doors in the estate, telling people 'Come along, this is the most amazin' thing.'" The group grew from fifteen to thirty-five, well-outgrowing the barber shop. After a failed stint at a Methodist church ("we freaked them out") they found a home with the Salvation Army. Northover speaks of the Monday Night Group as the greatest experience of church he could imagine. "I absolutely love it," he said. "I can't imagine going to church anywhere else." These are folks who've been kicked out of other churches, banned from whole cities, done hard time. Not a few are still addicts and alcoholics and have been for decades. They love God, love one another, and still slip up, and hate themselves for doing so, and with criminal convictions can't get proper work. There are no bootstraps to pull up. But for those who do want new patterns, there is help: a charity called Handcrafted teaches skills like woodworking, cooking, and carpentry. Rusty points me to his barstools: "One of our people made those for me. Later that year he slipped on the ice, drunk, hit his head, and was found dead the next morning." These are some of the most marginalized people in their communities. And this church is reaching them. No, this *is* them.

Every situation has challenges and opportunities.[13] There may be no SDF funding for the Monday Night Group, but there is also no one barging in to say, "You're doing this all wrong." Anglicans, evangelicals, all Christian churches have myriads of signals to tell these folks they're the wrong sorts of people. But none of that is on display at Sanctuary 21, their meeting place, when I attend. The vibe is welcoming, accepting: "We're not exactly safe, but we are welcoming." There are hard rules: no drink or drugs or sex or bullying, so that the weak are not preyed upon. And not only by other marginalized people. Other churches come with "suggestions": a band, a sermon, better doctrine, less doctrine. "But then we'd just be like every other church in the city," Northover says of their refusal of any golden handcuffs. The MNG has built something precious, with buy-in from its members, so Northover shields them: "I can be incredibly stubborn."

"They've had lots of evangelists, but no discipleship," Rusty told me. Everyone wants to do evangelism, Northover says. It's exciting and fun. "We had new commitments to the faith just last night." But instant conversion of one's whole life is not on the cards for these folks. "I learned early that our church is going to look more like Corinthians than Romans," Northover said, mustering the sort of patience no other pastor I know has.[14] The model is less St. Paul on the road to Damascus and more St. Paul in the desert for three years.[15] The MNG meets in small groups around scattered tables mostly, which keeps anyone from monopolizing the microphone, whether homeless or seminary-trained. Trained volunteers are at each table: "It looks like chaos, but there is structure there," Northover tells me. And insights from Scripture come out that wouldn't be seen elsewhere. The woman at the well, told by Jesus "everything I have ever done" (John 4:29) in a way that's good

---

13. This may be a truism, but I learned it from my friend J. J. Brown of Appalachian State University. In the UK, vicar Mark Miller of Stockton Parish Church also articulated a version of it.

14. Several sources point me to a talk by Andy Prime, "Struggles of a Middle-Class Pastor on a Council Estate," accessed on YouTube, 3 March 2020: https://www.youtube.com/watch?v=hoFxZZjI50Q. Dan Northover credits Prime with the distinction that your church among the poor will feel more like Corinthians than Romans.

15. That is, more Galatians 1:13–20 than Acts 9:1–19.

news, who goes back to evangelize the people who'd long rejected her. That rings the bell: "That's us," they say. Discussions often turn to suffering, but differently than with university students. "I got tired of hearing privileged people say, 'There's suffering so how can there be a God?' I heard people who'd suffered horrendously say 'Well I need God, because I'm suffering.'" Northover got involved as a university student uninterested in the party or Christian Union scene: "I preferred talking to homeless people." Now he's an accountant, working three days a week to support his ministry habit. "No one would ever choose me, a middle-class civil servant, to reach these guys." But God does have strange ways of reaching those he loves most.

And the church responsible for it—the one that handed out coffee at 1 am, that supervises the Monday Night Group, that provides advice and legal input and policies and money for food, is none other than King's Church Durham. One might accuse King's of being too focused on a university crowd, but here it is making possible an innovative form of church for folks otherwise not-reached. My own Methodists used to thrive with poorer people; Anglicans are desperate to do so now, but somehow class and erudition get in the way. Rusty, who came from poor people, had to step away from serving them. Northover describes Rusty as a man full of convictions, who could turn his life around, with God's help, who is perhaps less patient with those who cannot ("you're a Christian now. Stop it"). Northover describes members of the MNG who will vanish for months at a time, either for prison or a bender, will turn back up penitent, and have been doing the same for decades. Everyone they love or who once loved them has given up on them. Not God. And so not this church.

I can hear the natural questions: what can middle-class, mainline/liberal churches learn? They may be put off by the grandeur and grant money available to the Anglicans. But King's doesn't have that—Bonnington's and Rusty's and Northover's day jobs fund their ministry. In fact, Anglican money and prestige keeps folks like these vulnerable people far away—the cops come if they go any closer. All Rusty did was ask their story and bring pizza and video links. Dan did research and was ready to connect folks' stories back to the Bible. And he has a theology of conversion. "These folks aren't interested in liberal theology," he said, with gentleness, but also conviction. "They know they're sinners. They've been terribly hurt, they've hurt other people terribly. They want to hear about justice, sin, grace, forgiveness." Middle-class people may thrill to a gospel that we're all really alright deep down. "These folks know they're not. And they've been in the media for not being alright. So everyone else in town knows it too." When the woman in John 4 marvels that Jesus knows everything she's ever done, we can almost *hear* the townspeople murmur, "Lady, *everyone* knows everything you've ever done."[16] The only difference is that Jesus knows with mercy, not condemnation. Archbishop of York John Sentamu speaks well of another verse in John, "Go and sin no more." "Only Jesus has the power to say that," he says. You can look it up, chapter and verse: John 8:11.

Rusty suggests that people with no parents or only abusive ones need mentors. And what do elderly mainline churches have to spare? I suggest that the folks I've pastored wouldn't feel like they can relate to ex-cons, drug users, people who prostitute. Rusty is quick to respond: "That's why they're perfect. These folks want different sorts of people in their lives, different patterns to live by." Being able to make and save and budget money may not seem sexy, but it can be life-saving. So too can food. "Mining villagers are proud. They don't want handouts. So call it a celebration and invite everyone to come. They won't tell you they haven't eaten in days."

The church of Jesus Christ, Andrew Walls teaches, is the sort of thing that seems to die in the middle and renew itself on the edges. Poor Anglicanism is still fighting over the centre. But the edges are where the Holy Spirit is bringing new life, writ large in global Pentecostalism in Latin America, Africa, and Asia.[17] But in every community there are edges, margins, vulnerable and marginalized people. If all you can see is wealthy people, just ask who's doing their laundry, cleaning their houses and businesses, washing their cars—those are the lucky ones with jobs. Now look lower still. God is already with them, washing their feet, usually unnoticed, bringing new life. The church can join in, and then this is the remarkable thing: we can return to the centre *with new stories*. Stories of life and health and salvation that renew the very place that was previously dying.

Growing churches in the Northeast of England show us how this is so.

I'm loathe to dilute stories into principles, lives into how-to's, but there are some patterns in these churches' lives that can be pointed out.

Patterns

One, don't present your church as the only way to do things. The body of Christ is much wider than one congregation or denomination. This has been a truism in western Christianity for a century, but with the waning of the ecumenical movement, and splintering of liberal churches over inclusion questions, we seem to have lost it. Conservative churches are not the only ones that do this. In fact, many proudly liberal or mainline churches present

16. John 4:39–42 describes the Samaritan woman as the first Christian evangelist.

17. For a local vantage on Pentecostalism's growth, see Gavin Wakefield's *Alexander Boddy*.

themselves as over against some other form of more barbarous Christianity. No one cares. They can stay away from church altogether if the goal is to be not like *those people*, they don't need your church's help to do that.

Two, don't neglect your church's built-in advantages or disadvantages. Churches I spoke to in Durham all lamented their lack of resources, and had ways of suggesting someone else had all the resourcing they need. This may be a macro-pattern: no church has all the resources it wants or needs. This may be God's doing. Having not quite enough money or talent or volunteers or whatever may be a way of keeping us reliant on God, and not the bank account. WPC has the best spot in town. King's has a spot to worship on campus. Christchurch has its own building. Rusty and Northover have intuition about how to reach street people. What *do* we have? The gospel, and one another, and a world in need of saving. That's all the church has ever had. And it is enough.

Three, speak clearly and winsomely about who you are. Christchurch has a forthrightness about its faith that folks find attractive. More muddled obfuscation feels like a safe strategy, but it isn't. Churches unsure the way forward about inclusion questions often avoid them. This is because clearer answers seem divisive, and who needs another scandal? One longtime leader at King's worries her church has not been as articulate as it could about its teaching on sexuality. "Students don't know to keep their pants on," she said. Permissive culture has won, while the church has been distracted over what to say and do about gay marriage. No one else in our culture is saying that sexuality is a gift to be expressed in covenant relationship to one person. We fear seeming exclusive or intolerant—our era's lone remaining vices. But there is a cosmos through that narrow door. Not one that beckons by guilt or blame, but by invitation to a fidelity that matches Christ's faithfulness to the church.

4

DURHAM CATHEDRAL
This massive fascination

THERE IS A STORY around declining Christianity in Europe that we North Americans like to tell. Granted, Europe has fantastic cathedrals, loads of history, a heritage of Christendom's fables and failures. But those churches are *empty*. Two or three old ladies on a Sunday morning in a magnificent building designed for several hundred is a depressing sight at best, a funeral dirge at worst. It conforms to the most dire predictions folks have of Christianity evaporating from these shores, maybe in our lifetimes.

When I first attended Matins at Durham Cathedral, where I was later graciously invited to preach, I was struck by just how few people turned up. A building that can accommodate some 2,500 people had maybe twenty to thirty who were not in robes (i.e., paid or otherwise promised to be there). This doesn't augur well for the future. I've been part of Bible studies in living rooms that matched it in numbers. Duke Chapel, the imitation of Canterbury Cathedral at the heart of my alma mater's campus built in the 1920s, regularly drew more than a thousand people to worship when I was there. To look out on a building fit for thousands and see empty benches is to have every detail of the secularization thesis, the new atheists' broadsides, and American smug superiority confirmed at once.

The thing is, the stories of European church decline are not always true. Hence this book. Sometimes they are. Hence the need for this book. One vicar told me of palatial Victorian-era churches in his home city built by barons of industry making so much money they didn't know what to do with it. I know, I'll build a church! Some streets in Birmingham would have several preservation-worthy edifices on the same block. These were not sought out by the Church of England, they were built on the impetus of captains of industry wanting to unload taxable income, flatter a religious spouse, appease an angry God, or whatever. They're empty now—*just like they've always been*. Churches usually reach a little when they build, figuring ambition impresses donors. This suboptimal macro-level planning is no new phenomenon. In England, it is often the case that a genuinely magnificent cathedral will have a parish church literally a stone's throw away. The two I know best, Durham and York Cathedrals, both have an impressive parish church you could hit with a rock without too much difficulty.[1] Someone built that church to give thanks for a healing at that medieval shrine. The broader church said, "thank you very much" and proceeded to staff and try to fill it. What else are you going to do?

We North Americans fail to understand that English cathedrals were not always built with the intention to gather a congregation. In fact, the ancient ones were not at all built for that purpose. York Minster long hoped that their patron saint, one William of York, would attract pilgrims to his shrine, and money to the minster. He never managed to do either, apparently being unable to produce the miracles done at the graves of Thomas à Beckett in Canterbury or of Cuthbert in Durham. If you try to attend church at York Minster today, perhaps on a feast day to hear the Archbishop thunder forth from the pulpit, you'll be surprised how little you can see. There is a rood screen between the nave and the choir that's more like a wall than a screen, more "rude" than "rood." That's because the builders had no intention of a congregation gathering in that nave. There would have been no pews until the Reformation, no intention to sit in that cavernous space in rows and listen to a learned discourse. That gothic masterpiece was designed for monks and pilgrims, and for them to sing and to adore the blessed sacrament, looking up from their rosary beads when the bells rang for the consecration of the host, or to admire or pray in one of multiple chantry chapels throughout—that is, places where masses were said for the souls of the departed. Voluntarist gatherings of church people into congregations on the basis of individual belief are modern phenomena. York Minster has come into modernity and tried to make space (literally) for something like evangelical church growth alongside tourism (with a hefty entrance fee to boot), but they're fighting against their own architecture and history as they do so.

---

1. St Michael-Le-Belfry in York is actually one of the most creative evangelical churches in the region. The nearby parish church to Durham Cathedral is now a museum. Their different trajectories would tell a story worth telling.

How much more so in Durham Cathedral.[2] Words tire quickly here, trying to describe it. York Minster is nice—it's full of light, its towers and ceilings bright and cheerful, its archaeological museum good enough you almost forget the littering of private monuments and memorials around the quire that clutter up the spiritual atmosphere, its medieval stained glass intact. York is a beautiful day trip. If York Minster is nice, Durham stretches language, drags awe even from the unwilling, burrows into the imagination and refuses to leave. Its sandstone rock reflects a spectrum of colours broader than I knew existed. Its towers have towers: the west towers have spires that both lead you to try and count them and also leave you unsure you've ever got them all numbered. The building has often been voted the most beloved building *in England*. John Ruskin insisted that no view so spectacular as the one over the River Wear through trees up to the cathedral exists even in Oxford or Cambridge. There are legends of Queen Victoria ordering her train to slow as it rounded the bend and the Norman masterpiece came into sight, so she could admire its triple towers that much longer. Bill Bryson, the American author and former chancellor of Durham University, speaks of it simply as the "best cathedral on the planet." An art historian friend accosted me when I told her I would spend a semester in the city: "Do you *know* how important those gothic pillars are?" "Uh, no . . . ." Their decoration—a step beyond mere weight-bearing—is a first in Romanesque architecture. The monastic "fabric," as they call it, represents the best preserved of all the ancient monasteries dissolved by King Henry VIII. Most abbeys are in ruins now, but Durham's are part of the cathedral complex, still used for ministry or for university functions—I swear I can *smell* the fourteenth-century oak in the former monastic dormitory. The city's prebendary bridge has these words from Sir Walter Scott etched in stone that show precisely why his era is called "Romanticism":

> Grey towers of Durham! . . .
> Yet well I love thy mix'd and massive piles,
> Half church of God, half castle 'gainst the Scot,
> And long to roam these venerable ailes,
> With records stored of deeds long since forgot.

I might have been in more beautiful buildings before—Sainte-Chapelle in Paris comes to mind, or King's College Chapel in Cambridge. Those are nowhere near to Durham Cathedral's scale, nor do they have the waves of history inscribed on the building's very skin, nor do they tell the tale of

---

2. I am drawing here on David Brown, ed., *Durham Cathedral: History, Fabric, and Culture*, filled with essays by scholars in all kinds of fields, and its coffee-table companion, John Field's *Durham Cathedral*.

Christendom's fissures so clearly. One can see why folks want to be buried under it, or near it. It is a space on earth that approximates heaven, near as we can, a place where, as T. S. Eliot said, "prayer has been valid."

And it all starts with the guy buried under it. St. Cuthbert was a seventh-century monk, reluctant bishop, and wonder worker on the island of Lindisfarne, off the English coast just north of Durham. He was basically a desert father of the sort that retreated into Egypt or Palestine or Syria, especially after the alignment between church and state with Constantine the Great (first acclaimed emperor, it just so happens, in York, where he happened to be campaigning against Britons). Committed Christians thought faith should cost something, not make you rich or powerful, so when Constantine started pouring imperial favour on churches, these hardy souls made for the desert and promised poverty, chastity, and obedience while battling devils for their souls to catch a glimpse of God. Their ideas powered westward through such intellectual giants as St. John Cassian in France. Monks off the coast of what's now Ireland pursued the same sort of monastic life—sometimes in community, sometimes as hermits. The monks sought pure, undivided prayer, entire devotion to God, love of God's creation, and evangelism of others.

We tend to think of monks and nuns as devoted to their own salvation, and that's not wrong, but they read the Bible enough to know their salvation was indissolubly bound up with their neighbours. "If you live alone," St. Basil the Great wondered, "whose feet will you wash? Who will wash yours?" So these celibate, learned, prayer-filled monks evangelized. They did so from Iona, off the coast of Scotland, and from Lindisfarne, now called Holy Island. Their form of Christianity was Celtic rather than Roman, they were Irish, they came via Scotland, and they tried to share Jesus, a faithful Jew, with people who thought of themselves as Northumbrian (which was not yet clearly part of England or Scotland), with ideas from what we call the Middle East by way of the desert and the South of France. Talk about an international, cross-cultural body.

St. Aidan was the missionary bishop who evangelized King Oswald of the Northumbrians, who in turn humbly translated Aidan's preaching for his people before their conversion. The king ended up losing his head in battle, a Christian warrior-saint "martyr." Statuary of St. Cuthbert often portrays him holding Oswald's crowned, severed head. Upon Aidan's (more peaceful) death, a young shepherd boy named Cuthbert saw a phenomenon in the sky and went looking for an explanation. It turns out that was the moment of Aidan's death, and he was seeing Aidan's soul rocketing to heaven. Cuthbert joined the monastery at Melrose in what's now Scotland, now a ruin, then a daughter house of Lindisfarne. He ended up on Holy

Isle, where against his better judgment he let a king and his fellow monks talk him into being a bishop. As soon as he could, he retired to a more remote island, backed out of his episcopal duties, prayed, and soon died. He is remembered as England's version of St. Francis—his stories are full of nature miracles, such as when he went for a swim in the frigid North Sea, his fellow monks worried he would freeze, but then discovered seals keeping him warm. I've heard those seals' successors on Lindisfarne—their group caterwauling sounds entirely too human for comfort. Maybe they are singing of Cuthbert. Or wondering who else they might warm. Or maybe they're just glad the fishermen can't harm them, and that few orcas come around yet. The onetime monastic island and then fishing village is basically a tourist destination now, its visitors still constricted by the incoming tide that temporarily separates the island from the mainland still today, like it did in Cuthbert's time.

Upon Cuthbert's death, he was temporarily buried while the monks made plans for a suitably grand church for his remains. Once it was ready, he was dug up, with plans to place his bones in a new final resting place. Opening the old coffin, he was discovered intact, more like he was taking a nap than dead, still limber in his limbs. A miracle, and a sure sign of sainthood. Eamon Duffy, the dean of English church historians, explains why: to be incorrupt is a sign of the resurrection of the body. Jesus' holiness reverses death for the whole of humanity.[3] His holiness, shared with his saints, sometimes even preserves them from corruption in advance of their resurrection. The monks carved a new coffin for their patron and placed him in the new church, and pilgrims came, and many were healed of diseases. They left gifts of gratitude and the monastery became wealthy. When they had to leave the unprotected island under pressure from Viking raiders, they carried Cuthbert to the mainland, changing location every few hundred years to protect him and other treasures. Legends remain that the monks would clip the holy man's hair, beard, and nails. Another legend has it that they would hold locks of his hair in fire to show astonished visitors that it wouldn't burn. Yet another legend has it that the monks were halted in their wanderings in the late eleventh century on what's now the Durham peninsula. The body would not move, so apparently Cuthbert wanted to be

---

3. See here Duffy, "Treasures of Heaven: Saints and Their Relics" in *Royal Books and Holy Bones*. There were other incorrupt saints in England—the fearsome queen Etheldreda of Ely most famously. But it's not "required" that folks' bodies be incorrupt to be called "saint." Thomas à Beckett, England's most famous late medieval saint, was not incorrupt. When the tombs of Sts. Francis and Clare were rediscovered in Italy in the twentieth century, the universally-acknowledged saintliness of Francis was not diminished by his being only rag and bone, nor was the less-celebrated sanctity of Clare catapulted above his by her being bodily intact. It's a sign, not a sine qua non.

buried here. Anyone who's watched the Military or History channels can immediately tell why: the River Wear loops into a teardrop shape here, with a high flat rocky peak enclosed on three sides by a natural moat. When William the Conqueror sought to impose Norman ways on his ungrateful Anglo-Saxon subjects, one way he did so was by building a new cathedral on top of St. Cuthbert. So Norman architecture crowns an Anglo-Saxon shrine that was mobile for hundreds of years before its building was constructed—an original "fresh expression," as longtime Durham Cathedral Dean Michael Sadgrove put it.[4] Durham is not a cathedral with a shrine at its heart. It is a shrine with a cathedral built over and around it.

The Norman cathedral was meant to court Cuthbert's blessing for William's new Norman regime, in an act of what we would call cultural imperialism. The building was meant to be cavernous, awe-inspiring. It worked. Durham Cathedral is called, in the tourist brochures, the largest gothic building north of the alps. Its style is actually older than gothic though—it is "Romanesque," built by Normans to look Roman. Architects did not yet know exactly how much weight in stone could be held up by those arches, so they built their pillars massive, their windows small. York is full of light because it is later Gothic—they knew by then what weight the stone could support, and that they could afford to make the pillars more slender, the windows bigger, so light pours in. Yet Durham is not simply "dark," that would sound grim, and the building is anything but. Maybe "dark" works in another sense—like water that contains depths, or arts that work magic. The place just feels . . . holy. Parts of the early *Harry Potter* films were filmed here, as were some of the more recent *Avengers* movies, yet Durham has not sought to monetize its Hollywood connection the way Edinburgh has— you'd have to be "in the know" to know it was a film set, no plaque memorializes it. On more sacred terms, the building is a microcosm of heaven on earth. A Jesse tree window above its great west entrance begins one's journey through the holy space.[5] The nave and transept cross one another like in most cathedrals, making the whole the shape of Rome's torture device, the saviour's symbol of salvation. The great east window shows the end of all things—Christ in glory, surrounded by the twelve apostles, each carrying

---

4. Sadgrove said this often, including in the sermons edited by Carol Harrison, *Christ in a Choppie Box*.

5. These stained-glass windows are relatively recent. The medieval windows were smashed by Scottish prisoners, their fragments gathered and patched together, mosaic-like, on display now in the Galilee Chapel. Stained glass had to come back into favor with the Victorians, so these windows are from the nineteenth century. There are still windows with only clear glass, presumably waiting to be filled with colour once a funder agrees to spring for it.

the instrument of his martyrdom, who are in turn encircled by the twenty-four elders of Revelation. Wheels within wheels. The building tells the story of everything, from God's election of Israel to his consummation of creation. In a way, every church building does this. But a building as grand as Durham can make the story stick.

And none of that needs a congregation of any size for it to *work*. It needs only to be a pilgrimage site for folks to come, pay their respects to Cuthbert, and leave gifts. A medieval apparatus in the shrine would occasionally open a covering, ringing bells, drawing worshipers' attention. His body was not exposed, but his coffin was, along with the treasures others had left in tribute. The pilgrims' walking route to the shrine is still clear enough in the cathedral—one can proceed from the entrance to the shrine and back out again easily enough without setting foot in the nave or the quire. In the Middle Ages, folks would come on pilgrimage from all over Christendom. Stories tell of kings approaching barefoot. Cuthbert's was the real power in the North of England—earthly monarchs take the knee. In fact, Cuthbert's monks' wanderings are responsible for there being a notion of "the North" at all. The places they stayed mark a map of northernness more surely than any other: the Holy Island, Chester-le-Street, Melrose, Ripon, Jarrow (where St. Bede lived and worked and died and, for a long time, was buried), loads of caves and niches claim the body stayed there temporarily, with Durham as the crown jewel. More recently, bishops of Durham were "prince bishops" for hundreds of years. Durham was England's outpost against Scottish incursion and bishops ruled in the name of the king—they printed money, levied taxes, raised armies, even led them into battle. From kings' perspectives, the prince-bishops arrangement was perfect: bishops would have no legitimate descendants to compete for a hereditary position. Cuthbert is not alone in his coffin. The head of St. Oswald is in there with him. Who was it who said "the past is a foreign country, they do things differently there"? Holiness has always been bound up with secular power in the Cuthbert legend and in the North of England.

Durham Cathedral is more than a shrine, of course. It is also a monastery. From the laying of its cornerstone in 1093 to the dissolution of the monasteries in 1540, it was home to Benedictine monks. The monks predated the stone and even Cuthbert. He led them as a prior and then bishop on Lindisfarne. They hauled his incorrupt body around the North for a third of a millennium. Their bearing of their founder and patron is memorialized *in a mall* in Durham in a sculpture by local artist Fenwick Lawson (one wonders what shoppers make of it). And then for half a millennium they lived together in Durham Priory, keeping the Benedictines' traditions of prayer, work, and hospitality. They vowed poverty, chastity, and obedience (a friend who was a Benedictine for a while tells me the first two seem harder, but the last one actually is). Then they gathered for prayer in the monastery's quire four or five times a day, more on some holy days. They greeted every guest as Christ, as commanded to do in Benedict's *Rule*. In fact, they greeted some guests who had truly nefarious intentions: Durham was a sanctuary, in the most literal sense you can imagine. If an accused criminal managed to elude the law and grasp the door knocker on the cathedral's north door, they were granted immunity for thirty-seven days (!?) until they would face trial or agree to exile. What would they do during those days of asylum? Pray with the monks? Taunt the powerless police outside? The accused couldn't do whatever he wanted: the priory had its own system of justice, and not one, but two jails on site.[6] As far as the Benedictine tradition is concerned, even a guest so impious is still Jesus Christ, appearing in "distressing disguise" perhaps, as Mother Teresa would later put it. The 750 some odd volunteers in the cathedral are still taught Benedictine spirituality around welcome. Kelly Carlisle, an American academic and author spending a year writing about life in Durham Cathedral, speaks movingly of the way the place can offer welcome to the mentally disabled and otherwise ill people. People often shunted aside in public places, even churches, find a capaciousness in Cuthbert's cathedral, and for a moment are treated with the dignity God demands.

And monks sing. They chant the Psalms. A monk's life is devoted to this *opus dei*, this work of God, of sounding the praises of Israel in the heart of God's sanctuary. And again, Durham Cathedral still does this. A small but hardy group gathers for Morning and Evening Prayer every day. Evensong is led by a fantastic choir. Durham's choral school is world-renowned, and luminaries from Tony Blair to Rowan Atkinson (!) have attended. Folks of all faiths and none gather to hear the Psalms intoned. Quite a lot turn up for Evensong on Saturdays. Choral Evensong has had a revival of numbers in England in recent years, with one atheist commentator accusing the Church of England of criminal negligence: it has failed to tell the world just how magnificent this tradition is.[7] Durham likewise underpromises and overdelivers. Its grey spires have filled with choral praise since 1093. It is difficult to determine exactly how many monks there were at any point in time, but not a lot more than a hundred is likely. The last prior at the dissolution, Hugh Whitehead, became the first dean of the cathedral, and

---

6. The dungeons are not exactly the image the cathedral is hoping to convey to tourists, and so remain closed to the public, unmentioned in the glossy brochures. They should reconsider. They would draw interest.

7. Dick Gross, "Apostates for Evensong," in *The Sydney Morning Herald*, 5 September 2011: http://chantblog.blogspot.com/2012/02/apostates-for-evensong.html.

some fifteen of his former monks joined him in the cathedral chapter as canons. In some ways life in Durham continued as before the closing of the priory, with the chanting of psalms, life organized around the liturgy, and some lingering Catholic practices that new Reformers denounced as so much "popery." For good reason Catholics ruled this area for centuries. There *were* no non-Catholics (a Jewish community was violently chased out of York around the time Durham was founded). Monks did engage with the community in limited ways: on Sundays a two-hour service was held with a monk preaching in the Galilee Chapel at the cathedral's west entrance. On Corpus Christi, monks would process with a local shrine around town, into the cathedral for a service, and then back around town. But there was never the expectation that lay people would come here in numbers. Half of lay people weren't even allowed to come nearer than a marble blue line toward the back of the nave. Cuthbert was taken to be antagonistic to women— a relic of an accusation against him that he had fathered a child. Enough money could vault you over the blue line however: stories abound of rich patronesses approaching the shrine to leave gifts.

By now you're starting to notice a theme: not a lot of people were needed for Durham Cathedral. Even today at Matins or Evensong, the dark oak quire seems to swallow up those attending for worship. I watched a hundred or so people file out of a service I was sure had no more than twenty. Thomas Merton used to wonder if the prayers of just a few monks were diverting nuclear catastrophe during the Cold War. Jesus says only two or three need gather for his presence to be among them. In the whole of the nineteenth century, historians have managed to find exactly *one* non-aristocratic person who was baptized in Durham Cathedral: a gardener's child.[8]

Perhaps the largest "congregation" the place has ever hosted was that of two thousand Scottish prisoners captured in Dunbar in the English Civil War—just clearing the bar for a megachurch. Puritans of the sort Oliver Cromwell led had no place for cathedrals (where, exactly, are they mentioned in the Bible?). But they still had this massive building in the middle of Durham. Cromwell did some good for Durham—he seems to have been the first person to propose a university here as a third option other than Oxbridge. The suggestion came to nothing until the early 1800s. Cromwell had thousands of prisoners to warehouse, and an unused edifice, so *voila*: Durham Cathedral became a prison. One of the first thing visitors to the cathedral notice is the disfigured effigies of the tombs of the Neville family, husbands and wives, among the first lay people buried in the cathedral.

8. Alan Bartlett and David Goodhew, "Victorian to Modern 1832–2000," in *Durham Cathedral: History, Fabric, and Culture*, 116.

They'd given a lot by way of money and leadership (one Neville was a bishop, others raised armies) and cathedral beautification (the fourteenth-century Neville Screen still stands proudly between the high altar and Cuthbert's shrine). Bored Scottish prisoners had little more to do for years than hack away at the effigies of English heroes from previous centuries' battles against the Scots. You can sort of tell they used to be life-like, but they're mostly just indistinguishable lumps of stone now. The prisoners ripped out the cathedral's woodwork for fuel, trying to avert freezing to death. They smashed every ounce of stained glass they could reach. The only thing of beauty they left unmolested is a great wooden medieval clock. It happens to have a thistle as part of its woodwork. Perhaps this national symbol of Scotland averted its destruction—we don't know for sure. Around the time of the 2014 referendum on Scotland leaving the UK, remodeling on Palace Green led to the discovery of the graves of several dozen Scottish prisoners, some no older than boys.[9] Whether through malice or neglect, Cromwell starved and froze those people to death in the house of God, their remains discarded like refuse.

The story of the 1660 Restoration of the Church of England in Durham Cathedral is remarkable. Bishop John Cosin, facing a hulking cathedral stripped of beauty, took to re-beautifying it with aplomb. A forest of woodwork over the cathedral's baptismal font dates to Cosin's time. So too does a magnificent organ. The quire's ocean of woodwork comes from him also.[10] The Reformation might not have liked bones or glass or statues or saints, but they had no objection to beautifully carved wood, so there it still is, gracing every eye that looks upon it. The nineteenth century saw more beatification still. A new rood screen was put in. "Rood" is an older English word for cross—denoting the cross at the top of such screens, not the rudeness of blocking off monks from lay people! There are no monks to segregate now, and the screen does its work: it focuses our attention on the holy of holies at the high altar, and it looks beautiful. Medieval accounts of a pelican Christ image as part of a Corpus Christi shrine were recreated with a pelican lectern. Ancient Roman zoology thought that mother pelicans slay their young, then wound themselves, pour their blood on their young, who then revive. St. Augustine was dubious: he'd seen a lot of birds, and none of them act like that. But if it were true, what a perfect image for Christ: who slays us in our sins, wounds himself, baptizes us in his blood,

---

9. "Durham Palace Green Remains Were Scottish Prisoners," BBC News (2 September 2015): https://www.bbc.com/news/uk-england-tyne-34116842.

10. The fabric of the cathedral is far from Cosin's only widely known contribution to the wider church. "Come Holy Ghost, Our Hearts Inspire" is his hymn, still often sung in Anglican churches and beyond.

and we live. It's a maternal image for Jesus, and a recovery of the doctrine of creation: one bit of the created order reflects the God who makes it and redeems it in Christ. Now every time we see pelicans we thank God for his costly salvation. An ornate marble pulpit flanks the lectern. The nineteenth century saw the gothic revival, so buildings like Durham were appreciated anew. It was filled with stained glass again. The ancient smashed glass was reassembled—sometimes as a sort of kaleidoscope, but sometimes with its original subjects discernible. Chapels commemorating Durham's participation in Britain's wars and its miners' dangerous work under the earth went in. With the founding of Durham University in 1832, students would assemble in the Chapel of the Nine Altars. And with the naming of Durham as a UNESCO world heritage site in the 1980s its tourist facilities were improved: a café, a treasury museum, a bookstore, even Durham Cathedral in Lego. When folks marvel that they made that cathedral out of 300,000 Lego bricks, I always say the same thing: yeah, and they made the *actual* cathedral *out of stone*!

Archbishop of Canterbury Justin Welby spent a year in Durham as bishop on his way south. He is not, perhaps, remembered as fondly as Michael Ramsey, who taught at Durham, became its bishop, went to Canterbury, and then returned in retirement. Welby is not as scholarly as his Durham predecessor N. T. Wright, perhaps the greatest New Testament scholar presently walking around above ground. But Welby is fondly remembered for doing a good job here and now again in his current role. Welby used to say that for half a millennium the leaders of this community of monks were saints. Cuthbert, Bede, Aidan, Hild, and a remarkable cadre of praying ones and evangelists and communicants with God and nature marked this landscape with their lives. Then for half a millennium the leaders of Durham Cathedral were thugs. The prince bishops ruled in the king's stead and often more ruthlessly than he. Bishop Hatfield, for example, knew the rules against bishops carrying swords into battle. So he carried a club. His tomb sits underneath the bishop's chair (cathedra) to this day. Someone was dispatched to Rome to determine the height of St. Peter's chair. They returned with this needed information and proceeded to build Durham's cathedra just an inch or so higher. Then, Welby says, bishops of Durham became, for the last half millennium, scholars. The Reformation's legacy is one of learning. This legacy predates that too—Bede is the founding father of church history, doing world class scholarship at a time when Oxford was a forest and Cambridge was a bog. Durham University was founded when the last prince bishop, Van Mildert, deeded his palace, the old Durham Castle, to house the new university. It is the city's second tourist site—one lots of European cities would kill to have as their first. Van Mildert had ulterior motives. The vast wealth being made from Durham's coal and tin mines was enriching the bishop and his friends the cathedral canons grotesquely, the media hammering such "idle curates" for holding multiple bishoprics and pastorates that they needn't even visit, treating "livings" like aristocratic entitlements rather than pastoral charges. The church needed a PR move and they got it, and the world has benefited since. Of course, one critic's "idleness" could be an academic's actual *work*. Bishop Joseph Butler was a leading intellect of the eighteenth-century church. Wright's luminous scholar predecessors include B. F. Westcott, J. B. Lightfoot, Michael Ramsey, and others. Durham's seat has a deserved reputation for being filled by scholar-bishops. St. Bede's tomb rests now in the Galilee Chapel, where it was moved in 1370. It was crowding the pilgrims' walkway to venerate St. Cuthbert, the real prize. But when I got to preach in the cathedral it was to St. Bede's tomb that I repaired. I put my hand on his tomb and asked for his prayers for my sermon. As a saint, part of the eternal body of Christ, he's not gone. He's not raised bodily yet, as Jesus was, as we all one day will be, as Cuthbert's incorrupt body reminds us. St. Bede is at Christ's side, praying for us, as all the saints do, diffusing Christ's grace, refracted through his particular life. His life was as a scholar, a Bible interpreter, a preacher. Perfect one to pray for what I needed just then. He came through. No one else was in the building at the time. Just him and me. And Christ and all the angels and saints.

Are you seeing the pattern here? Nobody much has to come to church much for this all to *work*. Kelly Carlisle put this to me succinctly: Durham Cathedral was not built to fill pews with worshipers once a week. It is not a failed American megachurch. It was built "to dazzle Saxons."

Simon Oliver, a canon at the cathedral and Van Mildert Professor at the university, is one of the finest preachers I've ever heard. And I've watched him preach to a nearly empty nave. A Dean Hensley Henson in the early twentieth century had a reputation as a fine wordsmith. He earned Durham partially on the basis of his reputation as a preacher. While in Durham he regularly complained in his journal about preaching to empty pews. Where was everybody?[11] The cathedral has made a hire of a new canon who will start soon, part of whose work will be to grow the congregation here. That says several things: one, with a dean and two canons paid for from London, that was not central to anyone's portfolio before. Two, the cathedral *wants* to grow. Now it's somebody's primary job to work on that. They will have their work cut out for them. When I first turned up for Matins (leftover Benedictine language for what we North Americans would just call "the early

---

11. And so he often took preaching invitations elsewhere. Bartlett & Goodhew describe this in part of their essay on the modern history of the cathedral in Brown's *Durham Cathedral*, 117.

service"), I noted how ancillary we lay attenders are to the whole proceeding. We were sitting in the nave, away from whatever action there was. We were not greeted or made to feel welcome, whether from the microphone or by a human being. There was some visiting choir on whom the person at the PA draped praise. The sermon went on at length on some story about a fourth magi who brought some unexpected gift or other. The liturgy seemed flawless as far as I could tell, but also bloodless. It could carry on without anyone else in the building. Which is precisely the point. It usually has. On the other end of the attendance spectrum, the Christian Union's Christmas carol service packs the place with university students, not an empty seat around, as evangelicals use medieval space to evangelize their friends (it's a strange world out there). Evangelicals are, in some ways, theological heirs to the puritans of the Reformation who had no place for cathedrals. But they find the building *works* in a residually Christian country where folks feel they should turn up once a year and sing carols, and would be more bored doing so at Gran's church back home. On the other hand, at a packed Christmas service not designed by the CU, a friend said he saw a wasted opportunity. There was no invitation for visitors to come back, no warmth extended in gratitude for their brave appearing that day. Evangelicals I know back in the US use crowded Christmas churches to announce a new sermon series in the coming year that will entice some of them to return. None of that boosterism here. The liturgy was, again, flawlessly performed, but not directed to any human being in particular, only to God. It felt there was no difference whether anyone else was in the room. The cathedral's worship is still more for monks than for imitating any megachurch.

You'll notice a pattern in the paragraph above: there *are* times when the cathedral is packed. Lots of times. Christmas is one. Canon Oliver told me the cathedral had counted twenty thousand worshipers through its doors between December 1st and 23rd—that's *not* including the Christmas crowds. These are folks who don't *have* to be there for any reason, yet there they are. Why? A cynical response would be they count school groups who don't exactly have full volition in the matter. Tourists turn up for reasons no more noble than their attendance at Cirque du Soleil or Euro Disney. But that twenty thousand represents *worshipers*, not tour groups or pilgrims. So the point stands. Oliver has written critically of any hard distinction between a pilgrim and a tourist, whether in the Middle Ages or now.[12] Whose motives are *pure* in approaching God, or anything else? Yet God has drawn people to himself in uncountable numbers through the

---

12. Simon Oliver, "The Cathedral and Rooted Growth," in Platten, ed., *Holy Ground*, 32.

years by this massive fascination. The prayers that tourists leave show they have often transformed into something more like pilgrims, whether that was in their original plans or not. Durham Cathedral still does not charge an entrance fee—for a reason. Benedictines welcome people. Holiness still fascinates, whether uncorrupt bones or cavernous pillars or choral music or a Harry Potter background scenery. God has worked through worse motivations before.

There are plenty of other times the building is full. Cuthbert himself has not one, but two feast days—the day of his death, March 20th, and the day of the translation of his relics to their current resting place, on September 2nd. They could multiply this, it seems to me, by celebrating all the times they moved his dead but surprisingly resilient body around England, but two is generous. I had trouble finding a seat for one of them, as the whole congregation was invited to process to the shrine and pray. The line between medieval and modern fell away a bit.

The building can be full during Holy Week. Good Friday goes on for a full three hours, commemorating Jesus' passion. In a move clearly designed to terrorize any remaining puritans, parishioners take turns venerating a cross. That is, they walk up to it, some on their knees, and kiss that thing. Physically. With lips. The sermon when I'm there reflects on the burning of Notre Dame cathedral, and the worldwide outcry of pain even from nonreligious people. There is something to these spaces, something far beyond or below our powers of speech, something that makes you do weird things, like kiss a wooden torture device. "One thing we can do really well in the cathedral is symbolic gestures," Canon Sophie Jelley told me, before she became Bishop of Doncaster. Easter sunrise service saw between five hundred and six hundred people gathered this year. "That's not bad for 5 a.m."

You can see Jelley's point. The cathedral hosts an annual miners' gala, recalling the way of life of pit mining which dominated the economy of this area for centuries but is now no more. The former mining communities all around the county process in with their banners representing their fraternal organizations. They pay homage at the cathedral's memorial to those who died in mining accidents. The relationship between cathedral and pit villages was often tense. Cathedral canons often made rich livings off the church's ownership of the mines—villagers worked back-breaking labour in the dark while parsons were seen to be doing very little indeed for huge incomes. Resentment at the establishment runs deep in the North—it owned the mines, it collected rent on folks' houses, it embodied "the man." Not surprisingly, bishops and deans often opposed organization of workers into unions (which opposition has been regularly apologized for since). Methodists did great ministry in those places since they were freer of those particular economic entanglements, more able to be *for* the workers. But with the mines closed and money gone that used to course through those villages, Methodists struggle to pay for leadership. Anglicans are still there—still collecting rent in some cases (it is, I'm told, harder to close an Anglican church than a Methodist one!). Anglicans struggle with how to close the gap between social classes. The gala is one success story. Cathedral staff tell tales of the building being full that weekend with folks covered in tattoos, with jewelry through ever-more creative facial orifices, leaving empty beer bottles overflowing rubbish bins. That's working-class England. Its members are not often in church. There was a day when their forebears avoided the cathedral but repaired to modest middle-class Methodist village churches. No more. Now, wonder of wonders, they still come up to Durham and up Palace Green into the cathedral once a year. How to attract them back more often? Or is that not the right question? "I would prefer they have a good experience at the cathedral and then go back and get involved in their parish church," Oliver told me.

On the other end of the social spectrum, the cathedral also hosts a weekend where the region's judiciary is invited. "It looks like a scene from Gilbert & Sullivan," Jelley told me, with judges in their long wigs and robes, a phalanx of costumed soldiers carrying pikes designed to pull knights off horses. The place is packed with these literal big wigs. This is another longstanding legacy—one medieval function of the prince bishop was to dispense justice. He set up a throne in the Galilee Chapel and held court, with a verse from the psalm about God's justice in Latin on the wall above him. Those who see to justice for the rest of us deserve our prayers, and at times, even our advice or criticism—it is good that they be recognized. Back across the socioeconomic spectrum again, Remembrance Day services are packed. There is a new generation of Brits who have fought in Afghanistan and Iraq, suffering (and inflicting) loss and trauma. World War I's end was recently commemorated and the seventy-fifth anniversary of World War II is coming. The latter generation of soldiers still has a few members around, and children and grandchildren remember their stories. One of the institutions with which the C of E has traditionally aligned itself closely is the military, and this one carries fewer upper-class affectations than its allegiances with the royal family or Oxbridge colleges, as long as ordinary people are doing the dying. And it fills the building. Not that they come back the week after November 11th.

These one-off events are a marvel. They show the cathedral still has summoning power. Even long-abandoned Methodist chapels still fill for a funeral, so religion has *some* residual cultural power still. Further, this was the region of the prince-bishops. If the Bishop of Durham wants to meet with someone, they take that meeting. That residual power can be brokered for significant good, and often is. If a group is invited, honoured, prayed for, they'll turn up. It's *their* cathedral in some sense, without them feeling obliged to turn up on other days. But their presence at those special events is carefully recorded, and then their hundreds are averaged in with ordinary Sundays attendance and so counts as "growth." Everyone who monitors such numbers knows they can lie. And yet we have to count. This is more than "bums on seats," as I often hear it derided. Bums, as I've already mentioned, have this stubborn habit of being attached to people. And God loves people, longs for them to reciprocate his love, and to be knitted together to one another in the body of Christ. Evangelism is the invitation into this divine-plus-human love that humanizes us, graces us, transfigures us slowly from sinner to saint. Beautiful churches with ancient stories become museums without this drama of the body of Christ, growing from grace to grace. Durham Cathedral is no mere museum.

Grace Davie, one of the great scholars of the secularization thesis, coined the description "believing without belonging." Statistics suggest Brits are not wholesale atheists. They're just not interested in joining the church, or subscribing to a neatly circumscribed creed of whatever sort. Some 70 percent of them will still say they are "Christian," but what does that mean?[13] That they're not Muslim or Jewish? Is it a simple conflation with Britishness of a reflexive sort? When soldiers signed up for service in World War I and said they had "no religion," the form filler-outers used to write in "Church of England." That was Christendom: "none" or default meant "C of E." Davie writes of Britain being glad for "vicarious religion": others can believe on my behalf. England does have the scars, and a memory, or religious extremism birthing civil wars—the 1600s feel not so long ago here. One fruit of the English Civil War and snide comments about puritans of the sort I've made in this chapter is to remember that extremism begets violence. Bishop Butler, mentioned above, famously took aside a young John Wesley and scolded him, that "enthusiasm" is "a very horrid thing indeed." England seems to know that. And when the situation calls for it, you can pray the Lord's Prayer in public, or trot out an American preacher for a royal wedding, or sing "God save the Queen" (especially at football matches, when things are going poorly!). The evangelical in me is sceptical about vicarious faith. We each have to answer for ourselves before God on judgment day. But the Benedictines did not harbor such doubt. They were glad to pray

---

13. The figure comes from Leslie J. Francis et al., "The Spiritual Revolution and the Spiritual Quest of Cathedral Visitors" in *Anglican Cathedrals in Modern Life*, 172. That 72 percent figure dates from 2001 and may be optimistic; national census figures in England and Wales taken in 2011 saw 59 percent check the Christian box.

for the world, to do their bit by being the praying ones in society as others did their bit in their work as kings, laborers, masons, or farm laborers. The weakness of evangelicalism is that it can think it exists for its own sake—to grow the church, to save souls. Its imagination is individualistic, not corporate. The Church of England, whatever its other flaws, knows it exists for all of England.[14] Vicars are charged with the spiritual health of their parish, not just their attendees. Cathedrals exist for a whole region. Cuthbert's cross adorns shopping centre marquees, car parks, and parking meters. Durham Cathedral exists for you. Whoever you are. You don't have to believe anything or even do anything. You can if you want. In fact, part of the appeal of cathedrals is that there are depths to explore—no one has found the bottom yet. But this is not for super special religious people out of reach of the rest of us, whatever images to the contrary may be conveyed. It is for *you*.

And that message has gotten through to some degree. If HTB-style church plants are the good news church-growth story on the evangelical side of the C of E, cathedrals and Evensong are the good news growth story on the liberal and high church side of the ledger. Some twelve million people paid a visit to an English cathedral in the last year, pumping some £150 million into local economies.[15] And 85 percent of Britons have visited a local church in the past year, compared to 51 percent who have been to a movie theatre. Cathedrals have recognized their civic importance, hosting secular events that some nine hundred thousand people attended in 2000, a figure that had grown to 1.6 million by 2010. And worship figures have soared in cathedrals. Not on Sunday mornings—those are steady at around fifteen thousand people across Britain. But midweek figures have taken off, from 4,900 to 11,600 from 2000 to 2010. The number of people volunteering in cathedrals rose by some 13 percent from 2005 to 2015, from 13,300 to 15,000 (a sort of gigachurch, that).[16] Churches have realized they are not just open for business on Sundays, and folks have responded, nearly doubling the worship figures for cathedrals as a whole. Some of this is no doubt the influence of Fresh Expressions, especially Messy Church. Cathedrals did not often seek to program for children aside from choral music have now expanded their offerings greatly. Some of the growth reflects other ministries profiled elsewhere in this book, like those to Farsi-speaking refugees. Some of it is smaller gatherings like midday Communion or Evensong

---

14. See here Sam Wells and Sarah Coakley, *Praying for England*.

15. See here Lynda Barley, "Stirrings in Barchester: Cathedrals and Church Growth," in *Church Growth in Britain 1980 to the Present*, 78 & 81. See also *Dreaming Spires* and *Anglican Cathedrals in Modern Life*.

16. Simon Oliver, "The Cathedral and Rooted Growth," in Platten, ed., *Holy Ground*, 23.

(Durham Cathedral offers lunchtime talks that promise to be no longer than ten minutes!). Some of it is just that these buildings are fantastic, and they offer something unavailable anywhere else. One source on cathedral growth quotes a "punk rock manager" saying the following: "Church is the most fantastic place. It's sanctuary. They should be open 24 hours a day. They're the only place left in London where you don't have to buy anything."[17]

As I've asked about these cathedral growth numbers around Britain, I've met with some furrowed brows. Folks working there know the figures but want to interrogate them a little. Stephen Hance and Paul Rattigan have conducted some more informal survey research of their fellow ministers in cathedrals, and found that of the twenty-five that responded, half report growth. Of those growing, most report they have some strategy to bring that growth about. Most interestingly, several myths fall aside in this research. One, I had assumed folks come to cathedrals looking for anonymity. They're big enough that you're not accosted with greetings, or asked to be on a rota to serve coffee or teach Sunday School. Hance and Rattigan insist otherwise, that warm welcome from a community ranks high on the list of what people seek as they attend cathedrals. Two, I had also assumed that cathedral growth siphons off people from local parishes that are already hurting. No one can say that never happens. Several folks with whom I spoke attend the cathedral for big spectacular events, but they stay at their parish ordinarily, and so too does their money and their service. Three, the charge has been levied that folks at cathedrals are not "spiritually hungry." They are there for an aesthetic experience, not for God. One sceptic pointed out that cathedrals tend to be high on the doctrine of creation (the aesthetics, the music, the building), and low on any need for salvation, a fall, Christology, or any sense of a world desperate for repair. "What's being preached implicitly: salvation by *music*?!" he asked. Such a question can betray jealousy, of course. Cathedrals have three full-time priests paid for by Church House: "*Imagine* what you could do with that sort of externally funded manpower!" And a budget north of £9 million on top of that externally funded staffing is jealousy-provoking indeed.[18] Yet Hance and Rattigan find that people mention hunger for God readily on their reasons for attending cathedral worship. In my own attendance in monasteries I notice a level of spiritual

---

17. Barley, "Stirrings in Barchester, 82, quoting Malcolm McLaren from *Faithful Cities*, 78. Of course he is referring to churches in general, not just cathedrals. London's St. Martin in the Fields functions more like a cathedral than many smaller and less prominent cathedrals among the forty-two throughout the country, though it has no bishop's seat technically.

18. Of course the cost of maintaining a thousand-year-old cathedral become UNESCO World Heritage sight gobbles up more money than we can imagine.

seriousness and depth possible there that often eludes us in parish ministry. Durham Cathedral and its erstwhile priory offer these, if you know where to look. Morning Prayer, Evensong, midday Eucharist, high holy day festivals, engagement with the civic life of the community—it's all there. Simon Oliver writes of cathedral ministry as middle-out, not top-down (an image that a middle-aged pot-bellied man can appreciate. I mean me, not Simon).[19] That is, it does not flow from God to the bishop to the priests and canons and thence to the people. The *via media*, or "middle way," often celebrated in the Church of England, is no limp compromise. It is rather Jesus Christ: *he* is the mediator, the middle, between God and humanity, between heaven and earth, between us and others. Between between between. The cathedral is appealing because of this betweenness of God that it signifies. Those attracted to the space may have no idea that's the reason why, or may even vehemently deny it. Yet Christians believe he is the one in whom all things hold together (Col 1:16). The cathedral is a sort of clasp on the fabric by which Jesus does this holding together.

Cathedrals are talking about growth again. There may have been a time when they could afford not to care whether anybody else turned up. A king would come with a kingly gift once in a while, or new monks would come every few years and devote their whole lives—no need for the rest of the city to turn up. But Durham Cathedral stewards a treasure that no other institution in this area, or in the world, quite does. Parking lots and shopping centres are not going to explain what that Cuthbert cross *means*. This story is too good for anyone to keep to themselves.

For the record: Henry VIII's commissioners ransacked Cuthbert's tomb ostensibly to end popish worship, but really looking for treasure to finance Henry's foreign wars. One scaled a ladder to Cuthbert's elevated tomb to smash it with a sledgehammer, and then looked inside to see that he'd broken the Anglo-Saxon saint's leg. The commissioners called up to the hammerer to just throw the bones down so they could climb up the ladder and find the treasure. He said he could not. The broken leg was still attached to the rest of his body. The commissioners scaled up too and looked, and in the most surprising pilgrimage moment ever, they saw an intact body. They took their treasure and left the body until the king could decide what to do with it. It was later reburied when the monarchy and the Church of England were restored after Cromwell.[20] Someone had the wisdom and courage to

19. Simon Oliver, "The Cathedral and Rooted Growth," in Platten, ed., *Holy Ground*, 26.

20. Apparently upon reburial it was mostly decomposed. Although some reports of the last exhumation in 1901 report some flesh still on those old bones. This is rather unlike what a pious Catholic professor (of something other than theology!) told me

hide a majestic work of Anglo-Saxon jewelsmithing back in the last place Henry's men would look for it: the coffin itself.[21] This could have meant the death penalty for the hider—disobeying Henry on such sensitive matters was considered treason, the penalty for which was being drawn and quartered. Later exhumations of Cuthbert found liturgical vestments and the like, not surprising. They also found, hidden in Cuthbert's clothes, that cross. It is more than merely a beautiful artifact. It is a sign of lost glory, somehow, perhaps miraculously, rediscovered. Miracles are ambiguous, of course. Ancient monks told stories of William the Conqueror being suspicious of Cuthbert's incorrupt status and being set upon by sudden intense heat. The saint was fighting back, and William fled in disgrace. Cuthbert failed to intervene during William's later vicious Harrowing of the North campaign, but never mind. Twentieth-century Durhamites tell of a mysterious fog that set in and covered the city when the Luftwaffe intended to bomb it during World War II. Cuthbert again, back up to his old tricks? But if he could play with nature, surely he could've, I don't know, *stopped the war*. Christian miracles are never mere conjuring tricks. They can't be summoned on demand to do what *we* want. But somehow, despite all our scepticism and cynicism, they happen. David Wilkinson, theologian at Durham, describes a miracle as a place where God surprises us. That happens to everybody paying attention all the time. And when it does, we give thanks, ambiguous though they often may be.

History can also handcuff you, of course. A friend tells me that pastors in one of the places where Cuthbert's body once lay hesitate to change anything. That's one of *Cuthbert's* churches after all—best leave it be. And history contains such ugly stories as Henry's lustful and bellicose destruction of his own church. After they were done looting the shrine, Henry's commissioners despoiled it best they could. The great medieval shrine, famous throughout Christendom, was destroyed, its place of literal grandeur reduced from above the "high" altar to flat with the level ground of the quire. The space was used as storage for centuries, and only in the nineteenth century returned to a sort of dignity. It's a much sparer space now. A marble slab over his grave proclaims, simply *Cuthbertus*. A small altar presides over the space, with kneelers surrounding it. A canopy cover has a painting of a (weirdly beardless) Jesus, cornered by the four evangelists. Banners for telling Cuthbert's and Oswald's stories loom in the corners. Surly beadsmen

---

back in North America: that every year they open the tomb to change the vestments around the intact saint. Uh, no they don't, and no he's not.

21. Willem, *St. Cuthbert's Corpse*, gives the grisly details.

will shush you if you talk too loud in that space.[22] I told one I understood being shushed if I talked in the reserve sacrament chapel, but not in Cuthbert's shrine. "For us, you see, he's as good as the other," he said. Both the saint and the sacrament are the body of Christ. So are you and I and the surly beadsman and the nice one, and one day so too will be all creation.

Patterns

I've written this book for the sorts of Protestants who mostly don't have cathedrals. Mainline denominations have some big churches, sure, and some (Anglicans) even have technical cathedrals. But most children of the Reformation know who they are, still, by rejecting such traditions as relics. We would be more aligned theologically with the Puritans and Scottish prisoners who smashed chantry chapels and scattered relics than with the medievals who built them and kissed them in hopes of lessening time in purgatory. I hope I have shown Durham Cathedral is not just an "important" church, in the snooty sense of "important"—the country club at prayer. It is a shrine, a pilgrimage site, a one-time monastery that still bears Benedictine gifts, a civic symbol and source of regional pride, a church for all people. The C of E has realized it has neglected these treasures in terms of their power for evangelism and is hard at work rectifying that neglect. What would be the equivalent in our traditions? What's the strange, unexpected gift we neglect in our very midst that could, once again, have summoning power? The hidden treasure waiting in plain sight to be exposed, to fascinate and attract once more?

Magisterial Protestantism was built on the power of theology. One thing that still holds us together, insofar as we are at all, is the importance of a learned clergy. We want pastors with masters' degrees. The goal is not wall art. It is learned preaching and teaching. Not esoteric or obscure preaching, but preaching that beautifully presents the gospel for the transformation of hearers and ultimately our communities. Simon Oliver suggests his own church has "lost confidence" in many of its historic treasures, and he's surely right. So have we, whatever Protestant group we are. We bear a treasure of great price too. It is not a World Heritage Site cathedral ordinarily. It is the gospel. Durham Cathedral has its own way of noticing that treasure,

---

22. Beadsmen were, in the Middle Ages, paid to say rosaries on behalf of dead bishops' souls, hoping to spring them from purgatory. This may not have worked. A cathedral in Toledo, Spain hangs the ridiculous red hats of dead cardinals over their graves in the nave. "Every time one gets out of purgatory, their hat falls," a tour guide told a group of visitors. We looked up. The hats were all firmly in place . . . . Now beadsmen include women and are glorified maintenance types. And shushers.

dusting it off, and placing it in a setting for all to see: these layers of history with their gaudy scars, from Saxons to Normans to high medievals to the Reformation to Cromwell's reaction to Restoration to gothic revival to now. We have similar layers, whoever "we" are. They're just not so obvious to the naked eye. What we have to do then is teach harder, better, more lovingly, beautifully. The cathedral tells the beautiful and flawed story that all Christians share. It is the only thing any of us ultimately has to offer the world. The story of a God wed to a particular, flawed people in history, transfiguring us from our present misery back into beauty. Medieval thought, such as Thomas Aquinas's, is often compared to medieval architecture, such as Durham Cathedral. Protestants who don't have the latter often still revere the glories of Christian orthodoxy, whether from John Calvin or Jonathan Edwards or Karl Barth or Marilynne Robinson. We shouldn't hide that treasure away—we should invite folks into its depths.

The cathedral shows us again the foolhardiness of any demand for a holy church. Bishop Hatfield, with his bloody club, still lies buried beneath the scholar-bishop's throne. Scottish prisoners starved to death in the space where angelic choristers now struggle to hit just the right note for tourists. Some of those beadsmen are downright mean. And that aging building has probably been replaced, stone by stone, at least once, if not more times over the years. Its wealth was built on the sacrifices and fears of ordinary people. Like most of our great human achievements, its grandeur masks outrages, not difficult to detect beneath the surface. The glory here, in fact, is that these scars are shown so visibly. There is no going back in time to stop the wounds from happening. But in Christian faith scars are transfigured, not effaced. They show glory, evince grace, identify Jesus, and make him known to others (John 20; Luke 24). The church shouldn't try to hide our scars, however eager we are to present well to new people. We're a flawed, broken, disabled body. That's ok, because so too are the bodies of those we seek to welcome. This is no country club. It is a hall of welcome for the undeserving. Mainline churches often worry about how clearly our faults show. We're too small. Our buildings are too post-World War II. Our worship isn't cool enough. We're fighting about inclusion questions. Scars are not necessarily abhorrent. They should not always be hidden. They can be humanizing: a source of grace rather than shame.

Finally, the cathedral is a laboratory for innovation. Something about its sturdiness allows creativity. Some experiments fail, no doubt. The military chapels are efforts to connect with society that I find tawdry, unhelpful, bellicose at best, fawning at worst. But Fenwick Lawson's sculpture is a marvel. His *Pietà* in the Chapel of the Nine Altars is massive, double life-sized, and rough, coarse, like the local wood from which it is carved. Jesus and

Mary are graced with bronze metal, which catches the sunlight, occasionally flashing forth, reminding us of a resurrection to come. Yet Mary's sorrow and Jesus' lifelessness are obvious, unmistakable. A friend of Lawson's tells me when his sculptures looked too smooth, he would take a chainsaw to them. Kelly Carlisle contrasts beautiful York with indescribable Durham: it's the rough edges that make a home, not the shininess. And Sophie Jelley notes that she asked if a lay canon could assist her at Communion. She went through all the proper channels, got permission, and presided. Then later she wondered: had she just changed a thousand years of tradition without stopping to consider?! Of course she had. Nothing stays the same, even a massive heap of stone. To stay true to the mission of the people of God, we have to change, to innovate, to risk failure, and occasionally, to catch "success," however debatable or ambiguous. Worship in the 2020s looks very little like it would have in the 1120s or 1620s in one way. In another they are recognizably in the same family—the same rambunctious, wounded, and wounding family that God makes for himself in the world. One sturdy enough to accommodate experimentation, failure, and maybe even success.

5

ALPHA

We're from London, here to help

IF YOU PAY ATTENTION to religion at all, Christian faith in particular, you may feel like Alpha is over-covered in the media. The ten-week introduction to Jesus, founded by Holy Trinity Brompton in Knightsbridge, West London, has some twenty million alumni since 1993. Alpha tends to grow big churches, and to broadcast its famous endorsers, which tend to draw media attention. I bet you see its advertising banners in your town, wherever you live. Its city-wide advertisements in London's capital drew the ultimate backhanded compliment: an atheist ad campaign in reprisal.

Alpha has been in the news so long now, more than three decades, that it feels like old news. It's not. Here's why. It has a spirituality that is groundbreaking, and should be copied elsewhere. Let me explain.

Alpha is one of those things that church leaders tend to have an opinion about. Some of those opinions are quite negative, perhaps born of jealousy, or of genuine theological disagreement (those allergic to "evangelicals" tend especially to grimace, though Alpha itself does not use the label). If a quarter of non-church-goers in the UK can successfully identify Alpha as a program of the Christian church, it can hardly be accused of media shyness.

Yet as a pastor and theologian I'm convinced that the story of Alpha's impact has been muted, if anything. Last year, one and a third million people worldwide gathered around meals to listen to ten weeks of videos about Jesus and discuss them. Mike Higton of Durham University told me that if you get non-Christians together over food to discuss faith in an open environment you've already done nine tenths of the work. As a

Methodist, it seems to me Alpha is a return to the Wesleyan movement of the eighteenth century. It has grown big by growing small. Christian faith is best practiced in small groups, face-to-face, without fear of rebuke for saying or doing something "wrong." If Alpha had accomplished this alone, it would be enough.

But it has done far more. Starting in the mid-1990s a creative relationship with then-Bishop of London Richard Chartres began to bear fruit. The Anglo-Catholic bishop had plenty of unused church buildings on his hands, and was disinclined (or if they were listed buildings, not easily able) to sell them for condos. HTB, Alpha's sponsoring congregation, was full-to-overflowing. Nicky Gumbel and friends approached the bishop to ask if they could use some of the disused space. Alpha would send a good leader, several dozen folks from the mother church would follow, and a church re-plant would ensue. Church planting has been in vogue in evangelicalism for a generation now, launching a new church in an area and under leadership likely to see it grow. Alpha's replants take a healthy graft from elsewhere and plant it anew. And it's worked. By the time Chartres retired from his office a few years ago he was out of empty churches. Church attendance has actually ticked *upwards* in London over the last twenty years, but not in the Diocese of Southwark across the Thames, which has not embraced the approach in the same way.[1] Some of London's uptick is due to immigration, no doubt, though that's present in Southwark too. Just as much is due to HTB's replanting efforts. In 2009 HTB did the same far outside of London, in Brighton, and subsequently it has done the same many times all over the UK. Recent C of E evangelism efforts invest money in "resource churches" in city centres that become hubs for mission-sending work in a region. Many of these are HTB-inspired. The first thing they do, often, is run Alpha. Mark Elsdon-Dew, longtime Alpha spokesperson, told me Alpha is key to planters' mission: they don't want to take church-members from others, so the goal is to invite non-Christians. "Our message to churches is this: if you have something working better, do it. Alpha is for people who can't find anything better."

Alpha has a certain spirituality to it that I'd not noticed before interviewing Elsdon-Dew, though it doesn't put things that way. Spirituality language is still vaguely Roman Catholic, and residual anti-Catholicism is alive and well in England. Elsdon-Dew told me both his raising in England and his evangelical faith taught him to be suspicious of the Church of Rome. No more. The number of Catholic parishes using Alpha increased more than 40

---

1. Jason Fout's book *Learning from London* charts this trend ably; the essays in David Goodhew's *The Desecularization of the City* add depth and academic rigor.

percent last year. Alpha often invites Catholic luminaries to speak at its conferences. Raniero Cantalamessa, longtime preacher to the pope, is a great Alpha fan and advocate. London's own Catholic cardinal noticed the utility of Alpha and adapted it to Catholic purposes. Christians of all kind have put Alpha to work for them, from mainline to Catholic to Pentecostal to liberal and back again. Just don't use any of those labels. "We never, ever, ever use them," Elsdon-Dew told me. "They tend to bring a 'boo/hurrah' response, where half the room boos and half hurrahs. We don't want that, we just want to be Christian." Gigachurches in America seem to succumb, eventually, to either moral failure or partisan allure. HTB's spirituality has it determined to avoid anything other than its narrow, and deep, mission.

In my own liberal mainline context, we hoped that ecumenism and post-Vatican II Catholicism would make for ecumenical rapprochement. It did, for a time. That time seems to have passed. The natural successor to the WCC's ecumenism is, surprisingly, Alpha. Working together for the gospel was seen as a social justice initiative on my side of the liberal/evangelical ledger. But the ecumenical baton has passed to an evangelical gigachurch in London. That's surprising. Alpha should crow about that more. But it does not. It's busy helping churches design small groups to reach new people for Jesus.

Alpha was an unintended evangelical success. In the 1980s it was simply the new member course that HTB designed for those considering baptism or joining the church. A new curate at the time named Nicky Gumbel reluctantly took it on (the dreaded job description bullet point for newbies everywhere: "other duties as assigned"). He wanted to reach new people for Jesus, not transfer around sheep from other flocks. But several early attenders were non-Christians. They experienced a new relationship with Jesus Christ during the course. They invited friends, who came like gangbusters. HTB is ridiculously good at events, the successor to the Billy Graham organization for its facility with promotion. "We have lots of young people at the door, flowers everywhere, lighting was different, it was fun, a night out," Elsdon-Dew said, understating things even. The show is really, really good. So people in trendy west London came. Soon churches were calling, asking if they could copy it. One early Alpha leaders meeting in the '80s saw a thousand people come.

"Alpha wasn't an invention, but a discovery," Elsdon-Dew told me. If they had intended to do an apologetics outreach for non-Christians, they wouldn't have started with the question "Who is Jesus?" That's already a churchy insider question. Or so they thought. They would have chosen "How can we believe in a God?" or some other, more speculative question. But this worked, and still does. One hallmark of Alpha is the weekend away.

Around week six they take a retreat and focus especially on the person and work of the Holy Spirit. Again, this would not likely have been part of an outreach course intended from scratch. But the weekend away has become so central Alpha begs people not to call their course "Alpha" if they don't use it. When people become Christian with Alpha it tends to happen on that weekend. The heavy emphasis is on the gifts of the Holy Spirit, appropriated in a charismatic vein, including speaking in tongues and laying on of hands for healing. They find sometimes folks receive the Holy Spirit before they're even Christians (a pattern in the book of Acts, if you look closely—see Acts 10:44 and elsewhere). As a non-charismatic, I'm tempted to quibble here. But again, it works. Folks want a God not elevated above their experience in the intellectual ether, but closer than their language, than their souls and bodies.

In fact, as a non-charismatic, a reluctant evangelical, and a convert to liturgy, I sometimes describe Alpha this way: I don't like it very much. But God seems to. Everywhere you look it's bearing fruit.

Alpha is also an accidental leadership pipeline. Gumbel has a practice of getting new converts up at the microphone before their euphoria has worn off. Elsdon-Dew told me that churches tend to acculturate people quickly. But "people can smell the real," as someone describes new life in Christ. Their friends notice too, as marriages are repaired, drugs and drink abandoned, joy experienced. New people will often bring a dozen or more friends to do Alpha next. And they become leaders at small groups offering Alpha to others right away. That pipeline led to another—St. Mellitus College, a seminary designed to train church planters. HTB couldn't find a school to raise up church-growth catalysts the way it wanted, so it made its own. "Nicky learned a lot at theological college, made great friends and learned a lot of theology, but that didn't necessarily help with the process of growing a church," Elsdon-Dew told me. So they started their own. It's among the largest theological colleges in the UK now, having expanded to some half a dozen sites.

Alpha's spirituality is one of discovery more than design. It's pragmatic—Elsdon-Dew keeps insisting they find Alpha "works," if something works better, by all means, do that (they will too). It's Jesus-centred, rather than Christianity-centred, perhaps more Barthian than evangelical Brits tend to be if left to their own devices. It's ecumenical despite itself, reminiscent of C. S. Lewis's "mere" Christianity. Cantalamessa explains it this way, according to Elsdon-Dew: "When the king is in trouble, people tend to rally around the king." In a hyper-modernity uncomfortable with strong religious commitment, Christians can either lash out in response (witness the Trump phenomenon), or they can grow closer to Christ and so to one another while taking risks together in mission. Not that there are not fissures in the king's defenses, of course. Catholics and higher Anglicans regret HTB's and Alpha's distancing themselves from traditional Anglican liturgy. Liberal Anglicans see in it a repackaging of American-style corporate and hierarchical faith, possibly anti-women and more likely anti-gay. Fundamentalists decry everything. But if you want to glimpse the future of Anglicanism, look perhaps not to Canterbury (though Archbishop Justin Welby is a product of HTB himself!), but to Knightsbridge. Or to your local Alpha group.

Another piece of Alpha spirituality I saw is, perhaps, the most counterintuitive. Its table leaders are taught to answer no questions. Remember these are non-Christians gathered for meals, watching videos, and asking questions. When I'm asked a question, I answer it. Not these folks. They simply facilitate as other first-timers respond, with nothing other than the videos and their personal experience (or lack thereof) to go on. As a pastor and theologian, I'm not sure I trust the Holy Spirit this much. "It is countercultural for a Christian *not* to answer a question. It is honouring of our guests to allow them to conclude for themselves. People don't like being told stuff they have to accept." Plus they'll be back next week, having done a little research and thinking and maybe even praying. That interrogative mood is essential—don't shut it down with declaration. Week 6 with the Holy Spirit weekend away is coming soon enough. In the meantime, let them think out loud. The Spirit is working, so you don't have to.

A final piece of Alpha spirituality for now: "love your bishop," Elsdon-Dew says. Evangelical outliers, especially those that grow big congregations, can be holier-than-thou toward their denominational machinery. Don't do it. Alpha has benefited from support from bishops across the Anglican spectrum, from Anglo-Catholic (Richard Chartres and Rowan Williams) to evangelical (Justin Welby) and back again. "Love your bishop, and you will be in the minority, because not many do, and if they know you love them, the world will open for you."

Alpha's impact is such that it now *has* bishops. A lot of them. I mentioned Welby above, who from his perch in Canterbury has funneled money and attention to HTB-style church plants. Ric Thorpe is another. He is a suffragan bishop in the Church of England in charge of encouraging church plants. His experience is hard-won. He was on staff at HTB as a curate. From the beginning HTB has heard the criticism that its model can only work with upwardly mobile people or aspirants in trendy neighbourhoods. Thorpe and friends set out to disprove that. They took on planting in an area that could not be more different than Knightsbridge—the East End of London—whose population was some 45 percent Muslim at the time. His church graft began and worked its way up to 150 people. Churches often struggle to move to the next level once they're that big, since staffing and relationships become more complex. So Thorpe's church did a remarkable thing. They planted again, sending twenty people and an ordained leader and £25,000. You know—the very money and volunteers with which they could have started a killer youth group. Gone. The *next week* they planted again, with ten people and an ordained leader and £170,000 over four years. Two years later they were up to two hundred people again. Time to plant. Two years on, back up to 250, and a fifth plant was launched. It was clear at Thorpe's church, as it is at HTB, that joining means preparedness to be sent elsewhere. Bishop Thorpe, speaking from his own experience as well as in coaching others, says the key thing with planting is not the size of the church. It is, rather, leader-readiness. When someone is ready to go, they should be sent—with not quite enough money and not quite enough people. The fruit of those four plants is five churches in a tough neighbourhood in London, each some 200–250 people strong, each looking to plant again, with Thorpe in an office where he can help make that happen.

It is important to note how shockingly new this approach to church is. My own Methodist movement was born in the eighteenth century as John Wesley asked people to take Jesus as seriously as he takes them. The result was a revolution in life: a whole new way of living, in disciplined relationship with Jesus and with all his weird friends—the poor, the surly neighbour, those in prison, even one's own disliked family. Wesley made clear being baptized as an infant was not enough. One had also to live in rigorous pursuit of Jesus now. He organized Methodists into bands and classes to ask rude questions about one another's discipleship ("who sinned this week? You first!"). And he found himself uninvited from Anglican pulpits. No matter, he would preach out of doors, to coal miners, on city squares, to whoever would listen. This was an affront—for an Anglican priest to do ministry in another's parish without permission. But those parishes were no longer reaching their people. Wesley was. Soon after his death his movement's separation from its Anglican roots was made official.

HTB-style plants are working in parishes that have failed, or are failing, and so could be viewed as an admission of the failure of the parish system writ large. Much of the opposition to church planting is a fulsome defense of the treasure of the parish system.[2] Yet with friendly bishops in place those who want revival no longer have to flaunt or work around or finagle space from the C of E's system. They *are* the system. While I was

---

2. See here Alison Milbank and Andrew Davidson, *For the Parish*. The book is so good in what it affirms I have used it to teach an introduction to parish ministry course. It's just wrong in what it denies (that there can be ways of doing ministry supplemental to the parish system).

in England an announcement had folks all aflutter. The Church's commissioners, managing its investment assets, were going to spend money not just from the interest earned, but the principle, on HTB-style plants, calling them "resource churches." They wanted more stories like Thorpe's, all over the UK, not just England. I asked Thorpe if this wasn't equivalent to pawning the family silver in a panic. "No—it's more like finding an odd spoon and parting with that." The commissioners are no longer willing to disperse money just so failing churches can hang on a little longer. They want to invest it in models that make for future sustainable growth, even multiplication. If numeric trends continue, the C of E will have billions of pounds in the bank and zero people in the pews within decades. This *is* the rainy day on which to spend the money. Thorpe is glad to show them how.

And so we come again to the North of England. Other chapters in this book profile resource churches in Durham (WPC in ch. 3) and Gateshead (St. George's in ch. 6). Resource churches were *the* talk of the C of E writ large while I was in England. Will they work? Why are they getting all the money and no one else? Can something imported from the South of England be effective in the North? One friend told me of a road sign outside of London on the A1 highway near Watford—still very much Greater London. It welcomes people to the North of England! The North is a mythic place, hard to identify precisely, but not therefore unreal. Cumbria and Northumberland were once part of Scotland. The football team in Berwick, England, actually plays in the Scottish league! The Christianity there started out Celtic before it became Roman, if it ever really did. And as with people in any region of any country made fun of for accents and economic and cultural backwardness, the North is highly sensitive to slights. "We're from London and we have the answers" is not a way to begin a conversation in the North of England.

Overseeing growth for decades

Thankfully, no one has to. Northern churches have had their own ways to approach church growth. St. Thomas Crookes in Sheffield did just fine in its growth before the world heard about Holy Trinity Brompton. STC's website credits its growth to a 1985-visit by John Wimber, a luminary charismatic evangelist from the Church of the Vineyard in the USA. They also benefited from visionary rectors like Robert Warren and Mike Breen, each an author and how-to speaker on church growth on both sides of the Atlantic. STC had a highly committed leadership training program, asking folks to work not more than three days a week in their job (quite an ask!), so they could spend the rest of their energy in practical mission at the church, with hands-on learning, some classroom instruction, but more interruption of consumerist lifestyle to immerse in more deeply Christian patterns. The church grew to some two thousand people and then sent five hundred of them to replant elsewhere. Think about that for a moment—sending a quarter of your most keen people away. St. Thomas Philadelphia, the resultant offspring, still thrives today. STC also pioneered "clusters," mid-sized gatherings off site from the church. "He freed up multiplication from the building," Bob Hopkins told me. And the original hole left by five hundred departures has been filled several times over. St. Thomas Crookes did more than what we would imagine possible in North America in response to growth—adding new services, each identical to the last, expanding the building multiple times to accommodate. It birthed new communities, with their own style and service and pastoral leadership. These met elsewhere than church and even became new churches, blessed and sent out by the sending church, and soon sending themselves.

In other words, HTB as a church and Alpha as its growth engine is a marvel, imitated and envied worldwide. But in the Church of England, it is first among equals. It is a large church, often imitated and learned from elsewhere. But it is not a one-off. Pastors hoping to catch lightning in a bottle have not just looked to London. They have looked north—to Sheffield, and elsewhere.

Bob Hopkins, quoted above, and his spouse Mary, are some of the quiet gurus behind church growth for the last two generations in England. Nearly everyone I talked to for this book said I must meet with them. I would not only learn a lot, I would leave changed. And sure enough. The couple met me at the train station and sat me down in their cozy, book-filled home, feeding me and regaling me with tales from their lives. Their unexpected conversion in their twenties. Their surprise at not having children. Their realizing that biological childlessness would make for greater effectiveness in ministry—many children by faith, if you will. And their front row seat—no, their driver's seat—for much of the growth in the church in their lifetime. They know everyone, and they've seen everything, and they're not bragging about it. They seem a little bemused, surprised at the unplannedness of the thing, and at the goodness of God.

First, they had a surprise conversion after living together while Bob was working for the oil industry in Brazil. Mary had an Anglo-Catholic upbringing, mostly left behind. Bob was disdainful of faith altogether. But her conversion, and the repair it wrought in their marriage, softened his disdain, and brought him to faith. They had once laughed at the revivals they witnessed among Brazilians. But coming to faith made them realize their home, England, was in greater need of revival than Brazil. And the great challenge was the youth, the next generation, whether sort-of-churched as she had been or more dismissive like him. They learned from stories of evangelists in Thailand, cycling from village to village to start new communities. They led in YWAM, Youth with a Mission, with a determined evangelistic approach and a genius for spotting and grooming the gifts of young leaders. They were surprised to learn on a tourist trip to Malta that Roman Catholics could be serious Christians too ("God was miraculously answering prayers—to what we thought were the wrong gods!"). "Our constant question," Bob told me, "was whether it was possible to have a planting missionary call and not be schismatic." Could you plant churches in the Church of England? Wesley tried, but could not finally. Could the Hopkins?

The answer came in layers. The Hopkins' co-conspirator, George Lings, told me the history. He has published it, eagerly and voluminously, for decades, from his research post at the Church Army in Sheffield ("George is the architect—Mary and I are the builders," Bob Hopkins said). There was a time when all growth had to be addition to the way the church was. Then in around 1975 Eddie Gibbs and others brought American-style entrepreneurial church growth to the UK. "That was helpful and shocking and brought 'growth' into the language, with a sense that the church needs to face outwards rather than inwards," Lings said. No reason C of E parishes can't become megachurches. Some even did—HTB, STC, and others. But not many. It is hard to replicate dozens of times over, though it will work in some places, with enough resources and a charismatic enough leader. The new thing that the Hopkins and others pioneered was a shift to church plants. The goal here is not to bring more people into the existing church, but to start more churches. "Not to go out and back with new people, but to go out *and stay out*, and to discover what is there," Lings said. Those Thai evangelists didn't tell villagers to go with them to the big church in the city. They started village churches, training local leaders, who would then do the same. The Hopkins didn't do this at a safe distance. They sold their house in London and plunged that money into one of the poorest parts of the UK—the Merseyside area, with its centre in Liverpool—and practiced kitchen table ministry there, along with running a school and training for YWAM. A vicar in Liverpool was connected with HTB and had planted nearby. HTB hatched and hosted the first national church-planting conference, in 1988. Looking around the planning room for who could organize the follow-up, all eyes turned to Bob. He wasn't a vicar—surely he had the time? He didn't, but he did.

Skip ahead a few years. One of the evangelical vicars in the North who was part of those church planting conversations was one George Carey, who became a surprise Archbishop of Canterbury in 1991. He was already slated to speak at the next planting conference, but had a rather significant enthronement ceremony the week before. Might he still come and speak? He did, bringing all the prestige of his new office. Suddenly evangelical church planters weren't the weird mavericks. They were the establishment. And everyone who wanted the new ABC's attention registered for the conference as well. A few years later, Bob Hopkins was in Monmouth, invited by then Bishop Rowan Williams to study places of growth in his diocese in Wales. Hopkins didn't want to go, but "this is one time we heard God right," so he spent ten days visiting twelve projects. Bishop Williams asked for a report, and later became the first modern Archbishop of Canterbury from outside England. Williams became a massive supporter of Fresh Expressions, which we will describe later in chapter 8. Hopkins called it "contextual church planting"—with his original report as its basis. *Mission Shaped Church*, published with Archbishop Rowan's glowing praise in a foreword in 2004, was still a hot topic of conversation when I studied in England in 2019.[3] Finally Justin Welby, a product of HTB and onetime Bishop of Durham, became ABC in 2013. He is a former oil executive, with sympathy for entrepreneurship. Lings describes his support of HTB-style church planting as a move back toward the church growth models of the 1990s. Yet another Archbishop of Canterbury is a friend of the Hopkins' and informed by Lings' research. Every holder of that office for the past thirty years has been influenced by the Hopkins and by Lings. Bob Hopkins remembers the supposedly "risky" days of bishops telling the press they hardly believed in God. There's quite a shift to now three straight ABC's supporting evangelical church planting.

Because of their long vantage on planting in the C of E, and their own transition from maverick outsiders to advisors to archbishops, the Hopkins can see long patterns. There was a day when bishops were allergic to church planting because it sounded like HTB. That is, it smelled entrepreneurial, its theology was evangelical, they probably hid their misogyny and antipathy to gay people, and they did not hide their upper-class aspirational culture. The Hopkins' and Ling's response was always the same: HTB is only one model of church planting. There are *dozens* more. Their research showed as much—they could regale you all day not just about St. Thomas Crookes but some thirty other approaches to starting or restarting churches. Now, things have changed. Bishops and other leaders looking at the dwindling numbers of Anglicans are frightened, even panicked at times. So they open

---

3. Graham Cray, ed., *Mission-Shaped Church: Church Planting and Fresh Expressions of a Church in a Changing Context*.

conversations *demanding* HTB-style church plants. The Hopkins and Ling's advice is the same: HTB is only one approach. There are dozens of other valid approaches. "They think that's *the* answer," Bob told me. "But they're twenty years late. That was the model then."

The Hopkins are plenty complimentary of HTB for being especially good at reaching "high powered and potentialed people in the city. Those people are wealthy and have well-resourced and influential positions in secular contexts." Hence HTB's visibility and resources. Yet there are problems with its model, as there are with all the others. HTB-style church plants do worship really well. So they tend to draw people from surrounding areas "because what they do is attractive," Hopkins said. "But we've discerned areas they come from grow darker and darker, because everyone is gathered at church, and not doing mission in their area. They're actually less equipped to because they commute for their spiritual life somewhere else." The Hopkins have long used the book of Acts to teach church growth. Bob Hopkins notes that the church did not stay and expand in Jerusalem. Instead it was driven out by persecution . . . and thrived (he points to Acts 6:7, 12:24, and 19:20). So too now the church shouldn't concentrate in one centre. We should push into new places, in small numbers at times, bigger in others. "The missional rhythm of the New Testament is to increase and spread, gather and disburse. We tend to hold on to what we have." The problem now is all the money and attention are going to those sorts of churches. Instead, HTB's model should be "kept in the right context with the rest of the models and synergized, instead of being singled out as *the* answer to our crisis."

George Lings agrees. Through sad eyes and a handlebar mustache, he tells me that HTB does many things well: "Life is extraordinarily attractive," he told me. Alpha is its secret. Its gifts include welcoming new people well, honouring their questions, treating them as individuals with gifts. But how often does the "normal" Sunday church do that? Alpha can be hard to "graduate" out of. That's the sort of accidental disconnect most churches would be glad to try and solve. Others may not be so soluble. It's not clear that plants do cultural diversity well. "These work well at upper-middle-class aspirational" places, Lings said. HTB-style plants can give the impression that if something isn't flourishing, it's failing. But Jesus does not just disciple life's winners. There is little place for darkness amidst church plants' driving guitars and light shows. The primary emotional note is happiness. But there are other emotions we experience, especially now. Lings seems almost physically weighed down by the church's scandals in recent decades—and not just the Anglicans'. Roman Catholics' troubles weigh on him. I ask if it doesn't help him sleep at night to remember that's not his communion. No, he says. We are one body in Christ. If one member suffers, we all suffer (not a theme likely to be preached at HTB). Lings borrows a line from a Catholic missiologist: "The new belongs elsewhere." That is, what is getting born needs protection from the ecclesial structure. A fragile new community, among, say, economically-deprived people or ethnic minorities, needs not to be held up for comparison to some success story from a very different demographic. In the Middle Ages, bishops and abbots had to protect something new on the edges of church life from being amalgamated by the power at the centre. So too now. Lings himself attends a Fresh Expression that meets during the week. He votes with his feet and his tithe and his prayers. It's small. No plans to grow big. But it might launch something new. That will also be small. Lings' research at the Church Army shows Fresh Expressions, this sort of micro-planting, has grown the equivalent of two new dioceses in the Church of England. HTB-style plants draw headlines and celebrities, and also now money, but it's not clear they're reaching new people: 60 percent of Fresh Expressions attenders are previously part of no church; 80 percent in a new resource church already are.[4] HTB-style plants may not be trying to steal sheep, they must just be "growing better grass," as apologists put it. But it's happening.

Holy Trinity Brompton and Alpha are amazing, gifts from God to the world, bearing fruit in ways both intended and unexpected, as detailed above. But they are not the only thing going. In my North American mainline world, we often notice what evangelicals were up to twenty years ago and try to copy it as our latest new thing. It only works usually to pick off disaffected evangelicals who liked those good ole' days. Non-Christians rarely find it edgy or interesting—if they were inclined to notice, they did already twenty years ago and weren't impressed. Ric Thorpe knows HTB need not only be upper-class aspirational—that's why he planted in the East End. The Church of England as a whole owes its life to people in poor places that others neglect and abandon. It is wise to target money to invest in places that can grow. But as variegated as those places are, so variegated must be the way to reach them. More on that in chapters to come.

---

4. See here the Church Growth Research Project, "An Analysis of Fresh Expressions of Church and Church Plants" (October 2013), 33.

6

DESPERATE IN NEWCASTLE

ONE OF THE PAINFUL things about studying church growth in the Northeast of England is to see the state of my own church here. British Methodism once thrived in the small mining villages and seafaring coastal towns in this region. The way our mythology tells it, the Wesleys' vision of the gospel's promise of new birth in the human heart and holiness across society appealed to those on Britain's margins in the 1700s and early 1800s. Priests in cathedrals had much to lose, and so they rejected Wesley. Coal-faced miners, some children, some elderly, had nothing to lose, and much to gain, and Methodism lit the region on fire. Wesley himself worried not that there would ever be no Methodist movement, it had grown so fast in his lifetime. He worried that there would be Methodism, but without the fire—that a gospel of conversion would yield respectable middle-class people no longer interested in Jesus.

It's not clear he had the right worry. Margaret Thatcher—a daughter of Methodism herself—closed England's coal mines and shipyards in the 1980s. There are still people living in those pit villages, sometimes several generations dependent on government assistance now. But there is often little to no presence of Methodism. Economically distressed people used to be *our* people, the people "no one else wants," as a South African Methodist once put it, but now there is no "we" to want them. Often there is still an Anglican church, tethered to eight or ten or twelve other churches in other villages who share a priest, only because it is so much more difficult to close an Anglican parish than a Methodist chapel. Methodism has evaporated as quickly as it once grew up. There were successes along the way—Methodism may have helped avert an eighteenth-century revolutionary crisis in Britain, as folks were more interested in converting than in revolutioning, and it certainly birthed the modern Labour party, with all its struggles and glories in the UK. But Methodism itself is today in even bigger trouble than the Anglican and charismatic churches we have treated so far in this book.

When Alison Wilkinson arrived at Jesmond Methodist Church in Newcastle in 2016, she might have had reason to despair. Jesmond is a booming university district in one of Northern England's hippest cities. The economic engine in the region, Newcastle is home to several leading universities, and is Britain's answer to Las Vegas, a European destination for stag and hen parties (though depressingly *not* the place where Newcastle Brown Ale is brewed anymore). Upon her arrival, Jesmond had some twenty or thirty people on a Sunday. This hearty remnant looked little like the surrounding university neigbhourhood: young and diverse. Instead, they looked older and whiter—more like England's past than its future. One early challenge was to take the congregation outside and ask them to look at their own building as if they had never been inside before. What do you see? There were still Christmas announcements out. This was in February. There were three sets of heavy doors to push through to even *see* inside, let alone to get inside. The building was half occupied by the congregation in what used to be its social hall, half occupied by a booming coffee shop and bakery leasing the church's old sanctuary space. One of these two establishments had a line outside to get in. The other did not. I'll let you guess which was which.

Not that there was no history of faithfulness there, far from it. JMC is slightly more Pentecostal than most Methodists I meet in Britain. They tell stories of folks attending because they'd seen a vision of the building, or a vision over the building, or some supernatural sense of God's own invitation. Previous pastoral innovations set up the partnership with the coffee shop and launched a Fresh Expression called the Holy Biscuit, located in a former cookie factory, aimed at local artists. And there were some students, befitting a city booming with university kids. But the trends overall were dire, as they are in Methodism writ large in the UK. Andrew Orton, a researcher on Methodism for the University of Durham's Sociology Department, reports that the British Methodist Church's membership declined 17 percent between 2009 and 2014. He says that 80 percent of congregations received no new members in 2014, and fewer than 5 percent received more than four.[1] A

---

1. Andrew Orton and Peter Hart, "Leading Together in Growing Methodist Churches: Learning from Research and Practice in the North East of England." Published by Durham University (2017): www.methodist.org.uk/learning/scholarship-research-and-innovation/research/connexional-research-projects/archive. One response

revivalist sect, with a structure and apparatus designed for rapid growth, is no longer reviving anybody, and its structure is in the way. "Lots of ministry in our church is about managing decline," Wilkinson told me. "We've lost belief in the gospel as transformative, in the good news as good news."

Wilkinson has been in similar circumstances before. A previous appointment sent her to Hartlepool, an industrial city on the coast without Newcastle's reputation for universities, knowledge economy, or innovation, and with louder tales of economic woe. She was sent to close the church, but it accidentally grew. "Folks would come for funerals and then come back," she said. Wilkinson is a fantastic preacher and conversationalist, and it is not hard to believe that she is a natural evangelist. With a track record of leading a church turnaround, she was sent to JMC, where she has seen similar results. In two and a half years, the 25–30 people she inherited has grown to 50 (nearly 100 percent growth!), with most of the growth coming from students. The five students are now 15–20, led by Wilkinson's son Adam, who is himself training for ministry. 70 percent of those students are in small groups, though Adam Wilkinson regrets that figure is not closer to 100 percent! Eight different nationalities are represented now, including Russia, Antigua, and Egypt, so the place has some diversity. The Holy Biscuit adds some 20 more people for its fortnightly meetings, most with no other connection to any church. "We are the fastest growing church in the Northeast," Wilkinson said of JMC's place among Methodists.

It is striking how often Wilkinson has to work against the memory of past triumphs as she works to lead JMC toward growth. I mention the story from old timers about folks seeing visions. The problem with such talk of prophecy, of God's blessing, is "it assumes God is blessing *us*. I'm trying to say it's not for us." When Wilkinson arrived, there was no engagement with the café *that met in the same building*. She wandered over and asked what they might do together. The café offered to bake mince pies for Christmas, and to serve them in church. Wilkinson suggested instead that the church go to them. Not a far journey—outside and down the sidewalk a few paces to reenter under the same roof. But the sojourn from a "come to us" to a "we'll go to you" church can be a long one indeed.

Some of the need to fight Methodist tradition has to do with polity. As I mentioned, Methodism in Britain is organized for rapid growth. Churches that grow pay more into the general church's funds. Those that do not receive money. This makes a sort of sense when most churches are growing. When they are not, it feels punitive to the few churches that are growing,

---

to the documentation of decline in British Methodism, Orton tells me, has been to . . . wait for it . . . stop documenting the decline.

and disincentivizes growth system-wide. Pastors do not preach to their own congregations very often. They preach on a rota in a circuit, perhaps to their own people only one Sunday in eight. Since Methodism is a dissenting tradition over against Anglicanism, it has a marked anti-hierarchical ethos, and a suspicion of celebrity pastors. That means that local churches often hear sermons from lay people. Sometimes from the same lay people preaching much the same sermons for years. A vital gospel opportunity then is lost, especially for casting vision, which has to be repeated over and over in creative ways so that lay leaders and members and even guests know it, own it, and can repeat it to others. Wilkinson has counteracted this thinning out of her voice partly with her family. Adam preaches on the rota also. So does her husband, David Wilkinson, Principal of St. John's College at Durham University and a leading Methodist theologian worldwide. "We have to fight our own structure," she said. "But there *is* someone named Wilkinson preaching three weeks out of four." One longtime couple at JMC bristled when I asked if Wilkinson is behind the recent growth. "Our previous pastor was quite energetic too," she said. But an eavesdropper and newcomer swooped in after to disagree: "I came and heard the Wilkinsons and I could listen to them for hours," he said. "I need to be preaching 50 percent of the time, if we're going to invest in growth" Alison Wilkinson said to me. "You're a bit player if you're only preaching one week in four."

When I visit, she preaches a fantastic sermon on the women who fund and lead Jesus' ministry in Luke (8:1–3), but the most important thing she does is to talk about membership. A young woman is joining, so Wilkinson says a bit about what this means. "Membership says 'I will serve God in this place, I want to announce that intention.'" She promotes another new membership class to prepare people to join. Several researchers of church growth intone the phraseology to me: "Churches that intend to grow tend to grow." It's not automatic, of course. But a few miscues in trying to grow can lead a church to think it's impossible, that the only course is to manage decline as painlessly as possible. That might be fine for some, but Methodism is a revivalist sect. If we're not reviving anybody, what are we doing here?

One woman so revived told Wilkinson she felt compelled to come in as she walked by, glancing through the now open doors, seeing the friendly people inside ("when folks complain it's cold, I rejoice—it means the doors are open," Wilkinson says). She was struggling with finances, and the greeter who welcomed her is a mathematics professor, who offered help with her budgeting. She has been in surgery for cancer, and the church has stood by her, with visits and prayers and food. She speaks of a greater sense of peace. Friends comment that she *looks* physically different now. Methodist conversion can still be good news for people, for their loved ones, for the neighbourhood. We used to tell those stories by the thousandfold. That we can still tell them at all is good. There are lots more like her who have not yet wandered in.

The Holy Biscuit is another example of vitality at JMC. This Fresh Expression of church is a place where many non-Christians come and talk about their art and its significance. There are rough patches. One longtime church member asked a trans-gendered person about their sexual identity, trying to name the obvious and be welcoming, and got an earful about not having to explain oneself to anybody. One show on femininity had an artist waxing eloquent about her depiction of a clitoris. Artists will be disruptive—that's part of the job description. But the Holy Biscuit has credibility in the arts community in Newcastle—which, one assumes, it would not have if there were pious boundaries imposed around what can be expressed. Funding from central Methodism allowed HB to hire "proper artists" to lead. Wilkinson offers some theological commentary sometimes, but mostly she steps out of the way: "I'm a sophisticated cheerleader," she said. And HB has more folks on Tuesdays than lots of churches do on Sundays, disproportionately non-believers.

Hillsong: Welcome home

Another church that's growing in Newcastle is in a building that was once Methodist, but is no longer. The handsome former auditorium seats some 550 people comfortably, and is in a neighbourhood that still has a dodgy feel to it—panhandlers outside, rubbish untended to, tourists nowhere in sight. If parts of Newcastle feel like Vegas, this part feels like the part of town they leave off the tourist brochure.

When I mention the sketchiness of the neighbourhood, pastor Jonny Ferguson asks me "Where else would you want the church to be?"

The church is now Hillsong Newcastle, part of the network of congregations begun in Australia that has rocketed around the globe. It has turned up in media accounts in North America mostly for attracting celebrities in New York and southern California.[2] Ferguson, however, is also interested in the more modest question of the building's Methodist roots. "We have a ninety-year-old Methodist lay woman who still worships here," he said, a holdover from the previous congregation. "She and her friends were praying that this building would be full of young people again, and now it is." When

---

2. See, for example, Taffy Brodesser-Akner, "Inside Hillsong: The Church of Choice for Justin Beiber and Kevin Durant," in *GQ*, December 2015: https://www.gq.com/story/inside-hillsong-church-of-justin-bieber-kevin-durant.

I tell folks anywhere in the area that I am studying growing churches, they all assume Hillsong will be among them. And why not? The afternoon I am there some three hundred young people bop along to the music. I sing loud, and yet I can't hear myself over the din. That was one of four worship services that Sunday, totaling some eight hundred to nine hundred people. Hillsong has worked in London and has slowly expanded north, with Newcastle its farthest point north in England, though smaller experiments are afoot in Edinburgh, Birmingham, Liverpool, and elsewhere (without the music or lasers!). "We're doing what the Methodists once did: we have Sunday service, small groups, great music, and ministry with the poor. It's just all updated now," Ferguson said. And how. The congregation is far more diverse than any I've seen in the UK, with large swaths clearly from Africa and Asia. The greeter who welcomes me, I'm told later, is a former homeless man and drug addict. That same Sunday one of Newcastle United Football Club's star players attends, and remains relatively unbothered apparently. This is a church for all kinds in a city of both achievers and those left behind.

The music is the secret, it seems to me.[3] Churches I have pastored in North Carolina and Vancouver have played Hillsong's original tunes, with some degree of success even. They are technically difficult, they require excellent sound systems and musicians, the Sunday I'm there the screens provide their own sort of accompanying light show. It feels not a little like a rock concert. I can feel the music physically pounding in my chest. Ferguson explains that the pre-service music is intentionally a bit too loud, encouraging people to speak loudly to one another as they chat. The vibe is more nightclub than church-as-usual. Hillsong's lyrics are biblically rich, attempting to tell the story from creation to consummation and to locate us within it. My favourite recent tune is called "So Will I"—look it up, if you don't mind having the song invade your skull for weeks. It describes God as the creator of countless galaxies. A subsequent stanza praises God as the forgiver of countless failures. Creation and redemption are intertwined, as they should be in our theology. Hillsong lyrics mention the resurrection more often than any hymnody I've ever come across. Mainliners and liberals might dismiss the music as "conservative" or "fundamentalist," and they wouldn't be wrong. Hillsong has a lyrics-control expert who, from an office in Sydney, decides whether songs pass official muster (in the feature-length film about the church, one of the bands waits anxiously backstage to see whether their song will be OK'd before church starts!). Hillsong's centralized control and the Holy Biscuit's strenuous effort to release control to

---

3. For a bit of the history of contemporary music and Hillsong's place in it, see Swee Hong Lim and Lester Ruth's *Lovin' on Jesus: A Concise History of Contemporary Music.*

local artists could not be more different. Hillsong has then a sort of grand inquisitor, like the Catholic head of the Congregation for the Doctrine of the Faith, Joseph Ratzinger's last job before becoming pope. But once the songs are released, wow. The first song that day started slow and meditative, then ripped into a chorus that saw the singers on stage spring into dancing. I confess tears flew out of my eyes, an involuntary gesture that embarrassed me. Grace is worth celebrating like that, isn't it? No one could see me. They were looking at the stage.

"There is a paradox of the stage," Ferguson tells me. Everyone is looking up there, sure. The musicians are talented, vetted well, and wouldn't stay long without musical skill. But that's not enough. They have to be worshiping. Somehow one can tell if they're not. "We don't just put anyone on the platform. Anyone up there would be willing to clean toilets too. If you're too big to do that, then you're too small to be up there." Protestant theologians in the wake of Stanley Hauerwas have been discussing character in a theoretical way for two generations now. Hillsong considers virtue communally as they decide who can be a background vocalist. "You do need gifting to get up there, but character will keep you there," Ferguson told me.

Hillsong has had an outsized effect on the worship of any church with a screen in its sanctuary or a guitar on its stage. Scholars will debate this effect for generations. Several outside observers lob critiques: HS has simply hoovered up Pentecostals from smaller churches in the city. This entertainment model can "work," but not in pit villages, nor can it be replicated throughout a city ("there can't be two hundred such churches in Newcastle," as one person said to me). Some Newcastle pastors suggest to me they could also entertain more people into their church, but when the music stopped, folks would simply drift away, rootless, zombies in search of the next cool show. They note new people have come to them from HS complaining about lack of community there. HS does invest in small groups, to the point that they only celebrate Communion in those groups, they speak in tongues more often there, all so as to not put off guests at Sunday worship who might not understand these practices: "otherwise folks might be confused—do I take this thing or not?" There is something to these critiques. Yet it should be noted in response that HS's emphasis on the resurrection in their music is a hope-filled theological turn. Half an hour before worship, lead pastor John Cook summons the forty or so volunteers present and gives them a little pep talk, interspersed with cheers and applause. There is a sermonette, a last-second appeal to pick up any rubbish, critical analysis of where the community is in its greeting practices ("We're good at hello. I'm not sure we're so good on goodbye," Ferguson told me). Their openness to outsiders, including allowing probing questions from a journalist, is a positive sign.

John Cook tells his church the day I'm there, "We want a church that asks questions. If the leader can't answer them, that's not *your* problem!" Ferguson explained to me HS's commitment to be "radically transparent, open to all questions, since the Scriptures say to be accountable."

Hillsong Newcastle has an unusual history. Jon and Dee Cook grew up in the Northeast (Stockton and Sunderland, respectively). They worshiped at Hillsong in London, but then felt called to return home, where they started New Life Christian Centre in Newcastle in 2006. They began, as one does, with a handful of people in a coffee shop. They were involved in Hillsong culture—going to conferences, using the music—and then were approached by HS brass a few years ago about becoming a location of the Australian behemoth. Folks often told me, mistakenly, that HS Newcastle had grown to near a thousand worshipers in just a few years. The Cooks actually grew NLCC much more slowly than that. Ferguson tells me they expected more of a bump in attendance by joining the HS label, but saw very little from that. They do use Hillsong's branding, including the slogan "welcome home!" emblazoned on every screen and much of the merchandise. John Drane famously decried the "McDonaldization of church" in response to the gigachurch phenomenon, and sure enough, stepping into any HS location in the world one sees similar logos, branding, and slogans.[4] But there are advantages. People go to McDonald's for a reason. Ferguson tells me the story of a former British marine who walked into Hillsong, saw that sign, and burst into tears. I confess I find myself moved by it far more than a sign that says, say, "worship centre," or "washrooms that way."

Hillsong does exist, as my Methodists once did, to invite people into new life in Christ. The day I'm there an American preacher is beamed in from another location overseas to talk about personal finances. I'm sceptical of this enterprise, having written critically about Dave Ramsey on the American scene before.[5] Yet he is a fine preacher, not surprisingly. He spent time as a teenager homeless on the streets in Chicago, and Horatio Alger-like, has made his money and given back on a vast scale, as he repeatedly indicates ("The first time God told me to put £10,000 in the offering plate, I didn't think it was God—I thought it was the devil!"). I am surprised to notice that people do "amen" back to the preacher on the screen. Video preaching is common in multi-site megachurches. We are used to living our lives on screens, and within moments this experience feels no different. Depressingly for us mainliners, for whom a preached sermon by a live body

---

4. Drane *The McDonaldization of the Church*.

5. Jason Byassee, "Counting the Cost: A Crusade against Consumer Debt," *Christian Century*, 7 August 2007, 18–22.

with a master's degree is the highlight of our work week, this video sermon is just as good or bad as any on which we spend dozens of hours. It is this man's boilerplate speech, after all, refined over years, surely superior to my off-the-top thoughts on a Synoptic Gospel text on a late Saturday night. "It takes no faith to be a non-tither!" he points out. And it's "easy for God to give money to you. The hard thing is to give money *through* you." The theology is not a million miles off what I try to say in tithing sermons, and it's all said much better. The man beside me eats a peanut butter and jelly (the Brits insist on calling it jam) sandwich during the sermon, repeats "yeah" a lot, and licks his fingers, over and over. In the dark one hardly notices. There may be more space for weirdos amidst the dark and noise than there is in most of our churches.

Here is a genuine surprise: Hillsong sees conversions to Christ even when it's not trying for them, as on the day I'm there. All human beings count what matters to us. I count my children obsessively when I'm in public to be sure I haven't lost one or more; VISA counts my debts just as obsessively. Hillsong counts conversions as closely as Methodists count money. "Decisions for Christ matter here. We want to stir faith." And they have some decisions that day. *In response to the tithing sermon!* Five exactly at the service previous to the one I attend. That's their average for a Sunday—more than the fastest growing British Methodist church in the region gets *in a year*. Yet Ferguson is not impressed: "We can get complacent, especially at a large church. We can let our strength become a weakness. We address those areas so as not to slide into just getting tasks done. We want to be desperate for folks to pray to know Jesus."

It's enough to make one ask: what is a mainline church *desperate* for?

Ferguson tries to introduce me to a woman named Sidney from Scotland, who is HS's designated person to pray with those who wish to respond to the gospel and make a decision for Christ. "She shouldn't be here," he says, describing a background with addiction, heroin use, being from the estates. Yet she found her way here and the Holy Spirit turned her life around. "She can really preach," he says, overturning my assumption that HS wouldn't welcome women preachers. He tries to introduce me, but fails. She's too busy praying with people. They're desperate for Jesus, she's desperate to introduce him to them, and so to meet him all over again herself.

And I'm more desperate for lunch on time.

Church grafting in Gateshead: "Not radical enough"

Another church that's desperate to introduce people to Jesus is called St. George's Gateshead, across the Tyne River from Newcastle, but part of the same metro region. Its handsome building is full of brilliant stained glass, and its hulking organ pipes look like weapons from *Game of Thrones*. Plenty of grand downtown churches look just like this and sit empty in England. In fact, this one did too, until the Bishop of Durham handed over the nearly empty building to a church graft from St. Thomas Crookes in Sheffield. Seventeen young people left that church and journeyed northeast to replant a church in a nearly failed building so as to reach people in Gateshead for Jesus. Vicar Rich Grant said to me, "We're the most evangelical church in our diocese, I'm not ashamed of that—we need to reach the 99 percent of folks in England who are dying in their sins."

St. George's is planted through the church planting network of Holy Trinity Brompton. One of the critiques of these resource churches is that they can work in a city of young ambitious professionals like London, but can they work in Gateshead? It is not even a city, properly speaking, the government has withheld that esteemed designation for reasons unclear. It supported Cromwell in the Civil War while Newcastle supported the crown (people remember this stuff!). St. George's occupies numerous edges: the evangelical edge of the C of E, the edge of Durham diocese, the edge of greater Newcastle. But edges and their overlap are where ecosystems birth life. Pastoral care director Louise Grant, Rich's wife, tells me Gateshead feels like the annoying little brother in comparison to Newcastle's aloof big brother. And not only civically—the diocese of Newcastle is resoundingly Anglo-Catholic in orientation, while St. George's, from the diocese of Durham across the river, is as low church as one could get: "I've always considered myself a lifelong Baptist," Rich Grant tells me. "I've always been non-denominational, but I went to a church that happened to be in this tradition." St. George's is the first HTB-style plant in the Northeast, a pioneer among pioneers, so its success or failure is being watched carefully by many. "Justin Welby told me 'if we can't make it there, we can't make it anywhere,'" Rich Grant said. One vicar in the Newcastle diocese suggested to me that St. George's is receiving millions of pounds per year from HTB: "If I had that kind of money I could grow a church half the size of the diocese," he said. Not so, the Grants insist. They got an initial grant of £150,000 from HTB and a free building from Durham diocese, which immediately needed £400,000 in renovations, then St. George's hired a staff team at £150,000 per year, "So the diocese has, so far, made £500,000 off its investment in us," Grant said. The gossip about the money has been hard for Grant, who describes going to meetings where he's met with a certain vibe, "We hate you, but we're not sure why."[6]

Some of it, it has to be said, is jealousy. HTB has grown a church of more than ten thousand members in an era where many churches are closing (and then being given over to be replanted by HTB kids). Its catechesis resource, Alpha, has been used millions of times over around the globe by churches from Pentecostal to Catholic. Its vicar, Nicky Gumbel, is far more recognized worldwide than most bishops in the Anglican Communion. And HTB does have money. Its own church-planting wing is well-funded. Welby's encouragement has meant more HTB-style endeavours get money from the Church of England broadly, leaving less for other sorts of endeavours. St. George's has been in Gateshead for two and a half years when I visit and it's not exactly bursting at the seams—I count some eighty people not on payroll. There is a class-aspirational element both to HTB's appeal and to its detractors' laments. The first three lay people I chat to are all physicians of one sort or another, all refugees from some other church in town, all full of praise for St. George's. The fourth is a wife of a retired C of E vicar who has always felt the denomination was too liberal. But there are not only posh people here. One of St. George's straplines is that it is a church "For everyone. Always." The fifth person I talk with is a single mom who tells me of a near-death experience where, lying in a hospital bed, an Anglican vicar prayed with her. She told God if she got better she would raise her boy in church. She did get better, and kept her promise, finding her way to St. George's, where the little one in the mohawk haircut running around "loves it." They go together now every week. Some research suggests that four fifths of attendees at church plants like St. George's are indeed church people from elsewhere, but that fifth person, out of five, is often someone the C of E would not have reached otherwise. And in Jesus' stories, those few lost ones are enough.

The church's makeover is impressive. St. George's has left touches from the old congregation's life in place, the way a gentrifying makeover would do in a renovated urban loft. The hymn board showing numbers for the hymns on a given day still in place, plaques and memorials to otherwise forgotten leaders and parishioners dot but don't clutter the place. The music's production value is nothing compared to Hillsong's: "We're not the best show in town," Grant tells me. The music is competent, even good, but not flashy, with no light shows. The preaching is better. Louise Grant preaches

---

6. Just for the record, St. George's is not only hated. One of Rich's fellow priests in the diocese said this to me: "St. George's has made a beautiful building beautifully welcoming. It's hard work, but they're committed to one another and to Christ and to evangelism. There are lots of gifts in there, and Rich gets it."

the day I'm there. Rich is a brave vicar to allow his spouse to preach in his place—she's fantastic—accessible and funny and wise. She tells a story of growing up in Denmark and climbing a plumb tree to eat to her heart's content. Later that tree died, a victim of lack of pruning. Pruning can hurt, as otherwise healthy branches are cut off for the sake of the whole. Yet we submit to it because we trust the One pruning. The sermon is not meant to be a defense of HTB resource church style planting, but it could function that way. "If we succeed, we show the failure of the institution," Rich Grant tells me in an interview later. "That we exist highlights an issue. The Church of England has to fundamentally change to reach our community, and that's challenging." I think I know why he's hated. It's not because he's wrong.

Grant is in good company with others in the Anglican Communion who have challenged the system. "If the people you admire either challenged the state (like Wilberforce) or challenged the institutional church (like Wesley) or do so today (like Nicky Gumbel) then you're not an easy fit for the institution." You're not, that is, until you take the controls of said institution, as, arguably, HTB has done. Tired of seeing its candidates for ministry transformed into Oxbridge academics by going up to university, HTB helped plan its own seminary, St. Mellitus' College, named after the original church planter in London, a seventh-century Saxon bishop. The school focuses narrowly on training people to plant or replant churches and has on its faculty roster such luminaries as Jane and Rowan Williams. St. George's is in its ninth incarnation of teaching the Alpha Course, with its eight weeks of catechesis from God to the eschaton, with a noteworthy pinch of teaching about the Holy Spirit and the spiritual gifts, including speaking in tongues. "That's seventy-two sessions of Alpha," Grant said, "and for the first time I sat in the group and thought 'these people are all genuinely searching for faith.'" If HTB and Alpha are a challenge, it is because they are trying to teach the faith anew in an inviting manner. When I used Alpha at my Methodist church in North Carolina, I realized that while I might not like Alpha very much (it leans narrow and conservative and Pentecostal), it can be remarkably effective. Every year a dozen or more projects try to become a "liberal version" of Alpha, and each one so far has failed to have a fraction of the impact Alpha has had. St. George's may feel without friends in Durham and Newcastle for now, but more resource churches are coming. Others will be able to learn from its successes and failures, its glories and mistakes.

One of those, Grant tells me, is a failure of nerve. "We are trying to graft onto existing congregations too much," he said. "This is not radical enough." Churches in North America that take over existing buildings will often change the locks, repaint all the logos, and kick out any existing people, at least for a time. Grant inherited a parish counsel full of longtime church members whose church had been effectively closed. "I had to ask them all to resign six months in, which they did." Bishops can be reluctant to run people off, but those few who remain are often dysfunctional enough not to notice the building collapsing around them. They are just as clueless at recognizing the new direction the church is taking: "We have to play defense a lot," Grant said. In one way this is good—the oldtimers don't raise a fuss and go on volunteering. In another it is not helpful. With the old guard around, old patterns that led to closure remain in the room, and have to be triaged for, maneuvered around, shielded from new people. "It's problematic that in a town of two hundred thousand people, the C of E had no meaningful presence," Grant said. "Our conversation has yet to realize the scale of the challenge we face." He describes folks from other wings of the C of E carping at St. George's as "arguing over the scraps off the table. It's incredibly sad really."

What does he want to see instead? What is he desperate for? "I want to see Gateshead come alive. Like all HTB churches, I want to take part in the re-evangelization of the nation, the revitalization of the church, the transformation of society."

That's all.

Sometimes it all works. It only takes one church growing to give the lie to the despairing misperception that "nothing can work here." Sometimes the edges become a new centre. It happened before, as Irish monks transformed lonely, Godforsaken islands into hubs of mission and ministry across what would become the UK and Ireland. It's happened recently, as HTB went from an outlying success story to the Church of England's planting engine, as St. Thomas Crookes went from an ordinary parish church to a missionary-sending dynamo. Success and wisdom hard-won in Gateshead could transform St. George's from the edge into the centre again. Grant is not competing with other churches. Hillsong has the church refugee market cornered with its great show, other churches in town have their niches. He cites one of the online movie streaming services, asked if their competition was the other quite-similar service, saying no. Their competition is all the other ways people spend their leisure time. So too with church. "Most people are not thinking 'I want to go to church, I just haven't found the right one'. If someone comes to us, it's hard-won." St. George's has caught up with the reality of church in twenty-first century England, as the Wesleys did in the late eighteenth century before them. Whether they can help incite a revival similar to the Wesleyan one from which they take inspiration remains to be seen. But stranger things have happened.

"A bunch of misfits"

I didn't want to attend Connect at St. Luke's Anglican Church in Newcastle. This mother church of Sanctuary 21 in Durham was designed for ex-offenders, addicts, and other human wreckage, launched by Junction 42, a prison ministry in the area. I expected I'd learn something and leave sad. These are not folks with whom I go out of my way to spend my time. But Rusty, who we met in chapter 3, insisted on it. I'd miss something vital about ministry in the Northeast of England without seeing it. So I went. Unwillingly.

My first surprise was that I could hear the singing from the car park. That is, through the basement they were gathering in, through the modest brick exterior of the once-handsome parish church, and through the crisp spring air. This didn't sound like human wreckage. It sounded like the singing of the redeemed. Entering the press of humanity felt more like joining a frat party than a church. And they were just getting going. The next song, "Nothing but the Blood"—much derided as a an old-timey hymn with retrograde theology in North America—felt like something went off in the room. Folks rushed toward the front. A few leaped up on chairs. Half had their hands up, swaying. Several in the back looked nervous, like they'd wandered into a room full of the wrong sorts of wackos. People covered in tattoos, whom you wouldn't be surprised to learn had done hard time, looked genuinely frightened. This was a song of free people.

It is unsettling. In the best sense.

Connect, and St. Luke's Church that hosts it, shouldn't exist. St. Luke's actually closed its doors as a parish in 2006. The next year it was allowed to reopen as a Fresh Expression (FX), an effort to relate the gospel to a surrounding culture in creative ways, about which we will learn more in chapter eight. In response to the massive failure of church-as-usual to reach its neighbours, innovative efforts began in the 1990s to do church without the baggage and for the unreached, not for already-churched people. Some of these experiments were flat failures. One vicar in Newcastle told me of a £300,000 grant to open a Fresh Expression, in their case a coffee shop. It lost £1,000 a week, eight to ten people came, none unchurched, so it was given a good death. "It was a disaster," he said flatly. Gather enough such negative witnesses and FX looks like a poor investment indeed, especially for parishes that are already struggling with resources of money and energy and hope.

St. Luke's has had a rather different experience with Fresh Expressions. A similar grant funded a new vicar's salary. Instead of imposing a model from elsewhere, like cool worship with guitars or a café, Robert Ward set about listening. What does this community love? What does it long for? In response to what it'd learned, St. Luke's set about launching multiple cell groups to align with its new friends' needs. Aroos is a missional community in nearby Whitley Bay that meets at what seems, to me, the impossibly late hour of 9–10 pm. It meets not in a church, however, but in folks' homes, at open-mic nights, on basketball courts for cleanup, in local businesses. In prayer and worship it seeks "to create a vulnerable, deep, and sharing community between us." Another group is called Avodah, which seeks to create among its participants "a seamless life of work, worship, and service," meeting in one another's homes. Instead of hyping only attendance or converts, Avodah boasts of one of its group receiving an award for innovation in business, and another welcoming a new baby. A Christian motorcyclists group meets for churchy things like worship and discipleship, but also "meets" to ride—much farther afield than Newcastle! I could list a dozen more. Instead of starting a church and then begging people to join small groups, these small groups *are the thing*. And the least small of the small groups is Connect. It boasts some eighty to a hundred participants, it has gone on international mission trips as well as more predictable retreats and concerts. And its worship is more like an African-American church than any white church I've experienced in Britain.

On the way to Connect, Rusty tells me about a man named Reggie, whom he met fresh out of prison. The first time he saw him, Reggie was covered, head-to-foot, in tattoos, with his arms folded aggressively in the back. When time came to read Scripture, Rusty tilted his Bible toward Reggie to let him read along. The gruff retort came, "I can't read." Sometime later when Rusty attended he saw Reggie again. This time he was in a pink shirt—not a common fashion choice for ex-offenders. He wore a pair of thick reading glasses. When Reggie had said "I can't read," he meant not that he was illiterate. He simply can't see without glasses that made him feel self-conscious. But whatever had happened in the meantime that allowed him the confidence to wear pink also allowed him to wear those glasses.

Oh, and Reggie was reading the Bible. He hasn't stopped reading the Bible since.

Connect's worship is loud and participatory, as I said. So too are its announcements. A man rises to tell the group something "hard to hear." A young man who'd been part of Connect had committed suicide three weeks ago. He was baptized in the North Sea three years prior. He had been coming to Connect, but hadn't escaped his demons, and they overwhelmed him. There is hope: "we know he's with the Lord now." And a group from Connect was planning to caravan to his funeral. Prayers are asked for him, for those who miss him, and implicitly for all teetering on the edge of life. There is a reason this group preaches a life-and-death gospel.

And they are in-your-face about it. The group leader that night, one John O' Connor (not the guy in *The Terminator*, he specifies) is an ex-offender whose version of the gospel is all-in or all-out. He apologizes for this, sort of. In prayer he tells God "I know some here are not Christians." So he sets out to do something about it. At one point he asks who in the group has not yet been baptized. "Raise your hands." A few tentatively go up. Later he asks the same question again. More go up, with more confidence this time. "Come on, if you've not yet been baptized, stand up. We want to pray for you." A few do stand. He invites them to a course to prepare to be baptized in the North Sea in a few months' time. "Go see Kieran for details," and a small scrum ensues around Kieran, the detail-man.

Among the polite folk whom I've pastored, asking folks to identify as non-Christian would be a massive turnoff and land me in meetings about my employment future. But O'Connor has no time for politeness. He was in jail seven times. "I had to have smack every day," he said, before the Lord healed him of heroin addiction in 1999. He wants others similarly healed. And they need it. Rusty points out to me who is recently out of prison, who he thinks needs praying for, but then I realize I can spot them too. They're not singing or raising their hands or swaying. They're *there*, which is saying a lot. They're exploring. There is a frontier of faith being pointed out to them and they're contemplating whether to cross it. Other things have failed them. Will this? O'Connor and Reggie and others are insisting it will not. Try it. What do you have to lose?

One who has seen faith work is Cassie Hamilton, a student at Cranmer Hall in Durham, and Connect's worship coordinator. She leads beautifully from the front, and also quietly from the back. She is in her mid-twenties, and has been a part of Connect for its whole life, six years. Rusty says he's seen her grow as a leader from strength to strength, from precocious teen-aged rebellion to maturing and mellowing in wisdom. She's getting married soon, and plans to be ordained in the Church of England. If, that is, "they let me pastor my people. I have a heart for these people from the neighbourhood I grew up in."

It was a rough one. Her father was addicted to drugs, spending, he has said publicly, £400 a day on cocaine. He tried to be a father and husband, but Cassie and her mom tired of his promises to reform and do better and try harder. So they made the hard choice to close him out of their lives. He came back one more time, not insistent this time, just to tell them he'd changed. He'd met Jesus, he'd given up the chemicals, and they didn't have to let him back in at all. He just wanted them to know. They opened up, wary but interested, and found he really had changed. Jesus accomplished what nothing else could. Now Cassie is proud that her dad is "the best evangelist around." Folks in Connect trace their life there to his invitation. She has followed his lead into ministry, finding Jesus herself after Jesus found her father. Seminary has been wonderful, and she intends to offer what she learns there back to Connect, to her future ministry on an estate like the one she grew up on. But she has some lessons for the seminary too. "My classmates often ask whether the miraculous can happen. Not me. I've seen it. I've seen exorcisms and healings," she said.

The night I'm at Connect includes a testimony by a woman named Nina. "I tried to bottle this," she said to appreciative laughter, but O'Connor persisted in asking her to speak. She grew up depressed, attempting suicide, slashing herself, even "trying classier drugs," she said. But someone from Connect invited her to church. She would agree to come, only to "self-sabotage," and bail at the last second. Her friend persisted. When she finally came, she found something she never had before. "No offense," she said, "but this is a bunch of misfits, so I fit in!" Uproarious applause. She became a Christian while hungover. She didn't want to go to a church gathering she'd been invited to, so she got "mortal drunk." She woke up, and looked in the mirror, and felt the Lord ask her, "Are you the same person you were nine months ago?" No Lord. "Six months ago?" No. Last month? No. She'd changed. Just not all the way. So she went. She promised herself she wouldn't go in if she couldn't find a parking place up front. There were two. She went in, and one of the "prophets" on stage pointed to her, called her up to the microphone, and she went, and gave her testimony. When she was done, a woman in the congregation raced up to her. "You won't remember this, but you came here when you were five years old. I met you, and have prayed for you every day since." Nina concluded this way: "I had argued with God all day. But he's faithful. We're here for each other as family. There's no shame when we fall back. We seek the Lord's face and the sin falls off."

As an academically trained, upper-middle class theologian, all I have are questions and quibbles. Why are all her references to God masculine? Did God really orchestrate her parking place? Isn't this form of in-your-face evangelism more a turn-off than a model for others? Academics are good at asking questions—especially distancing questions. Sure, God might do that sort of thing for others, but I don't need that sort of dramatic turnaround. I'm good, thanks.

But need I even point this out? Nina's and Cassie's and O'Connor's and Reggie's versions of the gospel are more life-saving than mine. At the edge of life and death, they have no patience for quibbles and little time for nuancing. Something is at stake in what they offer. This is no academic exercise. It is a story of heaven and hell, angels and demons, life or its absence. They are on the hunt for God, and eager to find evidence that God has already been on the hunt for them. What we call "coincidence" or even "gullibility" they call *signs*. And signs stoke the search for a sign-giver, lover, friend. The gospel does its best work on the edges. Those of us who fancy ourselves safe in the middle naturally have little time for such a gospel. So is it any surprise our churches struggle, close, and board up, while Connect flourishes?

Trying to get my head around Connect—both my initial antipathy and subsequent delight—I met with Robert Ward, the vicar of St. Luke's Church. He hardly comes off as the gritty, social justice pastor. If some of the leaders in this book are whirlwinds, hurricanes of energy, Ward comes off more as an Eeyore, more Bilbo Baggins than Strider. He moves at a slow clip, he deliberately puts his cloth napkin into his neck before eating, and eating really matters to him. He made sure several times we were meeting at a good enough restaurant and that I was paying. This was before he was sure he had my name right or why I wanted to meet with him. Priorities. I respect them.

Whatever his personal speed, Robert is a Pentecostal Anglican. In this region of the Northeast of England, Pentecostalism broke out within an established denomination. Alexander Body learned about the Azusa Street revivals in the early 1900s and brought such strange new gifts as speaking in tongues to his Anglican parish in Sunderland, then the industrial heartland of this region. He and his wife preached and practiced laying on of hands for healing, they sponsored conferences internationally that included folks from all over the world. They were the early leaders of Pentecostalism in the UK, and they lived and died as Anglicans, not unlike John Wesley in a previous revival.

Ward grew up in the South of England and was a lawyer and a Pentecostal layman. He lost his job amidst political machinations and wondered if he should join the RAF or work for Rolls Royce, his other hobbies. But he heard a word from the Lord, as Pentecostals are wont to do, that his vocation would come clear in two weeks. Two weeks later he was back in church, grousing to God that he had ten minutes left, and the word came to him: what'd he like to do? Going to church, helping the poor, praying, reading Scripture. Oh God, he realized. God wants me to be ordained. He was miserable. The church seemed so often dead from the neck up, or down, or whatever way is more interesting. But the word he'd received was that he'd resist too, so that was part of it. He sought out info from the evangelical colleges in the country, and the least gauzy, most retrograde brochure came from Cranmer Hall in Durham. Someone who laid hands on him and prayed heard one word and gave it to Robert: Durham. He bought a train ticket and left, and has stayed in the Northeast ever since.

Ward noticed that Newcastle had no Pentecostal Anglican church, so he set out to start one. Newcastle is historically a liberal catholic diocese, though Ward insists how blessed he is to serve here, the bishops he's worked under and with love Jesus, they love the Bible, and they make space for him: "I'm so fond of the people who don't raise their hands, but honor the word and preach a darn good sermon, but don't pray expecting loads of people to get healed." His church rented space from an existing parish, and grew fairly quickly from six to twenty-five (when you're small a little growth is a lot). And the boiler went out on the host congregation. St. Luke's was down to a dozen or so old people, they didn't have £40,000 to fix it, so they closed up shop and the parish technically ceased to exist. The bishop called Robert: I have no salary for you, no pension, no house, and a building with no boiler. Do you want it? Why yes, he said. For years they met in the basement because it was less freezing than the sanctuary. It's amazing the freedom for ministry you have if you don't need a salary, isn't it?

For a time the church was the fastest growing in the diocese, from twenty-five to now 150 weekly, with those small groups or Fresh Expressions as the primary engine of growth. I ask Robert about the volume and intensity of worship among the ex-offenders at Connect, and he quotes a good source: "those who have been forgiven much love much." They do praise like Mary Magdalene, with perfume on Jesus' feet and all up in her hair. I tell him of the famous prayer, "Lord, send us the people no one else wants," and he says it's precisely that, these folks can't fit in easily in a middle-class church. They can't fit in easily anywhere. But they lead St. Luke's now. They're its largest cell group by far. And folks from five or six countries have come to learn from them; they've planted in other cities all over the UK. With onetime prisoners in the lead, St. Luke's is no longer near closure. It's been returned to parish status, which means it has the trappings of church life back: it has to fill committees: "My caretaker served seventeen years for murder," Ward told me, "My worship leader ten years for armed robbery." What can you say? Jesus has weird and demanding friends. And they eat together. Each Fresh Expression at St. Luke's meets over a proper meal. They used to meet over carbs and caffeine, but no longer. When you eat together, your metabolism changes, you get to laughing, new things are possible. It's just church. Ward mentions the buffet so often not just because he's hungry, it's because Jesus is hungry, and wants others to eat with him.

Robert Ward has found a pattern in ministry of what he calls "identificational repentance." I'd not heard of it, so I asked. He gave me an example. He and his wife's families both worked in civil service in India. So when he preached there he opened by saying how glad he was for the place—his family helped bring electricity to Bombay, his wife's sewer service to Calcutta. But that meant they were complicit in atrocities, not just the Amritsar massacre, but colonialism in general. He apologized. They cheered. Someone said, that's ok, you also brought us the language, civil service, railways, and cricket. Especially cricket. Then they listened. Robert had three or four other stories like that, including reconciliation between English and Germans and Japanese, folks from the North and South of England. In each case it seemed a child of Ward's ended up married to someone from the other place. Reconciliation is demanding, wedding altar stuff. Some years ago there was a vote for Scottish independence from the UK. Just before it, Ward invited a gathering of Scottish and English church leaders in the area to meet at Vindolanda, a Roman city now being excavated, with the ruins of the second oldest church in the UK. He read a list of atrocities committed against Scots by English people over the centuries. A Scottish leader did the same. They embraced, communed, forgave. And the vote turned out differently than many expected. Ward isn't saying the little gathering directly affected the outcome, though one can wonder. This was no direct political symbol. But he did expect the cross of Christ to affect where people put "the crosses in the ballot box." And who's to say that didn't happen? Here you affect politics not by telling people how to vote, much less telling Caesar how to do his job, but by repentance. For wrongs done centuries before in a holy place. And then you see what weird things God does, confident that God loves reconciliation.

Whether you're inclined to respect Pentecostalism or disdain it, Robert Ward has something that churches can't do without. He thinks God is alive, and active, and up to something. The way God called him into ministry might be particularly Pentecostal. But to say the living God works by discernible patterns is not Pentecostal, it's just Christian. Pentecostals have this that often mainline Christians have lost: a sense that God works and we can discern God's working. It's not automatic or simple to do so, but it's necessary and we have to be about it, otherwise let's give up pretending and go home. I love this about the Pentecostals; they think their God is alive. Often, when we object, we sound like we're saying 'nah, God doesn't work anymore.' Second, Ward has done what he's done with no denominational funding. I don't advocate this. I personally want a pension and to be overpaid, thank you very much. And there's some privilege in being able to say yes to no money. Ward was driven by wanting a Pentecostal Anglican church in town, even if there was nothing in it for him. He's paid a salary now, and a pension presumably, but there were no guarantees at first, as there are not for most pioneers in church history. Lord give us more like that. Third, and surprisingly, something Ward did have was networks. His church is part of Fresh Expressions nationally. It is linked up with Fusion, the most interesting student ministry in the UK. It's linked with New Wine, the most interesting charismatic-friendly network in the UK. Everywhere

I've seen something growing it's linked with such networks.[7] These provide conferences, ideas, encouragement, pools for recruitment. Scholars have begun to explore the rise in networked Christianity on both sides of the Atlantic. Our denominations were meant to serve this purpose but usually can't or don't anymore; we have to look elsewhere. And where they're absent Ward has grown them. How else, but with food! A group meets weekly for prayer in Newcastle. He founded it. They meet over a nice buffet for prayer. Bilbo would have it no other way. You are who you eat . . . with.

Patterns

I'm not proposing in these pages that we copy Jesmond Methodist, Hillsong, St. George's Gateshead, Connect, or St. Luke's. I am proposing that we do *something*. These stories of life are tentative, fragile, and beautiful. They are dramatically different from one another in scale, location, neighbourhood, socioeconomic status, worship style, and overall complexion. But they are each stories of churches that were not satisfied with their status quo. They innovated, tried something new for the area, and met with new life.

And one thing Jesus promises is that there is more life for those courageous, or foolish, enough to seek it.

These congregations in Newcastle open a number of questions. One, how do we pay attention to the history of our churches and deploy that history in fruitful ways? Jesmond Methodist has a history of charismatic visions—but their pastor, Allison Wilkinson, thinks that tradition can inhibit as well as help. Hillsong inherited a formerly Methodist building (and saint) and makes use of that in its self-understanding. St. George's represents an evangelical strand within Anglicanism, with all its gifts and inherited baggage, and puts it to use pioneering with a church replant in Gateshead. Traditions, like every other created good, bring both blessings and limitations (sometimes at the same time!). The question is how we understand our tradition in enough depth to deploy it for mission in a new day.

Secondly, these congregations raise the question of what we are *desperate* for. Connect has no time for nicety. Lives are at stake, and good news is dearly needed. St. George's and Hillsong are similarly desperate to reach new people for Jesus. What is our congregation desperate for? What is the thing that puts us into evasive action, sets our heart to beating fast, the thing we cannot do without? The converse question is also important to ask: where do we see complacency? Where do we see Christmas decorations left

---

7. Scholars have begun to take note: see, for example, Brad Christerson and Richard Flory, *The Rise of Network Christianity*.

out in February, or a connection with another institution *under our same roof* that's not being made? As leaders we have to be attentive to "low hanging fruit," to easy wins, to ways we can nudge mission forward and gain momentum, on the way to bigger challenges. Desperation and complacency are good gauges of where to find those things.

Third and finally this: who do you have in leadership, or in your congregation, who "shouldn't" be there at all? If Christ is drawing all the "wrong" people to himself, how is that displayed in the visual makeup of the folks up front, in the faces of those in the building, among those you're trying to reach? If the answer is nowhere, then we have work to do finding the frontier, the edge of our faith community, and inviting people across it to join us. I say that with confidence because churches *always* have work to do finding the outsider and inviting them in; leaving the security of being insiders and finding those farthest outside. Connect illustrates this most clearly in its work with ex-offenders and drug-abusers, but each church doing evangelism shows the same. New family members are added, with all the joy and distress that causes. Old ones are disaffected, fight, struggle for control. Amidst all of that churn, who do we have, like the recovered heroin addict at Hillsong who prays with those coming to Christ, whose story evokes admiration, awe, even imitation? That person needs to be up front, leading and praying others toward Jesus Christ.

7

BCP IN FARSI

The nations come to the North

THE BODY OF CHRIST speaks Farsi. And the English it learns has a discernible Geordie accent.

I shouldn't have been surprised to learn that churches in the North of England are doing ministry with displaced people from Persia. My wife did ministry with refugees from Iraq and Syria in Vancouver, helping them cope with the least friendly housing market in North America. If they would come to the Hong Kong of the Americas to be poor, they would come to the North of England, where one can still buy a flat for five figures. The typical path for a Farsi-speaking refugee is to be registered in Croydon and then shipped somewhere in England where the housing is most affordable (read: the North).

An even stronger reason than economics is theology. Churches welcome refugees. We are commanded to do so by Christ himself. And from Vietnamese boat people to Hmong in Minnesota to Syrians today, a displaced person should expect a welcome of some sort from whatever church they turn up at. The motives may be mixed: evangelicals welcome conversions while liberals may not encourage them (one welcoming Brit asked an Iranian would-be convert "Why convert? Islam is a beautiful religion!" The reply, from a refugee from a tyrannical theocracy: "No it's not"). But churches welcome people as commanded to by Christ. This is a political issue and often unpopular—in Italy and eastern Europe, "do gooders" are pilloried by a newly resurgent right wing with fascist sympathies. Trump in America and Brexit in the UK were, in part, powered by anti-immigrant,

Islamophobic, and often racist hysteria. There will be also be a backlash in English-speaking places against churches for their offering welcome when the local populace wants to build walls and shut borders. It is only a matter of time.

There are also colonialist and missionary reasons, difficult as these always are to distinguish from one another. Iran was once a British colony. There are still Anglican churches in Iran. They cannot proselytize, legally speaking, but they do conduct worship. The Bishop of Loughborough in the Church of England, Guli Francis-Dehqani, is the daughter of the first Iranian bishop in the Anglican Communion, Hassan Dehqani-Tafti. She, like many Iranians, fled the country after the 1979 revolution. Extremists targeted her family, murdering her brother and attempting to assassinate her father. The Dehqani's were Anglican in Iran, and they are Anglican now, with two generations of service to the episcopacy, signed in their own blood. As that wave of refugees and asylum-seekers in the aftermath of 1979 found homes in the West, some communicated with family back in Iran that they had found welcome among these nice Christian people, with some (limited, to be sure) links to Farsi language and culture and religious practices. With recent economic and environmental challenges in Iran, a new wave of refugees has left the country.[1] Because Iranians are generally Shi'a Muslims, culturally Persian and Farsi-speaking, they often do not find welcome in Sunni mosques in the West, which tend to be culturally and linguistically Arab and Arabic-speaking. Shi'a Islam has profound theological resonances with Christianity. Jesus is supposed to come back in Shi'a Islam just before the Mahdi does at the end of the world. Sharing an eschatology that is similar, not only in form, but even in content, Shi'a Muslims can make their way into Christianity more easily than into Sunni Islam at times. That these nice Christians will then help with the procurement of asylum-status is no negative.

Several churches I visited have seen large and sudden increases in Persian attendees, baptizands, confirmands, members, and leaders. For a church starved for people, this is a godsend. Not unilaterally—there can be resentment and backlash. One Catholic friend told me of a priest who invited Iranians to live in the church hall. The parish's longtimers felt like the church they had built was given away without their consent to other people. The priest doubled down, giving up his rectory as well. The stories we have of hospitality in the Christian tradition are extravagant, costly, and beautiful. They can be utterly opaque to those who are politically opposed to such

---

1. For some of the reasons why, see Amir Ahmadi Arian, "Why Are So Many Iranian Minors Seeking Sanctuary in Europe?" *Al Jazeera*, 18 January 2019): https://www.aljazeera.com/indepth/opinion/iranian-minors-seeking-asylum-europe-190109135539105.html.

acts of welcome, especially those who struggle with multi-generational poverty who are not receiving assistance from their government the same way "these new people" are. There are, of course, stories of immigrants playing the system, misleading government officials, coming with more assets than they let on, even offering cover for those who intend violence in the West. There are also stories of Home Office employees baselessly claiming to be able to see inside the souls of asylum seekers, insisting that their Christian conversions are not legitimate.[2] Queen Elizabeth I may have wanted a faith in England that refused to "peer into men's souls," but her descendants in government think they know better.

One can understand why. A baptism is a ticket to asylum status. Someone baptized in England, returned to Iran, is likely to be mistreated. The government may call it "religious repression," the church may call it martyrdom, but whatever it is, baptism means a step toward legal status in Britain. And yet that is not all that is going on with Farsi-speaking refugees. If the hope for asylum status were all they were after, we would see a similar rush of Muslim refugees from elsewhere, but Syrians and others are not joining churches in droves in the same way. Nevertheless, baptism can be a fast track. One priest tells me of an asylum-seeking atheist who sought status for reasons of political conscience, being opposed to a theocratic government in Iran. Her case is still unsettled. Meanwhile churches are hosting Farsi-speaking events and setting out extra chairs. In an era where being too immigrant-friendly can get you launched out of government, this is politically explosive.

For example, Liverpool Cathedral hosts a Sunday service called Sepas, conducted in Farsi, led by Iranians. There is an older generation present, made up of 1979-era refugees, including an Iranian-born priest. Then there is a younger generation with no memory of the overthrow of the Shah and the rise of Ayatollah Khomeini. They just know corruption, lack of economic opportunity, and climate-change induced eco-catastrophe are problems in Iran without foreseeable solutions. And they react against a government-imposed religion in ways that would make a western non-believer proud. One priest says this about that congregation: "You often find five or six young people passionately gathered around one Farsi Bible, in a way that you never see twenty-something young people from Britain."

I'll call this priest "Charlie."[3] Charlie was, himself, once a Muslim, and lived in Iran, before returning to the Anglican faith of his forebears and

2. Gabriella Swerling, "Church Attacks Home Office for Saying Christianity 'Not Peaceful' to Reject Asylum Seeker," *The Telegraph*, 21 March 2019): https://www.telegraph.co.uk/news/2019/03/21/church-attacks-home-office-saying-christianity-not-peaceful/.

3. Note: I much prefer to use actual names. Charlie originally spoke with me on record, but subsequently insisted he had not, and asked that I not use this material.

becoming a priest. He speaks from personal experience then when he says this: "Folks here assume Iranians don't know theology. But every conversation in Iran is theological. It's rife in the media, in commerce, so they have a deeper understanding of theology than Christians tend to assume at first."

So why convert, other than political expediency?

One reason is that they are here, now. Charlie has his numbers ready: there were 1,842 asylum claims in London as of our meeting in spring 2019, and 3,942 in much-smaller Liverpool. Those numbers may represent many more people, since whole families can be on one claim application. Liverpool has proclaimed itself a sanctuary city, positioning itself as a place of welcome, over against some more immigrant-wary parts of Britain. Industrial cities in the North of England are used to people leaving. They hope some newcomers will consider staying, after they see that "the Northwest is a blessing." There are deficits to living in the North. "They can be sent to places where there've been no Muslims, skinheads can react . . . ." Liverpool, however, has a history of welcoming newcomers from faiths that had previously been considered drastically (or even dangerously) *other*: Jews, Catholics, Muslims. Plus "new networks can spring up." There are push factors as well. Folks can have a sense of being let down by Islam, whether back home in Iran or by fellow Muslims in Britain. Oceans of Saudi money are being spent to promote Wahabi Islam around the globe, so there can be a pushback against that sort of fundamentalism, or at least against its accompanying Arabic culture and language. "Here they can be free to have a life with God *in Farsi*," Charlie said. He points to an Alpha course offered at the cathedral in Farsi that drew 120 people for its first meeting and had to break up into several smaller groups. The English-speaking Alpha drew four people.

Yet there are questions. Charlie is committed to interfaith dialogue and honouring the other: "Do we celebrate conversions? What does that do to our relationships with Muslims? Or to Christians in Iran?" He insists that the C of E has no evangelism program toward Iranian Muslims: "Our first calling is to care for the marginalized. We didn't set out to evangelize. We asked them in for tea, and asked how we could help." He tells the story of a young man named Faisal, who came to church upon a friend's invitation, but sat in the back, disengaged. A retired pastor from another denomination sat with him, engaged him in conversation, helped him procure food vouchers. Faisal asked why she was doing this: "They're surprised people who don't know them reach out to them." And there is a sense that this is

---

Since I had recorded his reflections accurately, I elected to use what he had said while changing his and others' names in this section.

the faith of the people who welcomed them, unlike the faith of the people who sent them fleeing from their homeland. "There is a sense of wanting to integrate," Charlie told me.

Nadine Daniel is a national coordinator for refugee relief across the C of E. I ask whether evangelicals in the Church of England might be especially enthusiastic about evangelizing Muslims. I have heard evangelicals in North America speak of the evangelistic opportunities on university campuses, where God brings the nations to study, and perhaps sends them home with a relationship with Jesus. She objects strenuously to any such strategy. Her own heritage is the Anglo-Catholic wing of the Church, more smells and bells than turn or burn. This nineteenth-century rediscovery of the catholicity of the Church of England was convinced that unlettered poor people would respond positively to sacraments and icons and incense in a way they never did to the Reformation's insistence on the Word alone. So they relocated churches to city centres, and conducted Corpus Christi processions around estate neighbourhoods. Its effectiveness is still debated, but inarguably there are still Anglo-Catholic parishes in poor neighbourhoods throughout the country. "Anglo-Catholics have always had a calling to city centres, so we minister to the folks who are there." She is also adamant that they do not evangelize: "Folks come in looking for community. The kind of worship there hardly matters. Liverpool has England's oldest purpose-built mosque, its second oldest synagogue. This isn't a stretch."

Here she pushes back against the fears of some in Europe about racial, cultural, or religious dilution. The right-wing press in Europe and North America has often suggested that refugees are a sort of Trojan horse, intending to make formerly Christian places Muslim. But culture is more complicated than that. People convert in multiple directions. Christianity has always worked at the edges of culture, revitalizing the centre. The gospel is given away at its missionary edges, and then those who receive it receive it in their own cultural categories, which are, in turn, transformed by the gospel. They bring their culture's gifts into the church in a way that blesses and revitalizes the centre. The C of E is aware of this reverse evangelism pattern in the ministry of John Sentamu, profiled earlier in this book. The entire Church of England and the society it serves has been blessed by his Uganda-born and persecution-forged form of Christianity. So too with Farsi-speaking Persians. I hear of newborn Christian faith filled with stories of dreams and visions, miracles and hopes for martyrdom. These are prominent themes in Shi'a Islam, of course, and now they are also in Anglicanism, through a stream of church growth that no one planned and few foresaw. Anglican missionaries once traveled to what's now Iran, protected by British guns and transported by British commercial routes. No longer. "The nations are coming to England," one vicar told me. Ready or not, they will change the church here, and not just the church.

Liberation in Sunderland

I had been told that Sunderland was the Detroit of England: a place with a great industrial heritage, now more than a little down in the mouth. Ancient Christians knew it as a glassblowing hub. More modern people knew it as a shipbuilding behemoth. But Margaret Thatcher closed the yards, same as she closed the mines outside Durham. Boats could be bought cheaper from elsewhere in Europe. Folks in Sunderland voted adamantly in favor of Brexit. They knew it would hurt them economically, but a Tory government and finance people from London shilling against it was enough to make them vote for it, so they did. One of Brexit's first casualties was Nissan's announcement it would not go forward with a planned expansion of its automobile factory in Sunderland.

The housing stock in Sunderland does not shout with despair. Someone once built handsome homes here, and sauntered off Sundays to churches with proud steeples. Of the seven church buildings I pass, one is now a homeless resource centre, one a Gudwara, two seem only to open once per week for worship, one is an evangelical church (Alpha: a dead giveaway), and one a private home bought by an organ aficionado who really wanted the instrument and space to practice whenever he wanted. The seventh is the Sunderland Minster, so-called once Sunderland became an official city in government eyes only a few decades ago. Sunderland was a Republican town in the English Civil Wars, but this church was a royalist parish, so the three Cromwell-era vicars have marked by their name the ignominious word, "intruder," etched in (literal) stone. As one might expect from a glassblowing town, the stained glass is magnificent. One image is of Benedict Biscop, an activist abbot advocating for England in Rome, bringing back glass blowers and stonemasons and literary treasures from the continent to build city and church. The other shows St. Bede kneeling in prayer. The church needs both sorts of leaders: activists and contemplatives. And the minster has both in the Rev. Chris Howson.

If there is such a thing as a likely profile for a vicar, Howson fails to fit it. He grew up on estates in London in a non-Christian family: "I had no baggage to overcome," he grins. He does that a lot, pulling his long wavy gray hair back over his bald spot and tying it up, as if eager to make mischief. A vicar he met as a teen suggested he try talking to Jesus as one talks to another person in the room, out loud. He did, and felt a presence he has not been able to unfeel, "full of light." He tried evangelical and Pentecostal churches and found them spiritually empty compared to his experience of Jesus, so he left the church until he went into social work. There he realized he could not help address society's problems with no attention to their spiritual dimension. Field placement put him in a church, he found he was good at the work, so he sought out ordination. The Church of England has few priests indeed from his sort of blue-collar background, so he sailed into ordained ministry.

The Church of England still has few people like Chris Howson in ordained ministry.

It's not just his frenetic energy, though he could make cocaine nervous. It's his cheerful activism. He comes off as a man in full stride, gliding like a horse in easy harness. Activists can come across as angry—Howson as anything but. His book *Just Church* is a plea for Fresh Expressions-style experiments in ministry to meet and marry the anti-war and pro-justice movements of our time. He regales the reader with stories of being a happy warrior. Some of the activism seems stereotypical—protesting nuclear submarines at their harbor. Others are more surprising—serving cups of coffee to grieving cops in the spot where their colleague was killed. He is a community activist, taking note of where the pain is, noticing resources folks didn't know they had, and marshalling them into the cause of the common good. The successes are sometimes small indeed: few military installations have closed here or elsewhere for such activism. Yet one historic movie theatre was saved from developers. One local grocery store was kept from conversion into condos. These might be small-scale victories, but they matter in neighbourhoods, and neighbourhoods matter to Howson. He delights in discovering that activists could superglue their hands together, considerably slowing down efforts to arrest them. "I do exorcisms at arms fares in London and Scotland," he beams. "It's a media stunt, but I really do think the weapons are evil."

And he has grown a church. Twice. Howson's activist career is not just for the purposes of virtue signaling to other similarly left-minded folks with lighter arrest records. "The gospel really is *good news* to the poor," he said, surprised at my surprise that he wants to bring people to Jesus.

Howson was invited to plant a church in Bradford, a 24.7 percent Muslim city near York that tends to turn up in the news for made-for-TV religious protests of one sort or another. The city had no need of a "happy clappy" church, Howson thought, "so let's try Liberation, shall we?" He launched two Fresh Expressions. One, called SoulSpace, was committed to challenging "the perception of those who believe that churches rarely involve themselves in issues of social justice." SoulSpace would engage in "guerilla gardening," cleaning up unused plots, or throwing seedbombs over fences into green space they couldn't get to. They would volunteer as "street angels" in Bradford, wearing bright uniforms on party nights in town, linked on the radio, and "smiling a lot." Crime reduced by 22 percent due to their presence, Howson writes in *Just Church*, and a short-term loan shark was put out of business. Another Fresh Expression called JustChurch agitated for justice around the issues discovered in SoulSpace, meeting to write letters, press legislators, and learn about issues from all sides. Howson sought to instantiate what Walter Wink called "nonviolent third-way protests." There were surprising areas of overlap between these ministries—when national police suspected activists might protest, local police were sent to watch Howson and SoulSpace. These were, of course, the same cops who knew these guys reduced crime and brought coffee when cops were grieving. Pursuit of justice can make you strange friends. And it can grow a church. Both endeavours were thriving when Howson left. The bishop had promised him "room to make mistakes" and Howson took advantage of it—perhaps a bit more than the bishop expected. The search for his replacement dragged its feet and the communities eventually closed after Howson left. Howson is well-known in the C of E in this region. He cuts a distinctive figure, perhaps is even a *sui generis*—there is no one like him in the Church of England. Archbishop Justin Welby offered to pay Howson's salary if it couldn't be paid otherwise when he decamped for Sunderland.

Howson's day job is not to lead a church in Sunderland. He is rather a chaplain at Sunderland University, doing the sort of multifaith work that faith leaders at secular universities specialize in. But on the side he has, in fact, grown yet another church. His two children declared that they were bored at the minster on Sundays and didn't want to go. He told the vicar he shared their sentiment. The building is beautiful, the old people are friendly, but there is no life in it, he said. Howson's vicar didn't respond defensively, but instead had the wherewithal to ask him, "Well what would church look like if it weren't boring?" Howson took the opportunity to show her. Howson is committed to the educational approach of Paulo Freire, a '60s radical who believed poor people really had wisdom, yet it's often squelched, not by the malice of the rich, but by their benevolence. Freire can burrow into the skull of an educator, making them rethink seemingly obvious things. Howson tries not to read from the Bible in church, instead preferring to recreate the storytelling of an oral culture. He will preach, "if I have to," but prefers to gather up wisdom from those sitting in a circle. I have watched him do it, and he is a genius at it—constantly drawing out those not speaking, and returning comments and observations back to Jesus' liberating praxis in the Bible. This was a long way from the boring liturgy in the minster. When I visited, a giant yurt was set up in a side aisle. "Isn't it fab?" he gushes. "We use it as a nativity creche in Christmas, as a tomb in holy week." It is there to dramatize the plight of refugees worldwide, and to be a place of prayer. "And our Iranians love it."

Yes, the Iranians, they are here too. Sunderland is even cheaper to live in than Liverpool, so national government ships them to the Northeast, where they find their way to the minster. A church that was as down in the mouth as its city is full of new life now, some two thirds of it Iranian as far as I can tell. The coffee shop before church is buzzing with conversation and energy. Church starts a good fifteen minutes late, to Howson's chagrin. "Where is Hussein? Get him in here! Tell them your news!" Hussein has received the status he hoped for and everyone cheers. The music is not impressive—a chorus led by Howson himself with a synthesizer player behind him. This is no cooking show display by a master chef. Instead it is a potluck, with all contributing. We break into small groups and react to the miraculous drought of fishes story. Most haven't heard it. Some have heard a different version of it. "I didn't know it, but now I want some fish!" a woman from Portugal says. One delights in Jesus saying, "be not afraid." "He says that not just to Peter, but to all of us," Howson promises. They nod. They believe him.

This is not Howson's day job, to grow the minster, but it is growing. "There are ninety to a hundred in sung Eucharist now. There were seventy when I came, and half of them have died," he said. He has no hesitation baptizing Farsi-speaking folks. "We're about 50 percent Iranian now," he said. He is proud to have heard not a single negative comment from the long-timers at the minster, who seem to me proud to have their building full again. He has, however, drawn backlash from white nationalists in town: "they'll have a run at me if they see me in the streets," he said, and smashed the windows at the university chaplaincy centre one time. Howson quotes an activist friend: "if you're not in trouble with the law, you're not doing it right"—and, we might add, with racists. Howson has built something genuinely fresh multiple times now in cities that need it.

If only he had more imitators.

The nations are coming to Stockton

On the other end of the ideological spectrum from Howson is one Mark Miller at Stockton Parish Church. He would describe himself more as "apolitical," which, for Howson, would mean wrongly political. Miller describes his calling as one of growing churches, of "making disciples who make disciples." And he works at a church that had seen too little of that.

SPC is another down-on-its-luck northeastern city with few economic prospects and lots of great need. Miller's predecessor as vicar felt a calling while walking by the church building one day to go and lead there. Procuring jobs in the Church of England is not usually so straightforward, nor is it so visionary, but it came to pass, and the Rev. Alan Farish helped bring the place back from the brink. He hired Miller as his curate, who remembers Alan's leading this way: "We are going to speak the name of Jesus, to glorify it, and to expect signs and wonders." It has worked. The building is full of some 250 people the day I go for worship, one of two services that day, with around half of them seeming to be Iranian. Miller has often been in the *Church Times* and secular media for baptizing refugees. He also advises the Home Office on how to evaluate asylum claims from Christian converts. Even more remarkably, he is now vicar of Stockton Parish Church, and Alan is a retired priest who serves under Miller's authority: "I don't know if you realize how unusual that is," he said. He was right.

The day I'm there is not long after the massacre of Muslims in Christchurch, New Zealand. Miller has the congregation congregate for a group photo to be sent to the Muslim community there with well wishes and prayers. He instructs folks that they don't *have to* be in the picture, for whatever reason, and some Iranians duck out. Then he leads music on the guitar and he sings. Worship is more of a production at SPC than at the Sunderland Minster, but it would be wrong to call it a show or performance. "One of our most anointed musicians is Iranian. He doesn't know a chord. But he has such authenticity in leading people to the throne of grace," Miller said. It would also be wrong to suggest that SPC is some sort of reactionary political outfit, a conservative yin to Howson's yang. The sermon that day, preached by Miller's curate, is on climate change, and how the church can get involved in the work God is already doing to care for and defend creation. Words to songs are on a split screen in English and Farsi, and a man in a headset in the front row offers live translation into Farsi, listened to by dozens of others in headsets. "We only have one translator into Sorani, so we can't have translation every week yet," Miller sighs. "God is bringing the nations to Stockton," he said. All the church has to do is to receive these visitors as if they were Christ, and to love him in them.

There are obviously enormous theological and ecclesial differences between Howson's and Miller's visions of the church. Yet their ministry to Farsi-speakers means there are also surprising similarities. They both know the work can be ambiguous on several counts. Howson admits many come to church precisely for the help with asylum: "It's a mixed thing," he said. Yet he has no problem boasting that he has baptized "loads" of Iranians—friends who have sought political asylum instead have languished in the queue for years. Miller used to baptize whoever came, but "the reality is not everyone tells the truth." So he raised the bar higher. Someone seeking baptism has to attend all the sessions of Alpha, "*all* of them," he adds, for emphasis. Both pastors agree that it is hard to keep tabs on Iranians once they achieve asylum status and move away, and this saddens them. And both have to arbitrate disputes that sound straight out of the New Testament. Sunderland's minster puts on feasts, often where refugees eat more than their share and others complain there is not enough left—and folks from different parts of the world argue over what to cook and serve. Miller glances at a £20 note in the offering plate, looks around at the folks at the midweek meal for homeless and refugees and others, and pockets it. "No need to tempt anybody," he says, knowing he is likely breaking some rule against pastors handling cash, but it's still the right thing to do. Paul's demand that thieves stop thieving among those who are recently converted rarely sounds so appropo in my church as it does in Miller's (Eph 4:28). And, as ever, new cultures refresh the existing culture of the church in ways we could not have anticipated. Miller presides over the Eucharist before a midweek meal for refugees and street people, and then serves the loaves of bread and consecrated juice *as part of the meal*. I've never seen this before, and yet it conforms to New Testament patterns quite closely. How many old timers at both Sunderland and Stockton prayed for new people to come and fill their old pews? Miller tells a story from Bob Jackson, an early writer on church growth in the UK, about a church that put out prayer cards asking God to send new people, promising to love the ones he sends. "They had to stop putting out the cards and praying those prayers," Miller laughs. Too many people came. And they were, like all people, hard to love!

    Miller's ministry raises some questions for us. Are we willing to live anywhere? Stockton is one of the poorest places in the UK. One of Miller's key lay leaders is Miriam Swaffield, leader of Fusion's student ministry, called by God out of hip university living in York to live in Middlesbrough and worship in Stockton with poor and disabled and Iranian neighbors. She realized she made inroads for Jesus when she quit leaving town for holidays to go home. Stockton is her home, called by Jesus. Are we willing to relocate for mission, not just for money? When Miller began telling friends he was moving his young family to Stockton, they would object: what about the children? Think of their future, their schooling, their opportunities. This is an objection to take seriously, of course. We are all called to protect the most vulnerable, especially those in our own family. But Miller realized these well-meaning questions were actually requests *to protect his family from Jesus*. Sure, they could get a "better" education by some lights in other places in England. But would they learn to be a multi-cultural community in the same way? To serve Jesus by learning another difficult language? To be part of a church with folks so different than themselves? There are all sorts of ways to be educated—and Miller's children know what the church is at its best. That's nothing to protect anyone from.

Miraculous growth in Gateshead

Meg Gilley is a vicar nearing retirement after eight years leading St. Chad's Church in Gateshead, across the river from Newcastle. Her husband is an already-retired church historian from Durham. Like many pondering retirement, she looks forward to time with extended family, time to travel and write, time away from the weekly grind of parish ministry. And yet her ministry hardly looks like it's petering out. It's actually hitting a new gear unlike any it's been in before. "We've had as few as eleven people here in a Sunday," she tells me, looking around with a grin and sweeping her arm over a full room for Bible study. "Look at this now. We prayed people would come, and here they are. This is our future." There are some thirty-five people in the room for a midweek Bible study on Holy Week, the atonement, and the resurrection of Jesus Christ. They are all Iranian, except for the church lady working away in the kitchen serving everyone tea. They all claim to be Christian—some already baptized, some eagerly seeking baptism. They all need Farsi translation, so when Meg teaches she stops every few sentences for one of the better English speakers to put her words into folks' heart tongue. She knows she is sought out partly as an asset in seeking asylum. A lengthy intro announcement details her days off, apologizes that there may be days she cannot attend court, and at regular intervals during the Bible study she stops to suggest "this might be something the Home Office asks about." She is teaching to the test to some degree, and she knows it, and those in attendance know it. Someone sceptical is paid to play the government's and the devil's advocate about their conversion and they had better be ready if they want to stay in Britain. "You can't claim your conversion came too soon after your arrival," she insists. "We can't baptize you too quickly, if you want it to be believable to the Home Office." She knows this is ridiculous theologically. "Look, here is water, what is to prevent me from being baptized?" the Ethiopian eunuch asks St. Philip in the book of Acts (8:36), a passage presumably present also in the Bibles consulted by immigration officials.

Yet it doesn't *always* feel like the vicar is teaching to the test. Rev. Gilley frowns on the group's decision the week prior to show Mel Gibson's *Passion of the Christ* in her absence. Even though the film has Farsi subtitles, "it's not suitable for kids, and I'm not sure it's helpful for you. There has to be a balance between your own language and suitable teaching." When I mention the Alpha course, wondering why she re-creates the wheel, she agrees that she spends hours each week preparing for Bible study. "But I won't do Alpha. This is a high church, I won't teach from that tradition." So she uses the Christian Year, the liturgy that HTB won't pray anymore in Kensington, and the wood relief panels in her magnificent building, originally designed to guide the prayers of working-class Englishmen, now working to teach Iranians without English-language skills. The work on her Bible study pays off. Why does Jesus pray that God has abandoned him? "We all know what it feels like to be abandoned by God, don't we? God feels that too." They ask whether the tearing of the temple curtain represents a rupture in the relationship between God and Israel or an opening of that relationship to all people. She tells the history of the Church of the Holy Sepulchre—that Christian pilgrims began arriving soon after the resurrection, the Romans didn't like it, and so built a temple to Artemis on top of it, so that when Helen traveled to the Holy Land she could find right where the place was. They talk over one another in Farsi, vying to ask the next question, at times complaining when one of their number forgets to translate another's English into Farsi. They are hungry to learn, for whatever end, and these questions seem beyond the range of the average bureaucrat playing devil's advocate. Meg mentions the anointing of Jesus' feet as a preparation for his burial. Later, she suggests, Jesus shows himself the learner when he washes his disciples' feet. "He gets the idea from her," she says. This is a faith more sensuous, more egalitarian on gender, more equitable between teacher and disciple, than most Christian churches I visit.

Meg admits the work with asylum-seekers can be exhausting. "It can feel overwhelming, advocating for all fifty-six people" for whom she has written letters already. There are tensions in the parish: "They haven't got a bean," she says, and of course ministry costs money, and no church is wondering how to spend all its extra cash. Yet she recently had sixty-six people at Sunday liturgy, some six times her low point. She counts them all, like the woman in Luke's Parable of the Lost Coin, and rejoices over each (Luke 15:8–10). "I wanted to leave with more than fifty people in worship," she says, having raced past that ambitious goal of 500 percent growth. Despite all rumours to the contrary, high church Anglo-Catholics and liberal do-gooders do care about church growth, at least in one parish pulsing with new life in Gateshead. And clearly that work is rewarding for her personally. On Mother's Day, the Iranians surprised her with cards and flowers, calling her "Mother Meg," also gifting Margaret who serves them food each week as "Mother Margaret."

I get to listen in on some of her interviews of those for whom she is to write letters soon. One man was evangelized, invited to Wakefield Cathedral, and found himself coming back. He felt differently if he didn't attend church. "Christianity is different than I thought, I found prayer solved problems, and I felt called."

"Called?" she asks.

"Called. Drawn in, like to a home and family that had missed me. I felt drawn by forgiveness and sympathy. My faith increases every day. He's my Lord, crucified for my sins, he saves us."

I'd love for someone I pastored to speak so eloquently about their conversion.

Another man: "What attracts me is the love, the forgiveness," which, indeed, are not central themes in Islam in the same way as Christianity. "I was no atheist, but Islam made me feel separate from God. I had no opportunity to search out other religions because it was dangerous. I felt Islam was good and complete in Iran, but compared to what I see and hear here, I can tell the difference. People here love each other, and you can pray in your own language everywhere, not just in Arabic."

The architects of the Reformation would be pleased.

Love the ones I send you

I cannot fail to introduce you to Dave Burke, one of the most fascinating pastors I met in my time in the UK—and that's saying a lot. Burke is a Brethren pastor, and so as part of that hierarchy-averse tradition he has no formal theological training. He came through Christian Unions in Britain. He also trained in hard science, zoology as it happens. I tease him it's the same field as the arch atheist Richard Dawkins ("Right, but he's a lot cleverer than I am"). Burke helped launch Bethany City Church in Sunderland. The day I'm at his church there are apologies for low attendance. Sunderland FC is in a big match in London and that team's fan base travels. The local Catholic priest is on the front page of the paper praying for the team's success. It didn't work. Apologies aside there are some two hundred people in the room. The worship is mildly charismatic, a few hands up (not "charismaniac" as one friend puts it), but no one would have been surprised at speaking in tongues. It's not encouraged—some of these folks are refugees from Pentecostal places gone rogue. At one point in the service fifteen or so folks file out. Burke explains, they're Mandarin-speaking folks who work in the food industry. The church's Malaysian student population has reached out to them and is now offering a Bible study in Mandarin. None of this was planned. Malaysian students came through Burke's natural affinity with campus ministry and they evangelized the Chinese. And now the group is welcoming Iranians and Kurds. The week I'm there they celebrate that a man named Babek had been released from detention, where he spent his time evangelizing fellow Kurds. This is Pentecost in the obvious sense: it is a church for all nations, in what has long been one of the ethnically most homogenous places in Britain. Pentecostalism is its own multiculturalism.

I met Burke as he spoke at a one-day symposium on popular culture, his talk on popular music. He asked this: what if every love song you ever hear is a worship song directed to the wrong person?

Think of our culture's endless and vapid appetite for love songs. We even have love songs about love songs (Selena Gomez's "I love you like a love song, baby." Repeat). Maybe this is why I like songs from my native US South—they're occasionally about something other than some chick, some bloke. Burke quoted a book about relationships: "We have shifted our expectation for endless ecstasy from something we expect of God to something we expect of our partner." The only problem: no mere human being can do that for us. To read the Song of Songs as the rabbis and church fathers do, God doesn't even do that for us. Just read the text: there are ruptures, spaces of absence, longing for the other who is not there. Endless rapture doesn't happen in marriage, in religious life. The songs are lies. No one can maintain ecstasy all the time. Not in this life anyway. Just ask Teresa of Avila in Bernini's famous sculpture whether she felt that way *all the time*. Then read a little of her *Interior Castle* and you'll know the answer right away.

Burke contrasts our endless love songs with "You Say" by a certain Lauren Daigle. She sings the same way as Selena or Adele or any other of these one-name wonders and teenaged millionaires. By the time I'm back in North America, "You Say" is being straight-up sung in worship in evangelical churches. It requires little amending (perhaps this should worry us!). Burke plays the YouTube video of the song until he stops it ("She mostly just ponces around that kitchen from here on out"), but by then the point is unmissable: "she's not singing about a bloke." She's singing about God. In our culture, "I love you" often means "I love me, and want to use you to make me feel better about myself." No human being can give us ultimate meaning, purpose, ecstasy. Only God can. And even then, God often chooses not to. Prayers, mystics, seers of all kinds past any sort of adolescent spiritual level speak of brick walls, silence, darkness. We pray and pray, sometimes for years, with no response. It's a sign of maturity, mystics unanimously declare. There is no way to union with God without it.

In response to this plea for love, I've never seen English people so agitated. One objected that the expressions of love in our culture are so facile,

Christians can only ever say "no" to them. Another that perhaps we can talk about "agape," but surely not "eros." Another that talking about love just sounds "naff." For non-Anglophiles, "naff" seems to mean, roughly, "stupid." Here Burke shone. Is being "naff" all bad? Anyway, he suggested, our hesitation about talking about our passions has more to do with being English, with how we were brought up, than the gospel, which talks endlessly about love. As a North American, in the shadow of an empire of evangelicalism built on fear, I'd love to be known as ridiculous for being too expressive about love.

And to glimpse at Bethany City Church, it will build a congregation. The day I'm there Burke preaches on their history of launching out of a pre-existing congregation in another village in County Durham. He reminisces with longtime leaders about the bad bars they met in, the surly service, the beer and cigarette smells. Then they got a building—they're easy to come by in a city so down economically as Sunderland. And here Burke leans on his people: they immediately relaxed. God had used the time in exile to show them the church was not the building, it was the people. But right away they got into fights about the building: whether to display a cross, how to decorate, who has control over what. He preaches Acts 10 that Sunday, where Peter is told to eat unclean animals, despite his Jewish faith. He tells God no way. Burke points out how odd this is: Peter had lived with Jesus for three years, seen him resurrected and ascended, and still he sees a vision from God and says uh, no, thanks. We too are similarly resistant to change, aren't we? Burke uses some soft humour around the passage: noting the lizards and frogs that Peter is charged to eat he says, "This morning isn't brilliant for vegans I'm afraid." And he uses some hard theology: God is always at work creating community where we religious types say God shouldn't. God can't. Nope, God says, I will, watch me, they're perfect.

Burke tells the congregation a story from the church's café. He was encouraged at the new immigrants coming to the café, but then saw a pair of Arab men harass and drive off two French girls. He was boiling mad. He prayed like the psalmist a prayer of vengeance: Lord drive them all away. "I'm not proud of it," he confessed. Pastors, lead in this: confess sin to your people. Then he heard God say something: "Turn the wi fi off." So God was not above being mad too. And doing something about it. But God also said this to him: "You must learn to love the ones I send you." Arab men and French girls alike, and everyone else too. He asks his church to be open to change with him. "Father, shape us not by the prejudices we grew up with. We pray for Jesus' atmosphere, his fragrance, that all might find a home here."

It remains to be seen what will happen with this influx of Iranians and other recent immigrants into churches in England. New liturgies have been introduced, new converts are on the rolls, new church members, new flesh grafted onto an old wound. One thing is for sure: it is growth. Not the kind anyone would likely have predicted or planned for. But it is happening now. And that the church in the Northeast of England will not be the same for it.

Patterns

These churches doing ministry with Farsi-speakers raise several points for those who want to see their ministries thrive. One, as Henry Blackaby once taught, God speaks to the church by whom God sends to the church. Those arriving are a claim on those welcoming. So those welcoming have to listen very carefully: What is God saying? How do we respond? What sort of new people must we be in response to these summons from God? With these sorts of questions new people are not marks to be evangelized, nor are they objects of our largesse. They are divine missives, directives from on high. It begs the question: Who is new to your community that makes a similar claim on your church? If they're not coming to your church yet, how do you find them and invite them? What sort of different people would you have to be for that to happen?

Mainline and liberal churches in North America may think there is no comparable community to Farsi-speaking asylum seekers in the Northeast of England. I hear this often where I work on the West Coast of Canada. Yet what part of the world has seen more immigration than British Columbia?! Lots of Asia's immigrants are quite wealthy, and have been a political hot potato in BC for driving up housing costs. Yet often those folks are quite lonely. Some come from parts of the world where Reformed churches are quite strong—Korea especially, but not only there. Some aid to transitioning to Canada culturally would be something that Christian Canadians could provide. Other newer arrivals are folks who struggle with housing costs, even if they have good jobs. The house sales that made longtimers and their children rich are making me and my children poor. How can the church be a place to mediate this generational friction? Both in Canada and the US we have to remember that immigrants and refugees are not mere "issues." They are human beings. The churches calling to care for persons always trumps sociopolitical rationalizations for why others in our countries say we should not. And they are in your neighbourhood too, wherever you are. The world has never been this small.

And finally this: what sort of problems of biblical proportions might arise if God sends new and unexpected people to your church? Paul's instructions on theft, on the wealthy eating and leaving little for the working poor, on assimilation of different food cultures, all pop off the page amidst Farsi-speaking ministry in the UK. What sort of unexpected portions of the Scriptures might be illumined by the new people with whom God gifts you?

8

FRESH EXPRESSIONS
Church growth writ small

I THINK I STARTED a Fresh Expression. I didn't mean to. I just wanted to reach folks outside the church and support a talented pastor who could do so. Here's how it happened.

I was pastor of Boone United Methodist Church in the mountains of North Carolina during a period of growth from 2011–15. We were a church of fifteen hundred in a town of only twenty thousand, and yet we never felt big—we were the third largest church in town. This is still Christendom obviously: ushers come to church to be seen in suits because it helps business; kids can ask other kids on the playground *where* they go to church. And my church staff had a fantastic young pastor-in-the-making named Luke Edwards. He started new ministries and made it look easy and fun, so people joined in. I knew we could tap denominational money for him to plant a new service. He was eager.

There were a number of ways to do this. We could choose a time, a worship style, advertise, find a wicked bass player, and go. We'd done that before to great effect. But Luke was uninterested (and he could even play guitar!). His *people* would be repulsed by that. Folks on the margins, sceptical of faith, were not interested in skinny jeans and mood lighting in a gym. So Luke went away and "had a think," as the Brits say. And he came back with this: Fresh Expressions. It's a way of doing church designed for those not presently in any church. It was perfect. It would give Luke language for what he wanted to do: listen to Boone's disaffected youth (some of whom had grown up in our church!). He would design church *for* them, *around* what they cared about. The purpose was not to grow a single big service. It was to grow multiple small ones. So we planted King Street Church—a series of communities designed primarily for those outside the church. Luke has since moved on to lead Fresh Expressions across western North Carolina, but King Street Church's mini-communities still meet under new leadership. One is in a pub, one in the local jail, one in the homeless shelter, one at a coffee shop adjacent to the trailer park. These gave our tall steeple, moneyed church a way to do ministry among folks who would have *never* come to us. The outreach to the edges blessed and refreshed the center, and vice-versa.

Methodists are often pragmatists above all else. King Street Church *worked*, so we doubled down on our investment. Later, with the academic part of my brain, I was surprised to find that Fresh Expressions had theological depth. It was born in Britain, midwifed by my theological hero. When Rowan Williams became a bishop of the Church of Wales, he saw the dire figures that the church would be extinct in no time. So he asked folks what, if anything, was growing. And he was introduced to small missional communities gathering around shared affinities that seemed strange to him—motorcycling and gardening and punk rock and so on. The contrast couldn't be more stark. Williams is the smartest man alive, and maybe the holiest, inclined toward the sort of high church liturgy that you might imagine from a then-future and now-former Archbishop of Canterbury. No one could doubt his theological profundity or sympathy with the ancient church—the man learned Russian to write his dissertation on a specific Orthodox theologian for goodness sake. Others look at these sorts of missional communities and sneer—especially Williams' fellow liberals and Anglo-Catholics. One Oxbridge theologian friend, not knowing I was working on Fresh Expressions, said to me "The Church of England is panicking. We're spending money on skateboarding. Can you believe it?" But despite his own Oxbridge and smells and bells predilections, Williams saw in these creative new communities a fresh work of the Holy Spirit. As one who had extensively studied and participated in monastic communities, he knew "church" doesn't only work one way. It works in a vast myriad of ways through time and space and culture. And if this was what the Holy Spirit was doing in Wales, then who was he, Rowan Williams, to object? He blessed it with terminology. A "fresh" expression of church is on its way, perhaps, to being a "mature" expression of church: one with ordained leadership, right practice of the sacraments, a rota of flower ladies, and so on.[1] Likewise "mature" expressions are blessed

---

1. And even then an FX will look different from a traditional-looking church. King Street has ordained leadership presiding over sacraments, but still meets in pubs and jails.

by the experimentation in the laboratory of Fresh Expressions as we all learn together how to be church in an age bored with or hostile toward church-as-usual. Williams called what he envisaged a "mixed economy" of fresh and mature expressions. He threw his mantle of immense theological erudition and prestige over missional experiments, and as Archbishop of Canterbury threw a great deal more at it than that. He threw the machinery and money of his office into it. Fresh Expressions became *the* thing in the Church of England, with grant money and official energy and attention behind it. This official endorsement may have hurt the movement in one sense. Folks in traditional church settings or with traditionalist affinities burn FX with a disdain only the Brits seem capable of ("Look, those people are going swimming." "Ah, it must be a Fresh Expression!"). But with Williams' backing, for a time no one could credibly accuse Fresh Expressions of being a liturgical or theological sellout.

Not being above evangelism

How's it work?

One of the skater churches that my Oxbridge friend sneered at is called Sorted, meeting in a strongly Muslim city called Bradford in the diocese of Leeds in Yorkshire. Its founding pastor is a man named Andy Milne, whose book *The DNA of Pioneer Ministry* has been influential in helping the C of E spot and encourage and equip leaders of new forms of church. Milne has now gone to work seeding Fresh Expressions throughout the North of England. And he's perfect for it. He's quiet, intense, playful, and wise. He really listens. When I ask if he still skates, as a paid-up middle-aged man with actual gray in his hair now, he seems sad to say "No, only when me son and his mate invite me along." We all grow up and become less cool, though Milne is less less cool than the rest of us. Milne opens his book with a promise that if God wants you to pioneer—that is, to start a new ministry—God will have been preparing you, and the people you will reach, from long beforehand. If you look back at your past, you will see the patterns of fruitfulness that God can use in planting now.

Milne tells the story of Sorted around skating. (How else?) He was skating outside the University of Leeds not long after finishing his university study there. On my own recent trip to Leeds, I noticed at least three closed former churches within a block of that great university—the church may go out of business, but God does not. Some teenagers saw his board and teased him for stickers on it that mentioned God. This will be standard in post-Christendom culture—folks think they know what Christianity is enough to mock it, the way you might with Scientology or Pilates or Veganism. Anything that has earnest disciples is fair game. Note, Christians: this is *not* persecution. It is just "taking the mickey" out of someone. It's having a laugh. Take it as a sign of respect.

Milne did, and then switched from defense to offense (not a very skateboardy analogy, but never mind, it's the one he chose). No, he's no Bible-basher, but yes, he believes in God, and in fact, he thinks God works in response to prayer. Would you like to pray together? Taken aback, the lads *agreed*. The three prayed for folks they loved, for healing for those in need of it. Both attested to a sense of peace afterwards. Friends they prayed for said they felt ankle and wrist injuries—from skating, of course—to be healed. They would meet again to skate and ask to read the Bible together. They were on their way to Christian discipleship. So Andy encouraged them to go to church.

And then everything fell apart.

These newly converted disciples of Jesus would skateboard up to traditional Church of England parishes and find no place for themselves. It was boring. They hated it. The old ladies were sweet but had no point of connection to their lives. And they couldn't rightly go asking St. Dismal's in the Mire to change its thousand-year-old tradition for a couple of skate kids. So they didn't go back, no harm no foul. And when Andy asked them about going, they'd tell him as much. Couldn't they just meet as his house and pray and read the Bible and skate after?

Those requests were the seed of a new way of doing church. The answer was "yes," they could meet with Andy and pray and read the Bible and call it church and even skate after. There was no language for this yet, it was still to be developed. A Fresh Expression like Sorted could be church *in its own right*. It was no bridge to established church, no outreach to get the skate rads to become church ladies—even if such a thing were possible, why would it be desirable? No—you use someone's *existing* friendship networks to evangelize. Don't break them out of those—they will carry the current of the gospel.

Andy Milne has forgotten more than most of us ever knew about evangelism, so there are further questions from a mainline liberal church vantage in North America: *why would evangelizing skaters in the first place be a good idea?!* The easy part of imitating Andy's story, comparably speaking, would be to learn how to skate from scratch. The hard part would be learning how to evangelize from scratch. Andy comes from evangelicals (originally Quakers through Soul Survivor, an evangelistic summer festival, to proto-Pentecostalism), though he now works for the Archbishop of York, Primate of England (that's some serious travel up the candlestick). But he hasn't lost a sense that Jesus is out to save the whole world, you included, whoever you are. And his great joy is taking part in that saving work of God on behalf of the unlikely. Milne doesn't sound worried that people will go to hell if he doesn't evangelize them. He sounds summoned by God to take part in God's renewal of creation.

Notice again how far this is from models of church planting regnant in the 1990s, still alive in some people's minds as they think of this work: a big, splashy first service, announced beforehand with countless advertising ventures, then frantic attempts to keep the initial hundreds from diminishing down too far. Sorted had three people for its first gathering, and one for its second (Milne recommends not counting too closely too early!). A flashy band on stage, with women in tight shirts and men in ironic facial hair, and a rhythm guitar player so good you really should be paying her, were beyond their budget and would've scared off their demographic. Sorted started out life in a rented pod that a school was using for a homework club. Andy is a guy who loves skating, but loves Jesus more, and uses skating for an opportunity to talk about Jesus, and see who Jesus gathers to himself in what surprising configuration. "Lots has been written about a worship-first approach" to church planting, Milne told me in an interview. "It's built a body of expertise, but that is increasingly irrelevant."

Milne's book is a step-by-step description of how Sorted started multiple Fresh Expressions in just a few years' time. It is, avowedly, *not* a how-to. Even if you could clone Sorted it would be a mistake: "Folks tend to look at blingy success and try and copy it." Milne's book seems almost written to dissuade you from planting something. He insists that if you're pondering church planting, you won't have enough volunteers. Sorted never did. You "probably have the wrong team." And the work will "probably take longer than you want." Milne practices instead an approach to pioneering that was pioneered (did you see what I did there?) by Mike Breen, then a C of E vicar and planter in Sheffield, England: they read the book of Acts *missiologically*. Peter and Paul and Silas and Luke and friends would approach a new community and seek to pray with people. They would find there "people of peace"—prepared by God beforehand to receive the word. The gospel would take root in that place, then a planter would move on, relatively quickly, to seek out people of peace among whom to preach the gospel in a new place. If you're still keen, there is a progression: 1. listen, 2. love and serve, 3. build community, 4. explore discipleship, 5. church takes shape, and 6. do it again. *The DNA of Pioneer Ministry* is a case study in one planter's efforts to do these several times through, interspersed with mentions of other similar communities that have done likewise. Sorted does not seek for people a one-time, dramatic conversion experience. The naming of stages suggests that people become Christian slowly and more sceptically now than they once did in a residually Christian culture. (Billy Graham could count on hearers who had *some* church background before he flipped the switch.) They are in for a long haul, a slow procession (on fast wheels).

Sorted shows that you *listen* in your context to what those outside the church are saying. Lots of churches that try to reach out to skaters (and kudos for even trying) fail at this stage. They might, say, build a ramp. Which is a nice gesture. But did they *ask the kids* what they wanted? Love and serve: Luke Edwards is worried this can turn into noblesse oblige, though one FE planter insists not: if the DNA of a place is radical hospitality, then inviting new people includes inviting them also to *offer* radical hospitality. Listening doesn't mean providing what someone says they want. One of Milne's examples was of a mum of a skater on the phone with him describing her positive experience with spiritualism—communicating with the spirits of the dead. Here Milne could have sneered or debated. Instead he asked if she wanted to pray together for the Holy Spirit's peace. She did. So they prayed on the phone, and waited in silence for peace, which she said she indeed experienced. You listen and love and serve *with the gospel.* Milne admits a conundrum: do you study your area and people so deeply that you "get a PhD" first, or do you start something, anything, so that it will fail quickly enough that you can pivot to something new? (He inclines toward the latter.) Sorted first listened *for three years.* A peer church planter got going earlier, starting a public expression of worship after only 2.5 years! A bit hasty, that. Milne admits jealousy at the rapid pace. But Sorted got started as soon as it could. The runway for planting is longer than we once thought, if something is going to get genuinely airborne.

And think now of the church planter you know who was impatient to launch three weeks after moving somewhere brand new . . .

Sorted's kids needed something: a place to skate. Milne and his spouse and fellow planter Tracy found it: at a school playground after hours on Fridays. They were nervous—that's a heavy drinking night in Bradford! Yet they made it available and kids came. There were always challenges. Kids would be from rival gangs, expecting to skate together. When Milne and other leaders would conclude with something spiritual at the end, kids would sneak away early and skip it. So Sorted interspersed the religious bits throughout and so made them harder to excise. Kids would slip out in the middle for smoke breaks. So Sorted put a break in the middle—a practice it still honours. There was always trouble: a mum reported to Andy's superiors that a youth had come drunk. Andy had to do damage control: no, he's got ADHD, his mum abandoned him, our group has loved him, but he's always on the edge—he *seems* drunk even when he's not! Sorted is the only family he has. That's what it became for those to whom it listened, whom it loved and served. Family. Folks explored discipleship and sought baptism—and the Archbishop of York himself turned up to help with that.

Then it repeated. Another school approached Milne asking for a community like Sorted. He refused. Too much to do. They approached again. He listened for the Holy Spirit, wondering if God was in these repeated requests. And soon, in a very different sort of school (just a few miles away!), Sorted II was born. It was different, even if this community was nearby: "We had to hold off on saying 'we did it this way in Sorted I.'"[2] Luke Edwards notes that very quickly, folks in a Fresh Expression will become as pushy about "the way we've always done things," or "hey, that's my seat" as any veteran church lady. Sorted veterans also found they had to go outside their comfort zones. As fairly conservative Christians, they worry about Halloween. But residents in this new site asked for a Halloween party. Saying yes enabled them later to offer the community a Nativity play, then an Easter party. They'd earned trust. Sorted even had to be open to planting back where it started: Sorted I aged, and younger skaters wanted their own community, so Sorted III was planted back in the pod where Sorted I first started at a different time. A student from Kenya came to be part of Sorted, went back to Kenya, and planted a version of Sorted back home. Another came from Ghana via Northern Ireland and planted on the Sorted model in south London. "He described a conversation with soccer players on whether God would be best described as a referee, a coach, the best player, or the crowd?" Sorted has gone through massive shifts over its short life since 2006. "It feels like Joseph's seven years of plenty after seven years of famine," Milne said. And its external valuation has fluctuated wildly: "We were undervalued early on, and overvalued later." Sorted is now in the hands of Tracy Milne, Andy Milne's wife and one-time co-planter, who had less of a role while she was pursuing theological training and then pastoring a local church. Now that she's ordained, Sorted has its own priest, unlike Andy, who remains a lay person. Perhaps a "fresh" expression has "matured."

One virtue of Milne's book is the very detailed specifics of Sorted's situation: this shift in emphasis cost him that partnership, this student misbehavior resulted in that punishment. (He banned someone temporarily from Sorted. Imagine! A kid who wants to go to church so bad that banning them is considered a punishment!) His prime challenge however is to churchianity: that is, those convinced church as it is now is church as it *must* be in God's eyes. His work shows, on the contrary, that church happens in the midst of ordinary life: skating, teasing one another, handling disciplinary

---

2 Milne, *The DNA of Pioneer Ministry*, 184.

challenges, raising money. "Lots of church seems to be about imparting knowledge to members," he observes correctly. We sit in pews. We listen to a lecture. It's voluntary school without grades. Imagine a day when university is no longer compulsory, socially or professionally, for middle-class people. Some would continue to go for a while. Eventually most would realize the benefits don't outweigh the costs. So too with church. This is "school" that is no longer compulsory and costs too much time and aggravation. Is it any wonder folks quietly vanish? Sorted, by contrast, attends to the power of God loose in ordinary people's lives, to heal, create community, answer prayer, bring about a new way of life with enemies transfigured into friends. "We always have to ask, 'how does this help people come to faith and become disciples?'" Milne writes. Mainline churches can act like that question is ancillary, or even tawdry. Fresh-Expressions-become-mature show it is essential, not just for skater churches, but for the whole church of Jesus Christ.

What do we really need for "church"?

Fresh Expressions may have higher ambitions than the ones I let on here, high as those are. It is more than just an effective way to reach people today. It may even be a sign of what God wants from the church writ large.

Pete Atkins is a team coordinator for the National Team of FX. He is a medical doctor by training and still works as a GP, while he and his wife attend the church he planted a quarter century ago. He has also converted a historic barn into his home and into a sort of prayer house, and his son and daughter-in-law lead a Messy Church outside Manchester. He could not be more invested in FX. He sees, in traditional denominations, systems well-calibrated for an entirely different century. What was meant to harness and foster growth is now "killing life within it rather than supporting it." Those structures, now mostly tuned to managing decline, are not designed for the culture we currently inhabit. Occasionally folks break out of those structures and produce good fruit, but the level of heroic leadership required is extraordinary. To give just one humorous example of structures that don't adapt to changing circumstances, consider that the Anglican Church has a Bishop of Dunwich. You may be surprised, since you've not heard of a town called Dunwich in England. That's because it's been underwater for centuries!

My passing on of the sneer about swimming above may suggest some think FX may as well be an underwater bishopric for all its usefulness. Atkins relates to me a vignette I hear several other times—that some bishop early in FX funding days got money to sponsor his local cricket tournament.

The payoff in discipleship was not obvious, and the hangover around FX's perceived superficiality has done real damage. But as a planter and church consultant, Atkins sees reason for caution in the push to resource thriving, HTB-style megachurches—he calls himself a "cautious fan" of such efforts. Rather than try with herculean effort to grow one thing, he would prefer to "multiply thousands of small things." The way to do that is for many pioneers to listen to their local context. If a resource church fits, try that—especially in a population centre. It won't always or even usually. What else might take shape in a local setting? Such listening is the opposite of HTB's approach, which he describes with a borrowed phrase as a "McDonaldization approach." "Contextual mission is the thing FX has brought back to the church in this country." And the reason for this missiological shift has to do, primarily, with God: "God is not trying to arrest the decline of the church. God is creating a new imagining from a place of exile." He gives an example from the city of Halifax, where a pastor named Linda Maslin started an ecumenical foodbank to respond to the hunger needs in the community. Those coming to the foodbank found themselves fed in other ways—making friendships with one another, with Maslin, and with God. So a more intentional gathering for prayer, Bible study, and singing evolved out of the foodbank, starting with twelve people, growing to the point where hundreds have now been baptized. Listening and responding to one kind of hunger led the way, and church naturally grew up to respond to other hungers as a result—all in a setting where HTB would not have worked.

HTB-style churches are impressive. They draw media attention and have a widespread impact. HTB itself, as already discussed, has influenced churches around the world through its Alpha course, which patiently and compellingly presents the Christian faith for outsiders. A gathering of hundreds of people seems to be just what the C of E needs. Yet Michael Moynagh, a sort of canon theologian of Fresh Expressions, argues that some 80 percent of those who attend HTB-style churches were already involved in another church elsewhere.[3] Churches like that start with an end in mind and then reverse engineer to achieve that end. They are big, expensive, and inflexible—battleships, if you will. Fresh Expressions start with no particular end in mind. They listen and befriend and serve and cultivate Christian community and then tend it and multiply again. Speaking with one FX leader I mentioned the five full-time staffers already hired at a resource church elsewhere in the North—a church with exactly zero parishioners at this point, mind you. He did the math: "I could start 50 Fresh Expressions with that money," he said. FX has punched above its weight in terms of

---

3. Michael Moynagh, *Church in Life*, chapter 2 up to page 42.

research. Perhaps it has been over-sold, and so it has also been over-studied. George Lings is the architect of one such intensive sociological study, or was before he retired from the Church Army, a C of E evangelistic centre. His research, covering the years 2012–16, discovered some fifty thousand people involved with the church through a Fresh Expression—the equivalent of two small dioceses. Of those fifty thousand, 60 percent were not previously involved in church at all.[4] That is impressive growth of non-churched people. No equivalent research exists suggesting that HTB-style churches are growing so much or among so many non-churched people. Church Army is sometimes described as "the C of E's best-kept secret" (every marketer's nightmare). Likewise, Fresh Expressions may be the best kept secret of the church in England writ large. This will surprise, since FX suffered from over-exposure in the Rowan Williams-era. Yet it remains so. If you want to reach new people, design an expression of church that is intentional about reaching those people—*with their help and input*—not a knockoff of what reached people somewhere else. A navy may need a few battleships; but pity a navy with *only* battleships.

Tim Lea is a FX national coordinator and a lay person. I set before him some of the offhand critiques I've heard of his movement, and watch as the former rugby player tackles them one by one. Isn't it just a cul-de-sac movement, with a few weird people getting together to, say, knit on a Tuesday night? "Well that's just a cheap shot by lazy people." Wouldn't it be more advantageous numerically to plant only resource churches, on an HTB-model? "No actual research says resource churches work." This is a man who needs a Twitter handle (he has none). He tries to massage and nuance his strong answers. Yet he is committed to FX. He notes the groups he leads and participates in are often asked "when" they are "coming to church?" "Uh, never?" That approach he also calls "Churchianity": it wants, above all, to pack people into the building. By contrast, he suggests, Alpha works best in a pub. Gather friends old and new around beer, watch videos, discuss, and repeat. Why ask people to *go somewhere else*? Isn't it already church? Sure, there's no pension plan for the pastor as part of it, but such a Christendom model with career paths for vicars "isn't even that old really."

In resetting my expectations of church, Lea first offers a geography lesson. What *is* the North of England? Richard Passmore, an FX planter in Cumbria, says it's Watford, that aforementioned precipice outside London with the sign that welcomes motorists to "the North of England." York, by this definition, is only halfway up England. To most Brits, York is unimaginably far north (this in a country where if you plan to drive more than an

---

4. Lings "The Day of Small Things."

hour, concerned people will pack provisions and blankets for you). A pastor in rural Cumbria would say such a thing, since it boasts plenty of acreage and not a lot of economic output. Listening in that setting led Passmore to design a Fresh Expression called "Mountain Pilgrims," for those wanting to hike, camp, and talk about God. "They have ads on sheep," Lea says. "That's contextualized." Mountain Pilgrims is an expression of faith for all, not just Anglicans, not just Christians, but any of those seeking life outdoors. Think of your aunt or cousin or brother (or self) who would "rather meet God outside than in a church building." Are they entirely wrong? FX says it doesn't have to be an either/or. Folks will still meet God in buildings of all sizes; and folks can meet God on pilgrim trails. What were the monks doing as they hauled dead Cuthbert all over the country *for centuries*?! "It is inevitable that people don't all want to be the same, that's human nature," Lea said. FX multiplies opportunities for people to meet God in Christian community. That it doesn't look the same as what folks think of as "traditional" church just means folks need to expand their notion of "tradition." Lea means no disrespect to large churches—he just sees God stretching the definition of church from the more to less blingy, from "looks cool on Instagram" to advertising on sheep (which, admittedly, might play well on social media itself).

Lea gives an example from when he led a Fresh Expression for the Methodist Church in Great Britain. Like most churches with some roots in the ancient church catholic, Methodists reserve presiding over the sacraments for those who have been ordained. Yet Methodism has also been evaporating in Britain, and has thrown in with Fresh Expressions perhaps even more than the C of E. It is common now for a Methodist minister to be appointed both to a circuit and also to the leadership of a Fresh Expression. Lea was a second-generation leader of this faith community, and as a layman could not preside, so occasionally they would have a minister parachute in for the sacraments. This left the folks that the FX was attracting—mostly new to faith—confused. "'Tim, you're our leader, why don't you preside?'" they asked. Enough stories like this piled up to the point that the Methodists changed their book of discipline! To change the *Constitutional Practice and Discipline* is a herculean task, akin to getting parliament to change a law (which is what the C of E has to do to change its prayer book!). Churchianity can get in the way of people coming to Christ. But if the churchy apparatus is held lightly enough and made malleable enough, it can support mission once again, as it did in this instance. And leading an FX requires no great expertise. Café churches have become popular all over Britain. All one needs to start one is the guts to go into a Costa (or any other coffee shop, of local or chain variety) and ask to rent the place for two hours when it's not normally open. The owner will appreciate the business, the baristas will appreciate the polite customers, and you have a Fresh Expression. Now, what you *do* with the folks you invite is critical. Be sure it involves talking about God, forming community, heeding hurts, and eventually hopefully prayer together, worship, conversion, new life, and a willingness to plant similar communities elsewhere. This is a tricky balance—those who come get to set the agenda to some degree. Yet it cannot simply be like a "ministry" I saw on one campus in the US: a "listening post" with earnest faced church people sitting there while someone held forth, never responding. Listening in Jesus' way includes gently turning toward God and being made new, together.

Sunday School that children actually like

One of the best-known Fresh Expressions out there is called Messy Church. Its founder, Lucy Moore, was struck that her church outside Portsmouth in the South was not reaching children in its area. St. Wilfrid's was well-enough resourced, putting on good programs, but was not seeing children get involved or come to faith. So she designed a gathering for all ages. I sometimes describe Messy Church as Sunday School without the bad parts. It's not trite or cheesy, designed to be free childcare without imparting any sense of or taste for discipleship. When Moore presents on Messy Church around England she will ask older people to raise their hands if they once attended Sunday School. Something like 80 percent of hands will go up. Sunday School was phenomenally successful in drawing children up until fifty or so years ago, when it, like lots of other church programs, fell out of social favour. But Sunday School was designed so that parents would *drop off their children and leave*. Messy Church is not. It is designed for all ages to participate together. They do the good parts of Sunday School—they draw and colour and do skits and, perhaps most importantly, they eat together. In other words, they do things that nearly every church in existence already does, and sometimes does pretty well. "This isn't rocket science," Moore told me in an interview. "This is stuff we all already do." We just tend not to do it together stratified by age groups. We tend to compress it into a tiny time-slot as part of Sunday morning. And we don't tend to reach out to those not already in church. Churches are pretty good at reaching those who already claim to be Christian, Moore said. "But Messy Church is designed for those who don't believe in God, who think Jesus is a swear word, but they'll experience this and say 'Come on! This is the best thing!'" She gives an example of one church where a four-year old started posing questions about God which her parents couldn't answer. They had noticed advertising for a Messy Church, so they went, and eventually brought their extended family—nine people total. They were all baptized, mum joined the leadership team, she now attends Sunday service and Messy Church both, and "she's flying with it. That's a minority experience, of course," Moore said. But not entirely, surely. Messy Church meets in twenty countries, some 500,000 attend each month.

Notice those numbers for a moment. They're like early Methodists' conflagration across the globe; Lucy Moore, a new John Wesley.

Several pastors with whom I spoke said MC is its best attended *service*, not just its best attended children's ministry event. And Moore is convinced MC teaches us something about God. MC is not designed to arrest the decline of the church, but to engage more people in mission. Its semi-chaotic style, its openness to noise and delight, its languid pace (more like two hours than thirty minutes) all make it feel more like a party than a church service. No wonder it's catching on. Some three-quarters of its leaders are women, few are ordained—in fact, Moore says, MC sometimes happens "in the teeth of the clergy." It costs money, volunteers, and energy, after all. But it is making new disciples. "We're not interested in knowledge about the Bible, but in discipleship—how we're being transformed into Christ," Moore said. Lings' research at Church Army agrees. Half of FX attenders studied in 2018 said their journey of discipleship started with Messy Church.

Not afraid of noughts

A final example of a Fresh Expression for now has similarities with these previous ones in the chapter. It was started by accident. It's led by a non-ordained woman. And it shows us something about the character of the church God is bringing.

Lots of people feel ignored by their churches. The church limits itself to "religious" things, so if you don't want to preach, or be on a committee, or volunteer to make coffee, or be on the rota to arrange flowers, your services are not required. Is it any wonder our churches are disintegrating? Chester-le-Street Methodist is not so bad off though. Their one Sunday service is more than half full. Their 2010 building, funded through the UK's lottery, created space for the community and is rented out seven days a week. It's a busy church. And its youngest attenders look to be in their sixties. The guitar player up front in the band certainly is, she tells me she's sixty-one. She's been part of the church since she became a Christian at fifteen. Her youthful, open face looks younger than her age, and she leads well. She first tried to recruit her daughters to replace her in the band, but they grew up and left town for work. Members appreciate that she's been playing for them for parts of six decades now. Most attending are her mother's age. The church worries about its future, even with a capable minister and handsome facilities.

What the church seems not to realize is that Kate Welch is a superstar in the world of social entrepreneurship. British society at large knows it. She's a member in the Order of the British Empire—her daughters called her Obi Mom Kenobi, and she won the Queen's Prize for Enterprise in 2016. Honorific letters pour out after her name. Yet she's never been asked to lead anything other than the band in her church. "I'm still the fifteen-year old," she said, making a head-patting gesture. "You got married in our church, sure, but you're still *our* Kate. This is easier to do in some other church," she said. She plans to carry on for some time—her new hero is an actress still working after turning one hundred. Don't bet against her, she's a whirlwind, a superhero, exhausting even to listen to, let alone follow. It's remarkable the treasures we bury in mainline churches. Sam Wells argued years ago now that God has given us everything we need, to worship God, to serve God, and to be God's friends.[5] But like the talents in Jesus' parable we're better at burying than we are at investing.

Some terms first. Social enterprise is a business with a social purpose that reinvests its profits back into that purpose. This is different than mere charity, offering a handout, which can make the giver feel good, but leaves the recipient decapacitated. A new raft of publications like *Toxic Charity* and *When Helping Hurts* is calling Christians to rethink dramatically our models of giving.[6] Social enterprise conveys dignity, not dependency. And it works. Welch has loads of examples for me. The bottled water she's drinking doesn't just look sleek in design. It's the most virtuous bottle of water in the world. Belu exists to raise money for Water Aid, taking our first-world bottled water drinking habit and making money off it for those with no access to clean water or toilets (and the plastic is biodegradable). Madlug is an Irish enterprise designed by a Christian social worker who noticed his kids carrying their things in tattered plastic bags, the sort desecrating our natural world. He designed a bag that you or I would fork out 30 quid for, and for each we buy a bag goes to a kid in care, "so there's a bit of a widows and orphans model there." She points to a Scottish company that's employing visually impaired former soldiers. Another that's designing a theme park for disabled people. Then other endeavours she herself has led directly, not just advised. She has designed job-training progress for workless people in the

---

5. Wells, *God's Companions*.

6. Steve Corbett and Brian Fikkert, *When Helping Hurts* and Robert Lupton *Toxic Charity*.

poorest parts of England, for convicts and ex-offenders, for those who are sure they lack the dignity to be employable, let alone run a business. There is a profound recognition of the imago Dei at the heart of Welch's work. And a profound Methodism. She is John Wesley reincarnate, if we believed in such things, rushing to do good with all the effort she can muster.

She even planted a church, sort of. It's easier to start a Fresh Expression in Methodism than launch a new church, so she did that. The ReFuse Café in Chester-le-Street uses food that would otherwise be discarded for all its work. Some 40 percent of our food is wasted, with incalculable loss to the hungry, to our environment, to basic human decency. ReFuse refuses to participate in that wasteful food industry, and instead makes magnificent meals from what the rest of us discard. They cater weddings, they've garnered national attention, and they host ecclesial events on the side. Quietly. Chester-le-Street Methodist didn't want to start it as an official ministry. The board was nervous, it was too much to take on, they're getting older, how could they be sure it would work? You can't, Kate said, and instead of despairing, she just got their ok and helped launch it herself. She didn't want to go rogue, so she went through official channels, asking nothing but permission, and then launched. She can see how the church ladies, now her mother's age, could start a café church with no difficulty. Instead of complaining about getting tired of volunteering they could make it a business and turn over a handsome profit. Welch designs businesses that turn over millions of pounds, she could do this while multitasking three other things. But the church ladies pat her on the head and don't ask the OBE holder to help them. We're like the disciples surrounded by hungry crowds who don't hear Jesus' admonition to give the crowd something to eat, don't notice the boy with the loaves and the fish right in our midst, let alone imagine he could do anything with them, or feed this many people. Here we Methodists have this entrepreneurial giant right in our midst, and we're not even asking her help to reimagine church for a new day, funded by enterprise, asking people for their best ideas and energy. We would rather fund ourselves on the handout model, please, can you give to meet budget? Rather than, well, whatever we might dream up together with Kate's leading.

It's clear what Kate Welch could bring if you were started a social enterprise—the expertise of running a small business (most get advice from bankers—don't do it! She warns), budgeting and capital and lawyering expertise, leadership of employees who aren't easy to lead, the works. But what do churches stand to learn? First, we don't have to always operate in a "deficit space." Sound familiar? There's not enough of this, if we only had a little of that which that other church has. "Don't be afraid to see value in what we do," she counsels, as if talking to an illiterate person just out of prison who's never had a job. Churches offer what our world needs, not just Jesus, though he's everything! But community, connection, a cure for loneliness, meaninglessness. The gospel is free, and yet we have to give up everything for it. There's not just value in it, there's infinite value, and people will pay, not just in the plate, but otherwise, she thinks. Joining enterprise to ecclesia is also about evangelism. This Methodist insists she didn't set off to evangelize, but she's living her life as a disciple, and she finds that brings more people to faith than preaching at them. What I mostly appreciate is the hustle. Kate Welch is as active as any church lady you've ever met, but she's doing it as an entrepreneur, turning over millions of pounds ("I'm not afraid of noughts," she says simply). Where do our churches get that hustle back? Call it entrepreneurship if you like, call it urgency for the kingdom, or whatever you call it, just go get it. Our churches are disintegrating, our world is dying for good news, the field is white for harvest. Lord, give us energy like hers.

Patterns

One adage that has driven this present research project was reported to me by David Goodhew, though it seems not to have been coined by him: "Churches that intend to grow tend to grow." It's not ironclad, as the wording suggests. It does, however, say something important: intentionality and results tend to correlate. Fresh Expressions are designed for those who are not presently in any church. If they don't work—if they attract no one, or only existing church people—they adjust. Churches can fail to notice that they only attract church people (or even that they attract no one!). FX's single focus and enormous flexibility allow it to travel light, to "fail forward," learning from missteps, and to stay focused on its desire to reach new people for Christ and the gospel. It also foreswears "church as usual." Fresh Expressions need not change to be more churchy—they are rather a signal that the church needs to change to meet its neighbours with the gospel. Church, Rowan Williams often says, is what *happens* when people meet the risen Christ and then seek to deepen that encounter and share it with others. Williams often speaks of the proliferation of these communities as his greatest contribution to the C of E and the Anglican Communion. If that were his *only* contribution, it would be more than enough.

The obvious question to ask yourself and your community is this: what would church look like if we designed it only for those who are presently not a part of its life? You may have to protect this. Church people will want to show up—they must be guided away, a FX is not for them. Even more worrying, the new people may very quickly start acting like old church people! That's my seat, I "always" sit there (in a church in a pub that's only been meeting for three weeks!). But it can be done. By accident even. With little or no money, astonishingly. And now the question you have to ask is this: what's keeping you from starting tomorrow?

9

CAN CHURCHES STILL *DO* THAT!?

THERE IS A RUMOUR afoot that medicine and religion are at odds with one another. People of faith have a way of attracting media attention for their purported certainty over complex problems like abortion, euthanasia, and contraception. Physicians and health bureaucrats get nervous about any approach to medicine that seems tangled up with one or the other strong religious belief, appropriately, for fear of discrimination. Yet such mutual acrimony is not long-lived. The church founded the first hospitals. Missionaries often established health clinics before they built schools or sanctuaries. Hospitals that may now worry about the influence of faith still bear names like St. this and denomination that, testimony to a previous, more religion-friendly age. Christians are presently struggling to overcome the loss of civic power that we gained with the favour of the Roman Empire in the fourth century and enjoyed until, approximately, the 1960s. Medicine knows that many people go into their field to help others, especially the less fortunate, yet is unsure how to replicate that sense of calling without the religious institutions that once seeded it.

In one sense, those nervous about faith's influence in medicine are right. The God of the Bible is irreducibly particular, and can't be boiled down to a least common denominator "religion," much less to some abstract principle to which all people of good will agree, like "equality," or even "health." The God of the Bible intends to bless the whole world. Yet he is committed to doing so *through* a specific people. God has no gifts that are unmediated, direct. They always come through others. So God chooses one people—Israel—through whom to bless all the nations (Gen 12:1–4). God chooses one people—the church—through whom to bring God's new creation. We don't know *why* God has this taste for the particular, this way of remaking what humanity has broken. The closest we get to an explanation is in Deuteronomy 7, where Scripture tells us it wasn't because Israel was more numerous than any other, but rather because the Lord loved Israel (Deut 7:6–7). God has a soft spot for Israel. He adores her, courts her, marries her, is jealous over her. God's penchant for the particular is certainly not because Israel or the church are "better" than anyone else. To read the prophets or Paul's letters, the church is, if anything, *worse* than any other people. Yet God maintains this stubborn habit of going through the particular to get to the general, through one people to get to everyone else. God's promises are shaped like an hourglass. Or like a womb.

One thing God's people keep confusing: God's gifts are not *for* God's people. They are *through* God's people *for* everyone else. The prepositions matter because God's people, like all people, forget and think the gifts are for them. But God's gifts are the sort that you cannot keep. Try to keep them and they rot, like manna. But give them away and they'll always be replenished. In church we are often worried whether there will be enough: people, money, energy, ideas, future, blessing. That's already a sign we are keeping God's gifts to ourselves. Give them all away and watch them multiply. Try to retain them and they run through your fingers like water.

I saw anew this peculiar way of God as I learned about Hope Citadel Healthcare (HCH) and its remarkable founder and CEO, Laura Neilson, in Manchester. In one sense, she's the wrong person to have tried her hand at entrepreneurship in medicine. She was a church planter's wife—she and her husband Chris started a Salvation Army church plant in 2004. They were doing the sort of work you do in church planting: listening to local needs, trying to draw a crowd, taking part with God in the ushering in of the kingdom on that particular corner. The newlyweds were running a youth club, a mums and toddlers group, a house cell gathering, retreats, putting on functions for the schools . . . : "It was creatively bonkers. Nothing works, so you might as well try another thing," Neilson said. Over time they did scratch out an existence for a congregation that still meets in Oldham called The Brew. It's now a pleasant café church, filled with lively customers the day I visit, with glass doors through which one can peer in or out. The Neilsons' successor, Tim Royales, was a chef, and turned those skills loose on leading The Brew in a more foodie direction. The next leader will pivot into her or his gifts, no doubt.

While the Neilsons were still in that role, they had a superior in the Salvation Army over for dinner. Cooking was chaotic. Laura Neilson cooks like she leads, with drama and intensity, and it all either goes spectacularly wrong, or a bit of kingdom light shines, or both. As Chris and his super were imagining what Oldham needs, Laura, then a medical student, trying "to be the nice wifey," plopped the evening's pudding down between the boys and, perhaps prompted into one frustration by another, said, "If I'd do anything here, I'd do a health centre. That's holding this community back." She hadn't planned to say anything like it, but the truth of what she'd said took hold of her, "and I became quite tenacious about that. A youth club and pool table were not enough."

There was, of course, a day when churches founded hospitals, health clinics, surgeries, and all the rest. We also used to found universities, colleges, secondary schools, public schools, orphanages, the YMCA. For that matter, we used to found countries and royal families and faiths. Since the 1960s' counter-culture, or maybe since the Age of Enlightenment's reaction against faith and its perceived privileges, or maybe since Dickens' skewering of the abuses of institutions, we have been reticent about this legacy of institution-building and maintaining. But I defy you to name for me a good in your life not mediated by an institution. You can't do it. Because there are none. In the West, we think of ourselves as individualists. That story, nay, that lie, was peddled to us by a whole heap of institutions: book publishers, movie makers, schools. And the right reaction to institutions' mediation of harm is to have institutions mediate grace, not to try to root them out altogether. The novelist Wallace Stegner said of the American old West, setting for so many individualist mythologies, that in real life the only individualist in the West was hanged at the end of a rope, hoisted up there by a group of communitarians. Human beings cannot get born, die, or anything good or bad in between without help from other people. Just try glimpsing the back of your own head.[1]

Laura Neilson does not look like an institution-founder of the sort memorialized in bronze in town squares or outside universities, any more than she looks like a pastor's wife or church planter. She deflects attention from herself so effortlessly you don't even notice she's being humble. But sister has skills. She is one-fourth of two sets of twins in her family of origin. She was doing her family's finances from her teens. She always had a sense of God's presence and care for her, which is why her family sent her to an Anglican church, "thinking that would cure me." It almost did. She was the only child in a service half in Latin, half from the 1662 Prayer Book: "I can regurgitate that for you, if you want." Her posh girls' school gave her

---

1. I take that last example from Rowan Williams, in an image he reuses often in speaking. For the institutionalist arguments in this paragraph see Hugh Heclo and the essays at https://faithandleadership.com/category/principles-practice-topics/traditioned-innovation.

such crucial entrepreneurial skills as flute, lacrosse, ballet, and embroidery. A friend in her teens brought her along to an evangelical church, where she first heard grousing about the length of women's skirts. She wasn't interested in the pious moralizing. But she also heard there about the fire in the prophets' bones, a Christ who brings good news to the poor. "I thought 'I can't do the skirt thing, but I can do that.' That was my proper 'I'm in.'" After university she took a mission stint with The Message Trust in Manchester— a mission strategy whose Eden communities invite people into places of deprivation to take part with God in blessing the poor (Isaiah 43:18–21). In Eden, she first heard grumbling against women preaching. But she also saw hierarchies leveled, as folks from different denominations and theologies worked together to bless the poor. And she learned trust, as she survived on money in envelopes pushed through her letter box. "I had never been in an estate before Eden," she said. "And I probably wouldn't be a Christian now without it." She notes that lots of folks from posh schools pass through Oxbridge on their way to leading in the NHS without firsthand familiarity with the way their policies and practices impact the poor, let alone *being* poor. Through her experience with Eden and as a church planter she had the poor as neighbours (sometimes aggravating ones!), church members (ditto), now employees, and friends. She saw how health policy affected them all. And, like the prophets, she demanded better. "I have a very simple faith," she said. "I can argue with people, sure. But for me it's as simple as a girl spinning and dancing with God." Laura Neilson spun her way into the office of those making decisions, assured enough of God's delight in her to demand better for others along with her.

 She led a public push to get a health centre in the neighbourhood. Oldham needed it, that could not be denied. The onetime industrial powerhouse outside Manchester had declined with the falling off of the cotton-spinning industry. Residents of Oldham die years earlier than the national average in the UK. Folks' problems are often complex. They might come to the doctor because they are lonely, or they might abuse emergency services (999 here—that's 911 back home) because they are drunk and bored, or schedule appointments and fail to keep them, or receive a medical plan and not even begin to follow it. The greatness of modern western medicine is its ability to drill down through symptoms to a diagnosable, treatable medical problem. But what if the symptoms won't allow the drill? It is a medical problem to be evicted from one's house—not one that can be fixed with a narrow, medical solution, but a health problem nonetheless. What if the person doesn't have the internet or phone access or bureaucratic wherewithal to gain the financial benefits that should be coming to them from the government? Doctors and nurses aren't trained for that. A more holistic approach was needed, something that regarded people as whole human beings.

But that wasn't going to happen at first. The health centre bid had gone out and was slotted for a for-profit company that would wring money out of the area and provide sub-standard care. When Neilson complained, she was told the company had a three-star rating from the NHS. This is where Neilson's *lack* of credentials helped. She was "just" a medical student. So she could take on a system against which she couldn't possibly win. "I wrote back nicely and said, 'Only 40 percent of your estate have a smear test, and this many patients die, you can't possibly have three stars, can you?'" Exasperated officials threw the ball into Laura's court. If she knew so much about medicine, she should do something about it herself. Ok, she said. She went home and entered "how to set up a company" into an internet search engine. She attacked the process of bidding for the clinic the way a nerd does a set of exams, and prayed about it the way a person of faith does about anything ("up till 2 am, asking for the words"). Her competitor company submitted a 700-page tender. But she got the bid, and set about establishing the sort of clinic she thought should exist for the sake of the neighbourhood. An unlikely church planter became an even more unlikely *surgery* planter. Now, Hope Citadel Health Clinic employs 120 people, sees 33,000 patients a year, and operates a budget of more than £5 million. It plows its profits not into the hands of shareholders or a board of directors or fully partnered-up doctors, but back into the work. And patients' outcomes have improved considerably. Visits to A&E (the emergency room) are down by 40 percent where HCH operates. Three of HCH's nine offices have received a rating of "excellent" from the Care Quality Commission, only given to 4 percent of surgeries across the country. Neilson was recognized as a "rising star" by a national journal of healthcare management. One of Neilson's bêtes noires is what's called "inverse law," which states that more physicians are distributed around the country in places of affluence, while places of greater need see fewer of them. Neilson thinks Christians, at least, should do better than that, and is leading the way. And a health company in the "proper backwater" of Manchester, not in Greater London or Oxbridge, is drawing external attention to how it's doing things. An ITV report wonders repeatedly whether Hope Citadel isn't the future of medicine in Britain, and if its approach couldn't in fact "save the NHS."[2]

So apparently the church can still found institutions, and perhaps show others how to have the sort of beating heart of mercy that they're all

---

2. From an ITV report on HCH, "Frontline Care: Saving the NHS?" 1 November 2018: https://https://www.itv.com/news/2018-11-01/frontline-care-saving-the-nhs-tonight.

supposed to have. It's enough to make you wonder, what other sorts of institutions should we be founding, tending, demonstrating to others? It is a hardy little plant, warm and inviting and full of light and good food with a chair set out for you. But its witness is not in its dramatic numbers. Its most dramatic public witness is that the church can, despite its manifest flaws, raise up a young woman of valor—an *eshet chayil* in Proverbs 31— who can take on an industry and win for the sake of marginalized people. Some describe HCH as "turning the church ladies loose on the neighbourhood." Neilson, veteran of not-a-few attempts to shoehorn HCH into either pro- or anti-religious propaganda, offers this correction: "I prefer to speak of turning good people loose on the neighbourhood." Some of the proudest wearers of the badge "Christian" treat people meanly; plenty of compassionate people without the signs of outward religion treat people the way Jesus asks. Not everyone who works for HCH is a Christian or a person of faith at all, and certainly not everyone it serves is. Yet this is a story that cannot be understood without the Christian faith, that faith's institution-building impetus, and a world in need of both.

Ruth Chorley is one of the church ladies. Her training is as a nurse, with a long stint in Tanzania, which she still considers a spiritual home. "Focused care," a term she proposed and HCH adopted, describes how she and forty other care workers at HCH treat a whole person. Focused care has been adopted by some fifty other surgery offices now around Greater Manchester. When I'm in Ruth's office, she introduces me to a young man named Scott. When she first saw him, his records were flagged throughout with warnings, "dangerous patient." He had a history of being abusive in doctors' offices. This was because he was having trouble navigating the bureaucracy to get his financial benefits from the government. And he was in terrible dental pain. Chorley had more time to listen as a focused care worker than she would have as a nurse, charged to find a cure for a patient in the shortest time possible. And as an employee of a GP surgery she had the power to refer him—in this case for dental care ("I referred someone to a neurosurgeon once. Little ole' me!"). Their first few meetings, Scott simply cried. Ruth listened. His mother had introduced him to using and selling cannabis at age seven. Their home was a no-go zone for police. Ruth sat with Scott through dental appointments, holding his hand. He has a fine set of dentures now. When he was beaten up recently by druggies, he protected those dentures. His ribs, not so much. When Ruth goes to hug him he warns, "I know I normally like a tight squeeze, but not today." His ribs were still sore.

That hug is a thing. Some professional protocols would guard against such contact, for some good reasons. This boundarying can lead to encounters that are more clinical than human at times. But Chorley respects those protocols, so she always asks if she can give a hug before she goes in for one. When she asked to hug Scott the first time, he seemed confused. "What do you mean?" It was as if he thought she was offering him sex in the surgery.

"Has your mum never hugged you?

No.

"Girlfriends?

No. We've had sex but not hugs.

"Here, let me show you. You stand like this . . . ."

Of course, this could confirm the worst suspicions of critics for whom religious approaches to medicine makes them nervous. Hugs *can* lead to abuse, and they are no substitute for proper medicine. Nurse Chorley would be the first to agree. Yet Scott is a human being before he is a medical problem. Human beings need hugs. They also need dental care, a proper diet, housing, government benefits if necessary, a way off drugs, and work through which they give back to their community. The absence of those basic human things makes for an absence of health. The social welfare state makes it its responsibility to provide for its citizens. Yet none could deny there are gaps, holes, unintended obstacles that leave those goods just out of reach. Arguably the state was never meant to function without institutions of compassion like churches helping fill those gaps. And less arguably, the church should have never abdicated its responsibility to care for the whole person.

Focused care allows a professional like Ruth to be nimble, to listen deeply enough to know the pain behind the pain, and to marshal resources to heal at multiple levels. It is medicine informed by faith, made effective through profound levels of compassion. Neilson has seen faith get caught up in skirt lengths, the gender of a preacher, and social hot-button issues. "I often see more of the glory of God outside the church than in," she said. Jesus Christ is a healer, though he is only an infrequent dispenser of moral counsel or doctrine. When he does dip into ethics, he takes his cues from the prophets: God hates it when the powerful crush the poor. A day is coming when those who are crushed will be exalted. I catch a glimpse of that as Ruth (gently) hugs Scott, and his pain-free teeth beam back at her.

"I never leave a patient without hope," Chorley told me.

Nurse Chorley tells me of another person whom focused care has recently aided. An older woman with mental health problems who neglects herself and her house, so each is a mess. Her cats leave fur and fungus and worse things, which makes it difficult for an asthmatic like Chorley to be there. Chorley asked what she wanted. To go to the library to get some books, she said. What would it take to invite people into her house and life? "Look at it," the woman said. She was ashamed at the state of her house. So

Chorley had a deep cleaning crew coming in, after which the woman was open to more regular cleanings. Chorley is picking her up soon for a trip to the library, "but only five minutes, because I don't want to be around people," the woman said. And a physician from the surgery is coming by to adjust her depression medication. There is a sort of barter going on here. To get to the woman's medical problems—a prescription change—Chorley had to go see her, listen to her, ask direct, even intrusive questions, and listen again. And then get busy helping. The medical outcome was reached, but only by going through the "mess" of this woman's quite ordinary, but for her insurmountable, problems. And something had to motivate Chorley, and HCH's physician, to go to the lengths they did to achieve their medical outcome.

Another of the church ladies/good people set loose in Oldham is Carol Hill. She's a healthcare assistant, the person whom patients see after reception, whose job it is to listen. "I do have a gift of making people feel comfortable and open up," she said. "Coming here, people say, is not like going to the doctor, but like going to a friend." This is crucial. One piece of negative baggage to the "church ladies" description is the stereotype that they demand Victorian morality, but a whiff of judgmentalism would shut down any sort of honesty here. Folks have to be willing to trust someone like Carol with stories of drug abuse, domestic violence, all sources of deep pain for which victims often blame themselves. HCH finds it has to convince its patients that they are *worth* healing, not only capable of but *deserving of* a better life. Judgment will never achieve this. Only grace can. And Carol Hill has grace to spare: "We have a church where we don't judge. I don't know my tomorrows. I could end up an alcoholic tomorrow." Chorley agrees that the building of trust is crucial for this sort of work. Some would say that HCH's foundation in faith means they have ulterior motives for treating patients—a desire for conversion or whatever. Chorley insists the opposite. The faith she holds builds a trust that she has *no* ulterior motives. "It comes across if you have no hidden agenda. You can just be *for* them. I think that's why we have a good response."

Carol Hill's sort of probing attentiveness is crucial. She's an "arrow," she said, pointing people in the right direction—either to the right physician, to focused care, or elsewhere. They may come in with back or leg pain, but they might go on and say "I don't normally talk about this," before adding stories of depression, alcoholism, appalling living conditions, and other things doctors alone usually can't fix.

Hill tells me two stories of people who have come through Hilltop, her surgery on Fitton Hill in Oldham. One young man named Jamie was from a dysfunctional family, "being wasted on the estate," she said. HCH's feeding project helped him understand the basics of diet, cooking, and self-care.

He found his way to church, to the clinic, and eventually into an improved life. He's nearly finished training to be a physician himself. Another young woman, Nicki, was "known to police," as the Brits say. She also found her way first to the church, and through it to the clinic. Her father was an alcoholic who would be encouraged by his fellow terrible fathers to physically abuse her. The clinic could go a step farther than any social worker or physician, who would also know to intervene for the defense of the vulnerable child. They could also work to bring about reconciliation, to get the father off alcohol, to propose a different way of being a family. Nicki is now trained as a community police officer, working in Canada with street people there.

The vulnerable who need care are not only "out there," on the estate. They are also "in here," in the surgery offices, like the Hilltop one on Fitton Hill where Carol works. "All of my daughters work for the NHS now," she said, including one child who had particular trouble finding a niche in school, but saw the good her mother was helping do through HCH. That daughter is working in end-of-life care now. One dementia patient was in particular distress, upsetting visitors, so Joanne went and sat with her and rubbed her arm. The woman asked, "Do you know Jesus?" Joanne did. She quieted down, and then drifted off to sleep. "That's from her having come and worked here," Carol said.

Carol herself had never done paid work before, she had mostly volunteered as a . . . wait for it . . . church lady. "But Laura seen something in me," she says to me several different ways. Carol has always been drawn to churches with trouble. "I never been to a church where things are easy. God always gives me the difficult ones—with problems." She works with baby boogies—a mums and toddler group, that allows her to see who needs extra help at home or for post-partum. She leads a meeting of older people as well, "they don't have a voice sometimes neither." Carol has "always been passionate about the homeless, about anyone who don't have a voice." That's basic bread and butter church do-gooding. Turning it loose in the clinic means Carol can offer more than a hug and ear to those in need (though she is quick to do that). She can direct them to exactly the right doctor, precisely the right government agency, perfectly the right sort of comment. John Patterson, HCH's medical director, often sites research that says the clearest determinant for how effective a surgery will be caring for patients is the depth with which employees care for one another. Carol loves this. "We need to look after one another first," she said. "If we don't we won't be any good for the patients."

That sense of a family at HCH starts with its founder and CEO. "I'm a CEO in a t-shirt and trainers," Neilson said of what North Americans call sneakers, with the sort of self-disparagement at which Brits seem to excel.

Don't let her fool you. Patterson calls her "one of the most impressive people I've ever met." Patterson only works for her due to her Laura's sheer *chutzpah*. He was an instructor for her in medical school, and she'd written a paper on undoing the inverse law in medicine. He marked her down for poor grammar. After complaining about her mark, she invited him to work for her! The timing wasn't right just then, but not long after it was, and the pair have worked in tandem, as CEO and medical director, since Hope Citadel's founding. Sitting with the two of them shows how they work so well together. They order each other's food, finish each other's sentences. Patterson brought medical expertise to the partnership—he is now the chief clinical officer for the NHS in Oldham. He praises a program Neilson developed to offer better healthcare among Oldham's Asian immigrants. High diabetes rates and low smear test rates were endemic, and thought impossible to cure, for complicated cultural reasons. But Neilson designed a program to improve both. I turn to her and ask how. She deflects praise instantly: "The team did it." But she brags on them: they designed a way for women to communicate with the office via post-it notes without their husbands noticing, asking for help with contraception and emotional wellness as well. It started in Fitton Hill and now has worked in other places. Neilson quietly innovates; Patterson publicly praises by telling the story. Neither grabs credit for him- or herself. Unlike lots of practices, HCH's financial successes don't benefit them personally. This is a charity or social-benefit organization, not a business. Profits go back into helping with the mission, and the inverse care law is subverted a little. "I'm amazed how many doctors tell me they can't work for us because they could make more money elsewhere," Neilson said. "These are 'Christian' doctors." Some other motivation has to be found to help the poor than cash, obviously. Stories might do it—like a story of the poor being blessed, and the rich sent away empty.

HCH is not a one-off that can only work in one place, as the story above illustrates. They have acquired other surgeries and sought to inculcate HCH's values there too. Laura has partnered with other doctors to write a textbook on their sort of deprivation medical training. Not only that, they are helping offer the first medical training in deprivation care in the country. Students will study the "social determinants" of health, they will do some more medical training, more mental health, but also communication skills and cultural acclimatization. I ask what she means. "Bartering skills," she says. "Quid pro quo. You could never do this with middle-class folks, but it is culturally appropriate here. If you agree to write a housing letter about the person's horrible damp, you can get them to agree to come in for ear tests." Medical missionaries to another culture once knew they had to learn languages and mores unfamiliar to them to reach people. Medical students in this new program will learn something similar—how to navigate the economics of non-middle-class people.

Neilson is also working to give her power and authority away. She introduces me to a young administrator in the clinic without university training. Amy is creating a PSA order for a patient who hadn't had one in years. This man's PSA levels are high, and he should be tested annually. The fact that he has not been tested signaled to Amy that other patients likely have not been checked annually, so she's working to create a system in the computer to find them. She is nineteen years old, came to HCH as a sixteen-year-old intern. "Well done you," Neilson tells her, and when she leaves the room Neilson turns to me: "She's going to run a practice one day, in the not-too-distant future." Another talent Neilson spotted is in a woman named Lisa Nolan, who coordinates all of HCH's administration. She's an oddity at HCH for not being religious, and just so has tremendous importance: "Because she's not into redemption, she can be really good at speaking the truth." The church needs the world in order to hear the truth, not just vice-versa. Lisa used to roll her eyes when Neilson said she would have to pray on some difficult work conundrum. Now she just accepts Laura being Laura. "I haven't found it exclusive here at all," she said. "I believe in kindness, in looking after people, which is the same sort of thing really." Nolan reserves her stronger confessional zeal for the way HCH practices medicine: "I completely believe in it," she said, and she is working to replicate it in the most recently acquired surgeries among HCH's nine. She even pitches in personally: one patient bragged she'd made "homemade" spaghetti Bolognese. "Amazing!" Lisa crowed. "Yeah I got it out of the jar." Which is . . . sort of homemade. Don't patronize progress! On a more serious note: John Patterson tells a story of a certain patient who scheduled heart bypass multiple times and then failed to go through, occupying slots other patients could have used and endangering his own life. The appointment-skipper meant to phone his wife to tell her he was leaving the hospital, but accidentally phoned the surgery. Lisa answered. She was on a first-name basis with his wife, so she told him how annoyed they would *both* be if he left. The man turned around and went back in for the surgery. "Everyone in the office was owning the problem. It's a relational one, and Lisa worked on it a different way," Patterson said.

I framed the story of Laura Neilson and Hope Citadel above as a story about faith and medicine. But that may be far too narrow. It is, more profoundly, a *human* story. Sure, it has faith components, and these are essential. Neilson speaks of herself in priestly terms. To be a doctor is to engage in activities in which you stand between the patient and God, between God and the patient. This is why people of faith find it so natural to pray for patients, and patients find it so natural to ask for prayer. They know they are in holy, vulnerable, dangerous space, and they want to honour all parties. "I have sat with people as they died, and prayed with them. I have told them they are going to die. I have been at births. I have looked after people when they're at their most beaten up and bruised, when they're psychotic, when their relationship or house problems become public." She turns and gazes at me intently and says this: "*You can be a doctor in a priestly way.*"

John Patterson is quick to add that he does not offer to pray with patients. Neilson agrees—there is a power imbalance in the room, all the more so among socioeconomically and otherwise vulnerable people. But *someone* at HCH is praying for patients—on their own time. Doctors are too, just not necessarily in their presence. Patterson speaks of his own "gifts of discernment" when he wears the lab coat, rather than gifts of miraculous healing (though he doesn't discount those). The stories I hear are of prayer humming in the background of the place, more ambient music than concert. Above all, HCH wants to be known for the respect and dignity with which all its patients are treated. "If redemption is real, how do we put that into practice in how we do medicine?" Neilson asks out loud. She began her journey with a conversation with a senior gastroenterologist whose scepticism that patients ever recover from alcoholism was patent. Yet Neilson asked anyway: do patients ever recover from alcoholism? No. Never. She begged to differ. She had often seen people healed from this and worse maladies, usually in the church. She realized that the story you tell shapes what you believe is possible. "Once you hear the story of the gospel, and you sit troubled with patients, then like Mary you ponder this all in your heart, and ask, 'what do we do?'" She didn't just ask, and didn't just stay angry at the poor healthcare. She offered an alternative.

A priestly one at that.

Where else might the church offer an alternative? In what other spheres might we innovate so as to bless not just the church, but the neighbourhood, and even the world? Back home in Vancouver, I am struck by the number of churches founded in the early 1900s that once had swimming pools. Can you imagine?! One is now a theatre venue; another was long ago demolished and turned into a fellowship hall. But there was a time when the church was counted on for civic recreation. That baton passed at some point to parachurch organizations like the YMCA and YWCA, which still exist, without the Christian bit. Now in Vancouver we expect the city to offer us recreation, and it does. That's fine—the church likely need not innovate in that area. But we must innovate somewhere. HCH and Laura Nielson show us it can be done in an area as forbidding as healthcare. Where else can

God's people rashly, fool-hardily, and blessedly rush in, and thereby take part in God's work of making all things new?

BIBLIOGRAPHY

Barley, Lynda. "Stirrings in Barchester: Cathedrals and Church Growth." In *Church Growth in Britain 1980 to the Present*, edited by David Goodhew, 77–89. Farnham, UK: Ashgate, 2012.
Bartlett, Alan, and David Goodhew. "Victorian to Modern 1832–2000." In *Durham Cathedral: History, Fabric, and Culture*, edited by David Brown, 111–27. New Haven, CT: Yale University Press, 2015.
Blackaby, Henry. *Experiencing God*. Nashville: LifeWay Press, 2007.
Brown, David, ed. *Durham Cathedral: History, Fabric, and Culture*. New Haven, CT: Yale University Press, 2014.
Christerson, Brad, and Richard Flory. *The Rise of Network Christianity: How Independent Leaders are Changing the Religious Landscape*. Oxford: Oxford University Press, 2017.
Church Growth Research Project. "An Analysis of Fresh Expressions of Church and Church Plants." October 2013.
Church Growth Research Programme. "From Anecdote to Evidence: Findings from the Church Growth Research Programme 2011–2013." 2014: https://www.churchofengland.org/more/church-resources/church-growth-research-programme/anecdote-evidence.
———. "From Evidence to Action Leaders' Guide: A Parish Guide to the Findings of the Church Growth Research Programme." 2014: http://www.fromevidencetoaction.org.uk/leaders-guide
Commission on Urban Life and Faith. *Faithful Cities: A Call for Celebration, Vision, and Justice*. London: Methodist Publishing House/Church House Publishing, 2006.
Corbett, Steve, and Brian Fikkert. *When Helping Hurts: How to Alleviate Poverty without Hurting the Poor . . . and Yourself*. Chicago: Moody, 2014.
Cray, Graham, ed. *Mission-Shaped Church: Church Planting and Fresh Expressions of a Church in a Changing Context*. London: SCM, 2009.
Daniel, Lillian. *Tired of Apologizing for a Church I Don't Belong To: Faith without Stereotypes, Religion without Ranting*. Nasville: FaithWords, 2017.
Drane, John. *The McDonaldization of the Church: Consumer Culture and the Church's Future*. Macon, GA: Smyth & Helwys, 2012.
Duffy, Eamon. *John Henry Newman: A Very Brief History*. London: SPCK, 2019.
———. "Treasures of Heaven: Saints and Their Relics." In Eamon Duffy, *Royal Books and Holy Bones: Essays in Medieval Christianity*. London: Bloomsbury Continuum, 2018.

BIBLIOGRAPHY

Field, John. *Durham Cathedral: Light of the North.* London: Third Millennium, 2007.
Fox, Kate. *Watching the English.* 2nd ed. London: Nicholas Brealey, 2014.
Fout, Jason. *Learning from London: Church Growth in Unlikely Places.* Cincinnati, OH: 2019.
Francis, Leslie J. *Anglican Cathedrals in Modern Life: The Science of Cathedral Studies.* London: Palgrave MacMillan, 2015.
Francis, Leslie J., et al. "The Spiritual Revolution and the Spiritual Quest of Cathedral Visitors." In *Anglican Cathedrals in Modern Life: The Science of Cathedral Studies,* edited by Leslie Francis, 95–110. New York: Palgrave Macmillan, 2015.
Goodhew, David. *Church Growth in Britain: 1980 to the Present.* Farnham, UK: Ashgate, 2012.
———. *The Desecularization of the City: London's Churches, 1980 to the Present.* London: Routledge, 2019.
———. *Towards a Theology of Church Growth.* London: Routledge, 2015.
Jackson, Bob. *The Road to Growth: Towards a Thriving Church.* London: Church House, 2005.
Kelley, Dean M. *Why Conservative Churches Are Growing: A Study in Sociology of Religion.* New York: Harper & Rowe, 1972.
Ker, Ian. *John Henry Newman: A Biography.* Oxford: Oxford University Press, 2019.
Lim, Swee Hong, and Lester Ruth. *Lovin' on Jesus: A Concise History of Contemporary Music.* Nashville: Abingdon, 2017.
Lings, George. *Encountering the Day of Small Things.* Sheffield, UK: Church Army 2017: https://churcharmy.org/Publisher/File.aspx?ID=204262.
Lupton, Robert. *Toxic Charity: How Churches and Charities Hurt Those They Help (and How to Reverse This).* San Francisco: HarperOne, 2012.
McGavran, Donald. *Understanding Church Growth.* 3rd. ed. Grand Rapids: Eerdmans, 1990.
Milbank, Allison, and Andrew Davidson. *For the Parish: A Critique of Fresh Expressions.* London: SCM, 2010.
Millar, Sandy. *All I Want Is You: A Collection of Christian Reflections.* Edited by Mark Elsdon-Dew. London: Alpha International, 2005.
Milne, Andy. *The DNA of Pioneer Ministry.* London: SCM, 2016.
Moore, Lucy, and Jane Leadbetter. *Messy Church: Fresh Ideas for Building a Christ-Centered Community.* Downers Grove, IL: InterVarsity, 2017.
Moynagh, Michael. *Church in Life: Innovation, Mission and Ecclesiology.* London: SCM, 2017.
Myers, Ben, and Scott Stephens. "The Discipline of the Eyes." In *The HTML of Crucified Love,* edited by John Frederick, 27–72. Eugene, OR: Pickwick, 2019.
Orton, Andrew, and Peter Hart. "Leading Together in Growing Methodist Churches: Learning from Research and Practice in the North East of England." Published by Durham University 2017: www.methodist.org.uk/learning/scholarship-research-and-innovation/research/connexional-research-projects/archive.
Percy, Martyn. "Paradox and Persuasion: Alternative Perspectives on Liberal and Conservative Church Growth." In *Why Liberal Churches Are Growing,* edited by Martyn Percy and Ian Markham, 73–86. London: T. & T. Clark, 2006.
Peterson, Eugene. *Run with the Horses: The Quest for Life at Its Best.* 25th anniversary commemorative ed. Downers Grove, IL: InterVarsity, 2019.

Platten, Stephen, ed. *Holy Ground: Cathedrals in the Twenty-First Century.* Durham: Sacristy, 2017.

Platten, Stephen, and C. Lewis, eds. *Dreaming Spires: Cathedrals in a New Age.* London: SPCK 2006.

Rowlands, Anna. "The Fragility of Goodness." *Journal of Missional Practice* (Winter 2017): https://journalofmissionalpractice.com/fragility-of-goodness/.

Sadgrove, Michael. *Christ in a Choppie Box: Sermons from North East England.* Edited by Carol Harrison. Durham: Sacristy, 2015.

Somerville, Christopher. *Ships of Heaven: The Private Life of Britain's Cathedrals.* London: Penguin, 2019.

Tavinor, Michael. *Shrines of the Saints in England and Wales.* Norwich, UK: Canterbury, 2016.

Voas, David. "The Rise and Fall of Fuzzy Fidelity in Europe." *European Sociological Review* 25.2 (2009) 155–68.

Wakefield, Gavin. *Alexander Boddy: Pentecostal Anglican Pioneer.* Milton Keynes, UK: Paternoster, 2007.

Ward, Benedicta, SLG. *The Venerable Bede.* 2nd ed. London: Chapman, 1998.

Warren, Robert. *Developing Healthy Churches: Returning to the Heart of Mission and Ministry.* London: Church House, 2012.

Waugh, Evelyn. *Edmund Campion: Jesuit and Martyr.* London: Penguin, 2011.

Webb, Simon. *Bede's Life of St. Cuthbert.* Durham: Langley, 2016.

Wells, Samuel. *God's Companions: Reimagining Christian Ethics.* Oxford: Wiley-Blackwell, 2006.

Wells, Samuel, and Sarah Coakley. *Praying for England.* London: Continuum, 2008.

Willem, David. *St. Cuthbert's Corpse: A Life after Death.* Durham: Sacristy, 2013.

Made in the USA
Monee, IL
08 January 2023